ALAN R. YOUNG

ROADS
TAKEN

A memoir

ALAN R. YOUNG

ROADS TAKEN

A memoir

MEMOIRS

Cirencester

Mereo Books

1A The Wool Market Dyer Street Cirencester Gloucestershire GL7 2PR
An imprint of Memoirs Publishing www.mereobooks.com

Roads Taken: 978-1-86151-295-6

First published in Great Britain in 2014
by Mereo Books, an imprint of Memoirs Publishing

The address for Memoirs Publishing Group Limited can be found at
www.memoirspublishing.com

The Memoirs Publishing Group Ltd Reg. No. 7834348

The Memoirs Publishing Group supports both The Forest Stewardship Council® (FSC®)
and the PEFC® leading international forest-certification organisations. Our books
carrying both the FSC label and the PEFC® and are printed on FSC®-certified paper.
FSC® is the only
forest-certification scheme supported by the leading environmental organisations
including Greenpeace. Our paper procurement policy can be found at
www.memoirspublishing.com/environment

Typeset in 10/15pt Bembo
by Wiltshire Associates Publisher Services Ltd. Printed and bound in Great Britain by
Printondemand-Worldwide, Peterborough PE2 6XD

TO MY FAMILY

Two roads diverged in a yellow wood,
And sorry I could not travel both
And be one traveler...

Robert Frost

CONTENTS

CHAPTER ONE

A CHILD'S WAR

Krrumpfe…
Krrumpfe…
Krrumpfe… Krrumpfe…
KrrumpfeKrrumpfeKRRUMPFE!

The noise keeps on like this, but it doesn't wake my sister. She hardly ever wakes up, however noisy it is. Even when the windows are rattling. Even when the plane noise up there is so loud. And even when the floor is shaking.

Then the light is on. It's my mother. She never puts the light on; she always creeps in beside us, sneaky like Mrs Foster's cat. My mother always thinks I'm asleep, but I know when she comes in. I just pretend I'm asleep. She gets upset if she wakes me up.

She always has a torch so she won't trip in the dark. She flashes it over us so she won't knock into us. Not tonight, though. She has the torch, but it isn't on. Everything's lit up by the dining-room light instead. And she doesn't creep into the shelter. She comes in fast, not sneaky at all, and not caring about us. Right away she's kneeling on my leg. She never did that before. I yell at her:

"Heeeey, that hurts! My leg! My leg! You're on my LEG! You're hurting me! Mummy, my LEG!"

But she doesn't care. She's not even looking at us, and she's making noises. Strange noises in her throat. They aren't words, just noises. I don't understand.

She's off my leg now, so I just watch her without any more yelling. Then she gets out of the shelter. She's moving so fast. She never moves like that. It's more like she's a child than a grown-up. When she comes back, she's pulling the big fence behind her to close up the side of the shelter. It's heavy. I know - I once tried to move it. And she's still making those noises. Most times, we don't have the fence on the side where we get in and out. We close the side up only when my father's there. He makes us do that.

My father. That's how he is; he's fussy. But he's hardly ever here at night. My father's with the guns in the Rec (some people call it the Recreation Grounds), telling the soldiers where to point the guns. They shoot at the German planes. That's what he told me when he took me to see them.

I like the guns. Big, shiny, and green. But I'm disappointed with him. He has a uniform and a helmet like the men who fire the guns. But sometimes he doesn't seem like a real soldier. Also, he keeps telling me the guns aren't really guns, they're rocket launchers. I don't take any notice. I know they're guns, so why does he keep trying to spoil things?

When he's down at the Rec, he's indoors, in a building with big tables and big sheets of paper on top of them. He took me in there once. He says that because he's good with numbers, they make him do this job. I think it would be better if they let him fire the guns outside like the other soldiers. I'm sure he'd hit lots of planes. Maybe then the bombing would stop and we'd not have to be in this shelter. Anyway, it's my mother who's usually in charge when we're in the shelter. Like I said, she never bothers with the fence.

Sometimes my mother does fire watching. She goes out in the street at night and sits there on the kitchen stool. Mr. Archer from down the street goes too. But my mother doesn't have a uniform, and she doesn't even get a helmet. All she does is sit there with Mr. Archer, with her thermos flask and her gas mask. They also have a bucket of sand, a bucket of water and a stirrup pump. So far they've never seen a fire. She tells me all this because I don't get to watch her. That's because I'm indoors at the back of the house in the shelter. Also, all the windows have those blinds down, and we're not allowed to lift them up to see anything. It's because of the blackout. My father laughs at my mother sometimes, but I can tell she thinks she has an important job – fire watching. He wouldn't be laughing if she did find a fire bomb.

I can tell my mother's different from my father. She does things my father wouldn't allow. Sometimes, we don't have to sit up at the dining-room table. Well, it's not really a table - it's the shelter where my sister and I sleep at night. Instead, she lets us eat on the settee in the sitting room. We have to watch out for crumbs and be very careful with drinks. Sometimes she lets us go to bed late. Sometimes she lets me poke the fire. Once she even let me use the shovel beside the coal scuttle to put more coal on the fire. When she does those things, she smiles and says "Don't tell your father". We have fun with her when she's like that.

Tonight it's all different. She can't do the fence. I think she knows how to do it, but her hands won't do what she wants. They're moving about very fast, but the fence is still loose. I want to help, but when I get up, she grunts and pushes me back with her elbow, hard. But I don't yell. I just go over to the side where my sister's still sleeping. Though my mother lets me do lots of things, I know when I'm not allowed to do something. I'm doing what she says tonight. I know she's really wants me out of the way.

Through the squares of the wire fence, I see lots of dust falling from the ceiling. It's all lit up by the electric light. Too bad my younger sister is missing all this. I don't wake her. She'd only start crying. Then my mother would be over that side, cooing and telling her everything's all right. And she wouldn't be noticing me at all.

I think about how there must be dust on the top of the shelter. My mother's going to be cross about that. She's always complaining about all the cleaning. The dust will all have to be cleared away before breakfast. I look through the fence again. Yes, there's still white stuff falling from the ceiling. It's from all the shaking.

Then, in the middle of the noise and the dust, I see two things. First, she's done the fence. Thank goodness. Maybe my mother will stop jumping around and making those noises. I want her to talk to me. Often we have cosy times in the shelter. I pretend to wake up, and she gets under the covers, puts her arm round me, and we talk. Well, just for a bit. I think I must fall asleep quickly when we cuddle like that. That's because I can hardly ever remember what we talked about when I wake up.

On this night, the other thing I see besides the fence is my mother's face. There's something on it I've never seen before. I know what it is; it's fear. The sounds she's still making. That's fear, too.

And she's shaking. Also fear. It upsets me. Everything seems changed. I've never seen a grownup afraid. And now I don't know how to make my mother feel better so she won't be afraid any more.

After a bit, while she's still shaking, I put my arm round her and say: "Don't worry, Mummy. It'll stop soon. You'll see." I keep on like that. At first she doesn't notice, but then she takes hold of my hand and puts her head down on the pillow. We stay like that for a long time, both wide awake.

After a while, her shaking stops, and the house shaking stops, and she's not breathing so fast. And then the bombs sound farther away, and then they stop too. After everything's been quiet for a long time, we hear the "All Clear" siren. That's when we fall asleep. When the morning comes and I can see light round the sides of the blinds, my sister starts to wake up.

And there's a surprise. My mother's still with us. I think that's the first time she ever stayed all night like that. She usually goes back upstairs when we hear the "All Clear".

Now she gives us both a hug. Next, she takes down the fence and climbs out of the shelter. Her feet make scrunchy sounds because of all the dust and dirt on the dining room floor.

"Stay where you are, both of you, till I've cleaned up this mess," she says. "I'll just do the worst of it here and in the kitchen, then I'll do the rest in a little while."

Later: "I've checked upstairs. Be careful going to the bathroom. The stairs are still dirty."

Later still, my sister and I are having our breakfast. Suddenly the doorbell is ringing. It doesn't stop until my mother opens the door. It's my Nana. She's never been this early. She always comes in the afternoon. She and my mother have tea, and they talk. When that's over, my Nana says: "Well, I'd better get going. He'll be home soon and wanting his dinner." She's talking about my Granddad. After she's gone, my mother often says rude things about her to my father when he comes home.

"Can't she see how busy I am? I've got dinner to get too, and the kids' tea."

Once I said something rude about Nana. Just like my mother does, but then my mother got cross, and I was told off. It wasn't fair, but she wouldn't listen. I learned that sometimes I just have to keep quiet.

So here is my Nana at breakfast time. She makes a lot of noise as she comes down the hall and into the dining room where we're having breakfast.

"Oh, my God! My God! My God! Are you all right? Oh dear, dear, dear! I've been out of my mind worrying. Tell me you're all right."

"Well, you can see we're all right, can't you? And why are you here? What's happened? If you were that worried, why on earth didn't you use the phone? There's a phone box just a few doors down next to the pub, and I've showed you time and time again how to use it."

"Haven't you heard?"

"Heard what?"

"There's a bomb at the end of your street. A big one that didn't go off."

"What, here on Finchley Avenue? Well, nobody's been here to tell us. I'm sure the warden would have been round if there was anything to worry about. Who told you about this?"

"Maisy."

"But how would Maisy know? She lives next door to you. And how did you get here? There was no need to walk all that way. Besides, they wouldn't let you through if there was a bomb down there."

"Well, I don't know. But Maisy was so sure. She said it was a really big one. The whole street might go up."

"Oh, for God's sake! Just sit down and have a cup of tea. I don't want you scaring the kids. Last night was bad enough. Stories like this just make things worse. You understand? That Maisy's always causing problems with her stories. You know that."

"All right, all right. Just so long as there's no bomb."

"Just drink your tea, Mum, and then you can help me clear up some of the mess from all this dust. The whole house was shaking last night. I think they were after Crompton's. Some of that stuff sounded very close. Too close. It scared the heck out of me, I can tell you."

"Well, I keep thinking about those poor devils on Bridge Street, right next to the railway, and the other side of that is the factory. They've already lost houses on that street. D'you think they've been hit again?"

"Mum, I don't know, and I don't want to talk about this any more. We just have to be grateful that we're OK. Now, finish your tea, and let's get on and clear up this mess. Bob'll be home soon, and I don't want him doing any cleaning. You know how he is. He'll want to turn the whole house upside down just to get rid of a few specks of dust."

Turning to me, she says: "And why don't you take your sister out in the garden. Teach her how to catch with that red ball of hers.

And don't get into any mischief. Just let Nana and me get on with this."

On a different day, my Granddad and Nana are visiting. My father's away somewhere, perhaps doing music with someone. We're having lots of fun. I like my Granddad. He used to work on a farm and have bread and cheese for breakfast. He once told me he had beer for breakfast. I thought he was joking with me, but my mother said it was true. All the men on the farm did that. Granddad also worked with horses. One of them once stood on his finger, so now Granddad has this bent finger that won't do anything. The nail's funny too. I like asking him about his finger, and then he tells me about the horses. Now he doesn't work on a farm any more. He works in a place next to the market where they have farm machines.

When I'm with my Granddad, we always do things together. He can fix things and build things, and shows me what to do. Often, he has to fix my mother's bike. By watching, I learn how to take the wheel off, how to mend punctures, and how to do brakes. What I like best is when he oils the chain. He lets me help with this, even though it makes my hands dirty. Also, he makes me model ships out of pieces of wood. Sometimes, he takes me where I can put a ship in the water and pull it along with a piece of string. But today we are indoors, all of us in the sitting room. My mother and Nana are talking, and my sister and I are on Granddad's lap.

Then I have an idea. I know what'll make them laugh. I go out of the room and they think I've gone to the bathroom. Instead, I tiptoe into the hall and take off all my clothes. Then I put on my father's helmet. It's always on the table near the front door so he won't forget it when he's off to the Rec. It's heavy and hard, and it won't keep straight on my head. Then I walk back into the living room and shout out: "Now I'm a soldier! See, I'm a soldier!" They all start shouting and laughing, and there's tears coming out of Nana's eyes, she's laughing so much.

"Just look at him. Those Germans better watch out. Here comes someone who'll make 'em run."

"I like the uniform. If they all dressed like you, the army would save a lot of money."

"So, are you planning to go to the barracks this afternoon? I'm sure they need fellas like you."

They keep on like that for a nice long time. Then I think I'll make them laugh some more if I march up and down.

But everything then turns bad. The helmet falls off my head. The nasty bit is that the front of it smashes into my toe. I start yelling. I can't help it.

"Ohhhh! Ohhhhhh! It hurts! It hurts! Mummy, it hurts! Look, it's bleeding!"

I've never had hurt like this. I've never cried and screamed like this. Also, I'm afraid. What's happening to me? It must be bad, because my mother and Nana are yelling and screaming too. That's when my Granddad gives my sister to Nana. Then, he picks me up and sits down again with me on his lap. He's always quiet and never says much to other grown-ups. But now he's different, and his voice is loud.

"Now then, both of you, just stop the hysterics. The boy's going to be fine. You," he says to my mother, "you go and get a bowl of water. Cold water. And bring a flannel." Then to my Nana, he says, "Just sit over there with the girl. And no more hysterics, like I said."

Everyone does what he says. I've never seen him like this before. He has a quick look at my foot and he tells me I have to be a brave soldier. "Soldiers don't cry, remember. And I can tell you, even if it hurts now, it's gonna soon get better. You'll see."

The bowl comes, and he puts my foot in the cold water. It feels a bit better in the water. Soon, he lifts my foot out and gets some of the blood off with the flannel. But then he says to my mother, "From what I see here, I think we need to take this little man to the hospital. Just to let someone have a look at it. He's gonna lose that nail where the helmet hit." Then, as the hysterics start to return, "Don't worry, the nail'll grow right back, good as new. So let's get some clothes on him, and we'll take him down there in the pushchair."

And off we go, Granddad, my mother, and me. We leave Nana at home with my sister. As we go through our front gate, I'm wondering about something, but I don't dare say it out loud. I don't want to start my mother off again. This is what I want to know: "Will my toe be like Granddad's finger? Will my nail be like his?" I decide I won't mind if I'm like him. I could show people my toe, and I could tell them all about the helmet. It would be like him talking about the horses.

I already know the way to the hospital. I've been past it lots of times on the way to where my other Granddad lives on the High Street. So we go up to the top of the road, across Moulsham Street, up Elm Street, then a long walk down London Road to the hospital. My Granddad is doing the pushchair, and my mother is walking beside us.

"I don't know what Bob's going to say when he gets back. He

can get pretty upset. I've told him before about that helmet. It just sits there on the hall table. It could so easily fall off when the kids are monkeying around. Now look what's happened. He's going to have a fit."

"Well, don't you go worrying about Bob. When he hears what's happened, he's gonna find some other place for that blessed helmet. And don't you say nothing about it. You'll see. As for the boy here, don't worry about him neither. He'll be all fixed up by the time we're finished with the hospital and Bob gets home. Just stop worrying, will yer. You'll see. It'll be all right."

With that, I feel his hand reach over and give me a little squeeze. It's like he's telling me to stop worrying, too. Anyway, I'm not feeling so bad any more, even though my toe still hurts like anything.

We're rolling along quite fast. It's like I'm in an adventure. Soon we're inside the hospital, in a big room where all the hurt people are. There's also lots of people in green clothes that look like pyjamas. They work at the hospital. There's some nurses, too, with purple dresses and funny white hats. One of the pyjama men and one of the nurses look at my foot. They seem quite nice. When my mother tells them what happened, they laugh a bit, but not in a nasty way.

"Well, you're a brave little fella. Not crying at all. You know, I think you'll make a fine soldier. BUT… you're going to have to get just a bit older first. Now, we'll get the doctor over here for a quick look at you. I expect he'll just have us clean up that toe, and then you'll be on your way."

That was the nurse. Then, the pyjama man gets the doctor. The doctor's in a white coat. He doesn't say much to me. It's like he's in a real hurry. He doesn't smile or make any jokes. He looks mainly at my foot. He hardly looks at me at all. I don't like him very much. He's not friendly like the pyjama man and the nurse. Maybe he thinks there are other people here worse than me.

Then, without saying anything, he does something to my toe that really hurts. I try not to cry, but I can't help it. Suddenly, when I'm not really looking, the nurse sticks a long needle in me, and I cry even more, though the needle doesn't hurt much. Not like my toe. But soon, the pain is all over and the doctor is gone. Everyone is saying how brave I am. That makes me stop crying. The nurse washes my foot and puts a bandage on.

"Well, there you are, my wounded soldier. You can go home now. Sorry it hurt when the doctor took that bit of nail off. Tell your mother here to change the bandage every day. You'll be better in no time, but the new nail may take a while to come back."

"And no more playing with helmets, you hear," says the pyjama man.

At home, Nana has to know all about everything, and I show her my bandage. Later, when my father gets home, my mother takes him into the kitchen to tell him everything too. I try to hear what they're saying, but they're too quiet. At least he's not yelling or anything. Then he comes into the sitting room, but he doesn't tell me off about touching his helmet. He asks me to show him my bandage. He doesn't say anything at first. Then he smiles and rubs his hand on the top of my head like he does when he's pleased with me. After that, he sits me on his lap.

"So, looks like you've really been in the wars this time. Good job you're a brave boy. Did it hurt much at the hospital?"

"No. Only a little when the doctor did something with my toe."

"And now? How do you feel now?"

"I'm all right."

"Good. That's good to hear. Want to stay here for a bit while I have a smoke?

And that's how it goes. He lights his pipe, and I stay on his lap. I like the smell of his pipe, and it feels warm and comfy with his arm round me. I think I fall asleep there, because I don't remember going to bed at all. Just waking up in the morning, coming out of the shelter for breakfast, and showing everyone the bandage on my toe.

Another time, I see real wounded soldiers. We're on a bus going up to Danbury for a picnic. On the steep hill the bus stops. There are lots of cars in front. They're all stopped too. We don't move for a long time, and the bus driver turns off the engine. My father says that's to save petrol. Everyone on the bus wants to know what's going on. My father goes up to the front of the bus and talks to the bus driver through the little window behind the driver's seat. The two of them, with some other men, then get off the bus and start walking up the hill. They're gone a long time, so I want to get off the bus too, but my mother says "No".

When my father and the other men come back, they're talking very softly. To my mother, my father says, "It's bad. An army lorry full of soldiers. It's on its side right across the road." Now I really want to get off the bus to go and look. When I ask, my father says, "Absolutely not! Don't even think about such a thing. You're far too young to see such things." To my mother, he says, "We'd better eat right here. It's going to be a while before the road gets cleared." I like that idea. I've never had a picnic sitting in a bus.

But just as he says this, we see three soldiers walking down the hill. Well, two of them are walking. The other one is between them with his arms over their shoulders. His feet keep tripping on the ground. When they get nearer, I see his face. It's very white, but there's also lots of blood that's dripping from his head. It's all down the front of his uniform. My mother tells me and my sister not to look, but I want to see everything. She gives up after a bit. Because my father's telling other people on the bus what's happened up the hill, she has to look after my sister and stop her seeing anything. So I get to look all I want. My sister's too young to look at things like this.

Then there are more soldiers, not together, but two or three each time. I see lots and lots of blood. Every time some of them pass the bus, people hiss in their breath and say things.

"Oh, dear. Just look at that. I hope they get him to hospital really fast. They need to stop all that bleeding."

Another soldier. "The poor devil. That arm must really be smashed up. I can see it's really hurting him."

And another soldier. "I can't believe this. They just keep coming. Aren't there any ambulances?"

And yet another soldier. "Oh, that's the worst so far. I don't think I can look any more. They're all so young, too. They're in the army for the war, and then this happens. In their own country, too."

After there are no more soldiers coming down the hill, my father says, "OK. We'd better go ahead and have our grub right now. Time's getting on. There's no knowing when the road's going to be clear."

I like this idea of having a picnic on a bus. That's different. But first…

"Daddy, I need to piddle."

"Now that's not a bad idea. I was thinking the same thing. Come on then."

I'm pleased that he's not cross about this, and I'm pleased I can get off the bus at last. He finds a hole in the hedge beside the road. We wiggle through. Then he finds us a spot, and we both go at the same time, standing up next to each other. Before we can go back to the bus, other men come through the hedge and do the same thing. A bit later, after the men have all come back on the bus, some women do what the men did. No one can see them behind the hedge. My mother and my sister go with them. I don't pay much attention because I'm eating my sandwich, but I do know they're not standing up to go. Girls can't do that.

I watch to see if there's any more soldiers, but no more come down the hill. Just after we finish our lunch, the cars in front start moving. The bus driver climbs up and starts the engine. Slowly, we move up the hill. And there's the lorry. Still on its side. You can see the whole underneath. But there's no soldiers. I heard someone on the bus say there were dead ones. Where did they go? Anyway, I didn't want to see any dead soldiers. I'm not disappointed at all. Instead, what I see is a big breakdown lorry. It must have used its crane to pull the army lorry so it wouldn't be on our side of the road any more.

At last we get to Danbury village, but we don't stay long. We walk around for a little while. My father says we have to "stretch our legs". Then we get on another bus to go home. There's a policeman making traffic take turns coming up the hill or going down the hill.

My mother says, "Thank goodness we don't have to wait so long this time. And have you noticed? It's starting to get dark. This is going to be a long day."

We pass the army lorry one last time. The bus back to Chelmsford seems to take forever. I keep asking when we'll be home. My sister, she just falls asleep. She's always doing that. We get off the bus at the end of Baddow Road. Then we cross over to the Regent cinema to catch the bus to the bottom of Finchley Avenue.

After that, I never saw any more wounded soldiers, but I'll never forget the ones on Danbury Hill. Sometimes, I even have bad dreams about them, but I never talk about that. After all, I was told not to look.

On another day, my father and mother ask me to come into their bedroom. They're not smiling, so I get a bit scared. Last time they did this was when I took that silver half-crown off my father's dresser. I just liked it. I thought he'd never notice because he has lots of money, but he did. They didn't yell at me. That's because I think they thought it was such a bad thing I'd done. They both said things to me about how I mustn't steal. Then they made me promise never ever to do something like that again.

So, this time in their bedroom is scary. Before, I knew it was going to be about the half-crown. But on this morning, I can't think what I've done wrong. They make me sit on the side of the bed and they are standing in front of me.

My father says, "Well now, your mother and I have something to say to you. So listen carefully. We think you're old enough to sleep upstairs at night. You've got your own room and your own bed, but you have to promise us one thing. The first sound of the siren, you have to get yourself downstairs and into the shelter with your sister. No waiting for us. You have to do this on your own. What do you think?"

What do I think? I can't think of anything that's happened as good as this. I'm very excited, and I jump off the side of the bed. They start smiling when I say "Yes," but then they make me say "I promise". Now I feel grown up. I just know I'm going to hear the siren before they do. Perhaps I won't go to sleep. That way, I'm sure to be the first down. I'll be there before they're even out of bed. My sister's still going to be in the shelter. She's two years younger than me. She's not going to be upstairs at night for a long time.

One day, my mother and father tell us that there's going to be a baby. When I ask where it's coming from, they keep talking about storks. I think they're making some kind of joke. They keep smiling, but I just don't understand it. Later, my mother says it's in her tummy, but I don't understand that either. Then she tells me that to have the baby she's going to stay in the big house in Danbury Park. She says all the mothers go there to get their babies. She says the nurses are nice, but she doesn't like Lady Muck. That's the person whose house it is. This Lady Muck comes round and shows off in her fancy clothes when she's going out to a do.

"Who does she think she is? And where does she get those clothes. You can bet she doesn't have to worry about rationing. I have to scrape and scrimp to get enough coupons. I just can't believe what goes on."

I think a baby will be OK, but the best thing is that I'm going to sleep at my Gran and Granddad's house when it comes. My

Granddad has a grocery shop on the High Street. It's big. On one side, there's cheese and meat and sausages, and things like that. And on the other side, you get sugar and flour, and other stuff. The best thing is that when you pay for something, the money goes in a round glass box and flies along a wire to a little office where there's a woman who does the money. Then she pulls a handle, and your change comes flying back in the same glass box. I always like watching these glass things flying across the ceiling. Once the cheese man lifted me up and let me pull the handle so he could send money to the office. But that was when Granddad was in the cellar getting something. He wouldn't allow me to do things in the shop. He was always very strict, and he didn't smile much. My mother was always complaining about him.

"You'd think he could help his own family out a bit," she would say. "All that food. He could let us have a little bit of something from time to time. Anyone else would. But no, only what you can get with your coupons. He doesn't even give his own wife anything."

But Gran is not like that. She's always laughing and joking. I know she sometimes steals stuff out of the shop when my Granddad isn't looking. Then she gives it to my mother to hide in her handbag. "Mum's the word," she always says. That means "Don't tell Granddad."

Gran and Granddad live upstairs over the shop. Where they live is much bigger than our house. They have a huge kitchen with a long wooden table. Once Gran chased me round that table with a dead rabbit. Other times she makes me a toy. She puts the lid on an empty tin can and makes a hole in the top and bottom. Then she puts string through it. When she ties the ends of the string, I can pull the tin around. Sometimes I pretend it's a lorry, and sometimes it's a train. My mother always complains it's too noisy, but Gran just laughs and lets me carry on.

"Just remember, I had four boys," she says. "You get used to it. Besides, he'll be grown up soon enough. Then you'll really have things to worry about. Let him have his fun while he's got the chance."

Sometimes, Gran also lets me help make biscuits. She makes a whole lot of round ones, but she gives me some dough so I can make a big one in the shape of a man. She gives me raisins to make buttons for the man's coat. When everything comes out of the oven, she makes me wait till my special biscuit's not too hot. Then I can eat it. I like to eat the head first, and I always save the raisins till last.

My favourite time when I go to Gran and Granddad's house is when two uncles come back from the war to visit. I like my Uncle Eric. He's in the Navy and he has a beard. He smokes cigarettes. All the time. Once he let me hold a packet of his cigarettes. It had a picture of a sailor. The sailor had a blue uniform and a blue hat. I liked it because the sailor had a beard just like Uncle Eric's. I think that maybe all sailors have beards like that. In the picture there was also the sea and some ships, so you could tell that the man in the picture was a sailor.

Sometimes, I ask Uncle Eric about his ship, but every time he just laughs.

"No, there's no ship. I stay away from ships and water. Best to keep out of all that when there's a war on, you know. I've got a nice office, good grub, and I can come home sometimes like this. Those poor devils out at sea, it can be tough for them. That's no life for me."

I think he's having a joke with me. I'm sure he has a ship, and I can't understand why he won't tell me about it. How can you be a sailor if you don't go on the sea in a ship?

Then there's my Uncle Jack. He doesn't come very often, and I never see his uniform. Everyone gets excited when he's coming. He's lots of fun, and he likes to play with my sister and me. What I like best is when he throws me up in the air and then catches me. He'll do that over and over, and all the time he's laughing. I think he's in the army, but when I ask him if he's been fighting, he shakes his head. "No, no. I don't do that. I work on a farm. That way we'll all have food to eat."

He doesn't smile any more when he says this, so I stop asking him those sorts of questions. Besides, my mother says there's no need for me to keep on so. That's how I learned to stop asking him. But I do know there aren't any horses on the farm where he works.

Anyway, when my mother is away getting the baby and I'm with Gran, there are no uncles visiting. What's really good is I have my own bedroom while I'm staying here. Through the window you can see the High Street and the bottom of London Road. There's lots of cars and lorries and buses all day long. There's much more to see than on Finchley Avenue. Gran lets me look out of the window while she's cooking and doing other stuff. When it's Sunday, the High Street is not so busy, but I still like looking out of the window.

That night, Gran says I can stay up late. After I've had my food and cleaned my teeth – she's strict about that - she stays with me by the window. She says she has a treat for me. I soon find out what it is. She tells me to look up the High Street and listen hard. Then I see the Shire Hall. But also there's a band there, right in front of the Shire Hall. The band's playing music, and you can hear it if you listen hard, like she said. Gran tells me it's the Salvation Army. I didn't know about this army, and I didn't know soldiers could be in a band.

After a bit, they get in lines, and they march down the street. They're going to come right past us. When they come down the street, the music gets louder and louder. Even better is that they're still playing music right under our window. I see all kinds of trumpets, and there's a big drum right in the middle. I like the drum best. That's what I want to play when I'm old enough. Gran says they're marching to their place on Moulsham Street. I like the music, but I don't like their uniforms. They're not like the uniforms other soldiers have. I ask Gran when the Salvation Army is going to fight somewhere. She laughs.

"Well, they're not like the other soldiers. Didn't you see? They're all too old to fight. But they call themselves Christian soldiers. It's a different war they're fighting. You'll understand one day. Meanwhile, it's your bedtime. Into bed with you."

And that's the end. I'm sorry I can't stay at the window any more, but I'm not too upset. You can't see the band any more, and you can't hear the music. When Gran has drawn the curtains, it's dark in the room, and it's quiet outside. Never mind. I can still hear the music in my head. She's like that. She always has treats for me.

When I come back from Gran's, my mother and father are excited. They want to know if I behaved myself, and I tell them how I got to stay up late to watch the band. I don't tell them how yesterday I wanted to come home and Gran said I had to wait one more day till the baby was there. I cried a bit, but she gave me a saucepan and a wooden spoon to make a big drum with. I made a lot of noise, but she didn't care. Soon I didn't mind if there was one more day.

"Right," says my father, "your Gran says you had a good time and that you didn't miss us too much." I nod, and he seems pleased with that. "OK, so now, how would you like to see that new sister of yours? Come on, she's upstairs. But don't make any noise. She's just gone to sleep."

So upstairs we go – my mother, my father, and me. My older sister is still away with Nana, so I'm going to see the baby before she does. That's good. But just as I'm feeling excited and pleased about the baby, something bad happens. Right at the top of the stairs, my father opens the door to my room. I'm expecting to go into my sister's room. Instead, he's making us tiptoe into my room. Then, right away, I get very very upset. Everything's all wrong. My bed's gone, and the baby's cradle is standing there in the middle of the room. I don't even look at the baby. How could they do this to my room? Where have they put my bed? Why is the baby in my room? And where am I going to sleep?

I start to make a lot of noise. I can't help it, and I don't care if the baby wakes up. It's worse than that time when I went out in the garden to see my other sister in her pram. She wasn't a baby any more. She was sitting there in the pram with my favourite wooden lorry on her lap. Who gave her that? It wasn't hers, and I wanted it back. I made a lot of noise then. I can still remember what it was like. That time with the lorry, my father said, "Now, now, you've got to learn to share. Just let her have it for this little while. Then you can have it back. You're going to have to learn how to be a nice kind big brother."

So here with the new baby, they're messing things up again. Then they get me out from where the baby is, and they take me into my sister's room. Now I see they've put my bed there. Before I can start making a noise about that, my father puts his hands on my shoulders and makes me look right in his face.

"All right, now just stop the blubbering," he says. "I see we should've told you first about moving things around. Just calm down and listen to me carefully. You're going to sleep here in your sister's room, but only for a few days. Just until the baby gets used to the cradle and your mother gets some rest. Then the baby's coming in here, and we'll move your bed back. How does that sound?"

Well, this seems all right. As long as I get my room back soon.

While my father's talking to me, my mother's just standing there. I think she's upset. Maybe she thinks I don't want another sister. But that's not true. I stop crying. When she holds my hand, I let her do it. Then I look up at her face and I say, "Can we see the baby now?"

Both of them are smiling now, and they take me back to my room to see the baby. I keep quiet this time. I creep up to the side of the cradle and look in. The baby's still asleep. Even though I was so loud, it didn't wake up. I see that it's very small, and it's got black hair. A bit like mine. Now I feel pleased that I'm going to have another sister. I'm also pleased that she's in my room. As long as it's not for long.

With her black hair, she's not like my other sister, who's very fair. That's what my mother always says. When I say her hair is yellow, my mother says "No, it's blond." I still think it's yellow, and that's what I keep saying.

I think my sister with the yellow hair is pretty. When we meet people, they always look at her and say she's pretty. Sometimes they hardly notice me. Once, on Duke Street near the railway station, my mother was pushing my sister in the pram. That was before my other sister was born. Suddenly, some soldiers came and stood round the pram. They started laughing and saying nice things about my sister. Then two of them started talking to my mother. They were saying things I didn't understand. She got angry, and her face got red. She also started bashing the pram into the soldier that was standing in front of the pram and stopping us. After that, she yelled at them and said some bad words, just like my father sometimes does.

"Sod off, the lot of you. I thought you came over here to fight the bloody war. Look at you. You look like you're drunk. Get out of my damn way, else I'm going to get someone to call a policeman. Go on, let me through."

She goes on like that, and when she gives one more big push, they stop getting in the way.

When my Nana comes up for tea in the afternoon, my mother tells her all about it.

"Those bloody yanks. I don't know what they're doing here. They're drunk half the time. Then they go on like this. Doesn't matter if you have kids with you. Doesn't matter if you've got a ring on. I know it's gotta be hard for some of them, being away from home so long. But I must say, that's no excuse for behaving like that. You'd think I was a…"

I don't know what word she's going to say. She doesn't say it. That's because I'm there. I'm disappointed because I'm sure it's going to be like some of the bad words my father uses. I know a whole lot of those words, like "bloody", "bugger", "damn", "sod", and "shit". I'm not allowed to say them. They're grown-up words. I know this because one day when my mother and father are there, I said, "Daddy, do you know what you are?"

"No. Go on. Tell me."

"You're a bugger."

When I say that, they both laugh. They laugh for a long time and ever so loud. I never expected them to laugh like that. I didn't know it was going to be funny. But my mother can hardly stop laughing.

Then suddenly the laughing's over. They both start to look a bit cross, and my father's telling me I mustn't say such words. He tells me sometimes grown-ups say words like that but I'll get a clip around the ear if he hears me say one. This isn't fair. I just know it isn't. Why can't I say those words? And anyway, why did they laugh so much? Lots of times, they tell other people what I said, and they always laugh too. So it's not fair if he gives me a smack for doing something that's funny.

Anyway, when my mother said all those words to the soldiers, I could tell she was really cross. Before, I'd only heard her say "shit" a few times, mostly when she dropped something or when the wind blew things off the washing line in the garden. Stuff like that. I think she hates Yank soldiers now. I know she often talks about "damn Yanks" even though they said nice things about my sister.

I don't hate them. I think I like all soldiers. Of course, I suppose I hate German ones, but I've never seen any.

When I'm big enough and have two sisters, I do something with just me and my father. On Saturday afternoons, he takes me to the library. It's a long way, but we only get the bus when we're coming back. We walk up to New London Road and keep walking a little bit up Writtle Road but not as far as Crompton's, which is just over the railway bridge. Instead, we go down Bridge Street. All the way we play this game. We look for new places where there's been a bomb. When we first turn the corner at the top of Bridge Street, there's a big space where houses used to be, but that doesn't count because it was like that before. Only new spaces count. Often there's no new space, so I'm a bit disappointed. Sometimes, even when I do find a new space, my father won't let me count it. He says it was there before. He's very strict like that. He always decides. It doesn't matter what I say. I think maybe two times I find a new space, and he lets me count it.

Two other things I like about our walks to the Library. One is that if we are lucky, a train will come past. If it comes the same way as we're walking, I know it's coming from London to Chelmsford. The other way it's come from the station, and it's going to London. I'd like to go on a train one day. I'd like to go to London. That's where Uncle Alf works. He comes nearly every week to our house to play his violin with my father. He rides on the train straight from work, and we don't eat till he comes. But sometimes he's late, so my mother lets us eat and saves food for Uncle Alf. Every time he comes, my father and mother always ask him the same questions.

"So how was it this week? We heard the East End got it really bad. Was your place OK? What about the trains? Were they fixing the railway tracks? It seems like every time they fix them, they get bombed all over again. We just don't know how you stand it." That's how I learned that London was getting even more bombs than us.

The other thing I like about the walk to the Library is that after Bridge Street there's lots of other interesting things to see. First we come to the River and the Rec. Most times we see swans and ducks there. Then after that we walk close to where the guns are, the ones where my father is at night. Then we walk under the railway bridge, past the bus station and into the Library.

The Library is very big, and it smells funny. That's the books. My father takes me through this special gate to where all the books are. He takes me to where there are lots of books with pictures in them. I sit on the floor, and he gives me some of them to look at. Then he leaves me there while he goes to choose some books to take home for him and my mother to read. I think they're mostly for him to read, because I hardly ever see my mother reading one. I can't read yet, but I'm going to learn soon when I go to nursery school. My father says that when I can read, I will be able to take books home from the library like he does. He says there's a special place in the Library where there are lots of books just for children.

After the Library, we get the bus home. My mother always wants to know if I'm tired and if I want something to eat. Often she says to my father, "He looks really tired. You know, I think it's a bit too much for the boy. That's a long walk for someone his age."

"Nonsense," my father says. "He does really well. He's pretty tough. When he gets older, he's going to be walking me off my feet. You'll see."

I feel good when my father talks about me like that. When he asks me in front of my mother if the walk is too far for me, I say "No". I say that even though sometimes it does feel too far and I wish my father would carry me, like he sometimes used to on long walks.

Soon after my baby sister has had her first birthday, I learn about buzzbombs – Nana always calls them doodlebugs. People keep explaining to me that they're a bit like small planes. They make a buzzing sound. When you hear one, you have to listen carefully. If you can see it and it keeps buzzing across the sky, that's all right. If the buzzing stops, don't try and look up to see it any more. Run inside fast and get into the shelter.

I see a buzzbomb two different times when I'm in the garden. Each one keeps on going, so I don't find that very exciting. But on a different day, there's one that suddenly stops buzzing. I run into the house and yell to my mother to bring my sisters into the shelter right away. After we're all there, I keep waiting to hear the bomb go off, but nothing happens. Everything stays quiet, and there are no sirens. I'm worried that my mother thinks I've made it all up, but she never says anything. Even when my father comes home, she doesn't say anything. So, I just keep quiet about it, but I know it really was a buzzbomb and that its engine stopped. I know what I did was the right thing, even if nobody believed me.

One day - this is very exciting - my father gets everyone in the bedroom. That's the front bedroom where he and my mother sleep. It's early in the morning and I'm not dressed yet, but he is. He's wearing the same green jumper that he always wears. I think he's only got this one jumper. It's something my mother knitted for him. I can tell it's going to be something important that he's got to say, but I'm not worried because he looks very pleased about it. Then,

"All right. Here it is. I... just... heard... on... the... wireless. HITLER'S DEAD!"

Of course, I know who Hitler is. He's the one who started the war, and he's the one who sent all the planes to bomb us. He's really bad. I saw a picture of his face once. You could tell he was really bad and ugly. Also, people were always talking about the bad things he did. If they thought I couldn't hear, they'd use bad words about him and say "That bastard Hitler," or, "That damn Hitler, maybe the sod'll get what's coming to him." Well, now he's dead, and I can tell my father's really pleased.

"Maybe we'll get some peace and quiet now," he says. "The war's going to be over very soon, you can be sure of that. This'll be a day for you to remember when you grow up. You'll see. Just think of all the suffering that he's caused. And for what? All those people dead. And it's not just our people either. I'm sure most of those Germans had families just like us."

He keeps on like that, but the rest of us start to get fidgety. Even my mother. I want to have breakfast now. But I don't mind if he keeps talking for a little bit longer. That's because I can see that he's very happy that Hitler's dead. Often, he's so serious, or he's cross about something. So it's good when he's like this. Of course, I like it best when he's laughing or joking and especially when he plays with us. But this is still good.

CHAPTER TWO

A PASSION FOR READING

With the war over, I go to nursery school. That's when I start to learn reading. Every morning, my mother takes me to the end of the street and puts me on the bus. She tells the bus conductor where I'm going, and then she goes home. When we get to the bottom of Moulsham Street, I get off. My Nana's there to meet me and to take me to the door of the nursery school. I don't like this place very much. It smells.

Later, I go to a different nursery school. It's on London Road, much closer to our house. I like this school better, but it's a bit scary. Everyone has a desk and we learn reading and writing. I also start arithmetic. The teacher's quite strict, but she's also kind if you make mistakes. My mother walks with me to this school and is there to take me home in the afternoon. I could do it all on my own, but my mother doesn't think so.

"London Road's far too busy, and Moulsham Street can be busy too. You know, there was an accident on London Road a few weeks ago. I'm afraid you just can't be too careful."

Maybe she's right, so I only argue a little about this. Besides, after a whole day at the nursery school, I get quite excited to see my mother when school is over.

Then comes the time when I go to Moulsham School, first in the Infant School, and then in the Junior Boys. On the first day, my mother takes me. I'm scared but I don't cry, even when she leaves me. Some of the other new kids do cry and the teachers have to tell their mothers to leave. One kid even wets himself, but the teacher helps him put on some spare clothes that she has. She doesn't get cross at all. When we see this, we realise that this teacher is going to be nice to us.

All the time, I get better and better at reading and writing. By the time I'm in Mr. Hymas's class in the Junior Boys' school, I've read all the Enid Blyton books, all the Biggles books, and most of the William books. I've also read quite a few books by Alison Uttley. My father keeps urging me to read other things that are more grown up. I know he's right, but it's hard to find things. I keep looking at the books at home like *Crime and Punishment* and *Germinal* but they're a bit hard, although I know I'll be able to read them soon. There are also books by Howard Spring and H. E. Bates that my father gets from the library, but I don't find them very exciting.

At school, Mr. Petchey, who's the headmaster, comes to our classroom on Friday afternoons and tells us stories from books. Everyone is very excited when he comes because he makes the stories sound as though everything is happening just as he describes it. He tells us the story of *Treasure Island*. We like this a lot. When we're in the playground we all pretend to be Long John Silver. We hop around as though we've only got one leg, and we make squawking sounds to imitate the pirate's parrot. Like Silver and the sailors on the *Hispaniola*, we can sing "Fifteen men on the dead man's chest, yo ho ho and a bottle of rum!" We also pretend to be the parrot and squawk out "Pieces of eight! Pieces of eight!"

When I get the book out of the library, I'm very disappointed, because I find it quite hard to read. It's by Robert Louis Stevenson, and he also wrote *Kidnapped*. We have that at home because my father got it as a prize when he was at school. But *Kidnapped* is even harder to read than *Treasure Island*.

Another time at school, we have a mystery story, John Buchan's *The Thirty-Nine Steps*. This is quite complicated, but near the end, it gets really exciting. Richard Hannay has been hiding because people think he's a murderer. But Hannay helps capture a German spy and so stops important information getting to the Germans. The First World War starts, but Hannay is now a hero because of what he has done. Mr. Petchey was in the First World War, so he gets all worked up about this.

Mr. Petchey also tells us the story of *Pilgrim's Progress*. Poor Christian, he has this long journey, and he has to carry this heavy burden. He makes all kinds of mistakes, like when he falls into the Slough of Despond or when he takes the wrong path and is captured by Giant Despair. But in the end, after all his sufferings and all his adventures, he gets to the Celestial City. We have this book at home, and my father says I can read it (or anything else that's on the sitting room shelves). I look at it, but it seems hard, and the pictures are boring, not like the pictures I have in my head when Mr. Petchey tells the story.

Better than *Pilgrim's Progress* is *A Christmas Carol* by Charles Dickens. We all think that Mr. Scrooge is a horrible man, At first he hates Christmas, and calls everything "humbug". We like this word and the way Mr. Petchey says it, and we later go around saying "Bah humbug!" about everything we don't like. Scrooge (his first name is Ebenezer) is very mean to Bob Cratchit, who works for him but hardly gets any holidays. Nor does he get paid very much. Then Scrooge sees Jacob Marley's ghost and the ghosts of Christmas Past, Present, and To Come. You can tell how he gets scared and sees how bad he's been. That's when he changes from being mean and a miser. Instead of saying Christmas is humbug, he sends a big turkey to Bob Cratchit's house for Christmas dinner. When he does that, we all cheer and bang our desks. Then Mr. Petchey has to make us quieten down so we don't disturb the class next door.

My parents have *A Christmas Carol* at home, so I read it. More than once. Mr. Petchey has left some bits out, but that doesn't matter. When he tells us the story, it's like Bob Cratchit, Mr. Scrooge and Tiny Tim are all in the room with us. Even when Tiny Tim dies, he's sort of there because his crutch is still in the corner. That's the sad part. But when Mr. Scrooge changes, we find out that Tiny Tim has not died after all. This was confusing at first until Mr. Petchey explained everything.

Because I like *A Christmas Carol*, someone gives me *Oliver Twist*, and Aunty D gives me *David Copperfield*. That's a fat book, but she says I can read the first part about David's life and leave the rest for another time. Besides, it's *Oliver Twist* that I really like and I read it twice. It's quite scary in places when you read about Mr. Bumble, Fagin, and Bill Sikes. The worst part is when Nancy is murdered. I have a bad nightmare about that, only it's not Nancy that's being murdered, it's me. I don't see the murderer, just his shadow on my wall. I have this dream several times, but that doesn't stop me reading.

Aunty D lives on Rothesay Avenue. It's the next street to ours, and we can walk there without a grownup, even when we're quite small. She always has special biscuits or sweets for us, and she's always asking me about reading. One day, she tells me that she's going to get *Alice in Wonderland* for me, but I'll have to wait because she wants a copy that has the proper pictures in it. When it comes, I sit and look at it for a long time in her kitchen. I like the songs and poems best, and I'm glad she made me wait for the pictures, especially the Cheshire Cat up in the tree, the Mad Hatter at the tea party, the Caterpillar with his hookah, and the Queen of Hearts.

The next time we go to Grandma's house, I take *Alice in Wonderland* with me to show Uncle Jack. When the war finished, he stayed on in Grandma's house. Then Granddad retired and didn't have the shop any more, so they all three moved to a house on Galleywood Road. We go there nearly every other Sunday, walking up Longstomps Avenue and along Galleywood Road. Next to the house are allotments, and Granddad has a big one where he can grow all kinds of vegetables. I hear my father and uncles talking about him. They call him "the old man," but I'm not allowed to use that name. I have to say "Granddad".

"What's the old man been up to?"

"Well, he's been working on the garden and putting in potatoes in the allotment."

"I can see that's going to be a godsend. He just needs something to keep him busy and to keep him out of Mum's hair."

"Too bad he doesn't read or anything. The old man's never had any interest in that sort of thing."

In the house on Galleywood Road, Uncle Jack has his own room, and we spend a lot of time in there. We have to sit on his bed because the rest of the room is mostly books. He lets us look at books with pictures of paintings. Sometimes we giggle at these, because there are people without clothes. Then he tells us to stop being silly. We have to learn to appreciate beauty and art. I try to understand what he means, but sometimes it's hard not to giggle just a bit.

Always he reads to us, mostly poetry. If my sisters aren't there, he reads me some of *Masterman Ready*. But poetry is our favourite, especially one poem - "Macavity the Mystery Cat." Usually, we make him read this more than once, and we like to join in because we've learnt some of it by heart, just from listening to him. Even when we're not in his room, if someone can't find something, we'll say "Macavity's not there." When I show him *Alice in Wonderland*, he gets quite excited and starts reading some of the poems to us.

> *"You are old, Father William," the young man said,*
> *"And your hair has become very white;*
> *And yet you incessantly stand on your head—*
> *Do you think, at your age, it is right?"*
>
> *"In my youth," Father William replied to his son,*
> *"I feared it might injure the brain;*
> *But, now that I'm perfectly sure I have none,*

Why, I do it again and again."

Or

"Will you walk a little faster?" said a whiting to a snail.
"There's a porpoise close behind us, and he's treading on my tail.

See how eagerly the lobsters and the turtles all advance!
They are waiting on the shingle—will you come and join the dance?

Will you, won't you, will you, won't you, will you join the dance?
Will you, won't you, will you, won't you, won't you join the dance?"
Or

Beautiful Soup, so rich and green,
Waiting in a hot tureen!
Who for such dainties would not stoop?
Soup of the evening, beautiful Soup!
Soup of the evening, beautiful Soup!
Beau—ootiful Soo—oop!
Beau—ootiful Soo—oop!
Soo—oop of the e—e—evening,
Beautiful, beautiful Soup!

After a few more visits to Uncle Jack, we know some of these poems from memory, too.

Uncle Jack used to be a boy scout. When I join the Cubs, he likes me to tell him all the things we do. He also teaches me how to tie different knots. I can do a reef knot, and then he shows me a quick way to untie it. He also teaches me to tie a bowline (you need that to rescue someone from a fire), a slipknot, a clove hitch, and a sheepshank. He has a copy of Lord Baden Powell's *Scouting for Boys*. He had this when he was a scout. It has all kinds of pictures and all kinds of information about what a scout needs to know. I spend a lot of time in Uncle Jack's room reading this book. There are pictures of knots, and Uncle Jack gives me some very thick string so that I can practise tying them. I also read about finding the Pole Star, where north is. How to use a compass (someone gives me one). How to read a map. What Morse Code (I know how to do SOS) and what Semaphore is. How to build a fire. How to build a shelter. How to safely chop down a tree. How to make a toothbrush. How to carry someone who can't walk.

Granddad and Grandma don't seem to have any books, but Gran has interesting magazines with pictures. Every time we go there, she leaves out some copies of *Punch* for me. Mostly, I look at the cartoons. Some of them are really funny, and some I don't get at all, even when she tries to explain them. She also has *Country Life* Magazine. It has lots of pictures. My father makes jokes about this magazine because it's mostly about people with lots of money and people with titles like Lord and Lady or Duke and Duchess. It's the same with another magazine she has – *The Tatler*. Gran just ignores him when he teases about her magazines, and I can tell that anything he says won't make any difference.

Nana's house on Rochford Road is very different. Every time we go there we step off the street right into her parlour, because she has no front garden like Gran's on Galleywood Road. Nana only uses the parlour on Christmas Day and Boxing Day, as far as I can tell. We have to make sure our shoes are clean, and then we go through to the main room where there's a table and chairs, and a settee. There's a fireplace, too, that's also a stove where she cooks. On the wall next to the table is a big picture of Queen Victoria that my father's always teasing her about. But like Gran, Nana takes no notice of him.

Each time we go through the parlour, I see a pile of three or four small black books on her sideboard, but she won't let me touch them or look at them. They're for when she goes to church. She goes to St. John's Church on Moulsham Street. One day she sees me looking at her books (just looking, not touching), and she says, "When I'm gone, you shall have those." She says this in a very serious voice, so the books become even more important to me, even though I don't know what they're about. Whenever I remind her about her promise, she gets cross with me. "I told you, didn't I? Just stop pestering me. I don't want to hear any more about it. There's plenty of other books for you to read in your own home."

She's right about that. Books are very important in our house. It's not just books. It's newspapers and magazines. The main one is the *Times*. It comes Monday to Saturday, but *Reynolds News*, the *Listener*, and the *New Statesman* come only once a week. Oh, and there's the *Radio Times*, also once a week. My father reads them all, but my mother only reads *Reynolds News*, even though she says she reads the others. I don't read any of those newspapers, but I do read *The Children's Newspaper*, which comes every week. This has news, history, science, geography, stories, and poems. When I start getting my own newspaper, I feel a bit like a grownup. I sit on the settee in the sitting room and read it all the way through, just like my father reads the *Times* when he's sitting in his chair. I also read the *Eagle*. This is a comic, and it is far better than any of the other comics I have read. I got it the very first time it came out. Every week after that, I never miss a copy, and I save every one, in spite of what my mother says about keeping the house tidy. I especially like the adventures of Dan Dare, Pilot of the Future, and his enemy, the Mekon. Of course, my father doesn't like me reading the *Eagle*. He doesn't like any comics. He says, "If you want to read it, that's up to you. But don't expect me to pay for it. You'll have to use your pocket money for that."

And that's what I do. I get half-a-crown a week for pocket money. It's never enough, but I learn to save up for things, mostly stamps for my stamp collection. The best place to buy stamps is the "Junk Shop" in the street down beside the Shire Hall. Often my mother gives me extra money, especially if I want to go to the pictures or if I want to buy a book. I'm not supposed to tell my father about this.

My father's always asking visitors what they read. I don't think he likes people who don't read. After the war, when babysitters come to the house, he asks them questions about politics and about reading, and he's always got books ready for them. He likes them to read parts of *The Intelligent Woman's Guide to Socialism and Capitalism*. That's by George Bernard Shaw. He tells them he's going to give them a test when he gets back, but I think he's just teasing. The babysitters all seem to be from the convent school, which is strange, because that means they're Catholics. I thought he hated Catholics even more than other kinds of church people. Anyway, one girl tells him she does not have time to read his books; she has homework to do. She's very clear about that, and instead of getting cross, he just laughs. She becomes his favorite babysitter, and he never bothers her with books again.

One wall of our sitting room is all bookcases. Most of the books are too hard, or they're just boring, but there are some I do read: H. G. Wells's *The War of the Worlds* and his *Short History of the World*. My father really likes this writer, so he's pleased when I say I like him too. There's also George Eliot's *Silas Marner*. This was one of Mr. Petchey's stories, and that helps me understand what happens in the book. After reading this, I really see what being a miser is like and how money is not as important as things like caring for and loving other people. Silas learns this, just like Scrooge.

On the shelves at home, there's also a copy of the *Ingolsby Legends*. This has a lot of poetry. My father often reads to us from this. When he's not home, I read bits to myself, but I can't make it sound like he does.

The fire-flash shines from Reculver cliff,
And the answering light burns blue in the skiff,
And there they stand,
    That smuggling band,
    Some in the water and some on the sand,
    Ready those contraband goods to land:
    The night is dark, they are silent and still,
    At the head of the party is Smuggler Bill!

That's from "Smuggler's Leap."

I sing of a Shirt that never was new!!
In the course of the year Eighteen hundred and two,
Aunt Fanny began
Upon Grandmamma's plan,
To make one for me, then her 'dear little man.'
— At the epoch I speak about, I was between
A man and a boy,
A hobble-de-hoy,
A fat, little, punchy concern of sixteen,
—Just beginning to flirt,
And ogle,— so pert,
I'd been whipt every day had I had my desert,
— And Aunt Fan volunteer'd to make me a shirt!

And that's from *"Legend of a Shirt."*

There are a lot of books from the Left Book Club, most of them with soft orange covers. I can't find anything interesting among these, except one day I notice Hannah Stone's *A Marriage Manual: A Practical Guide-book to Sex and Marriage.* I start reading this, and I can't stop till I've finished. Over the next few weeks, I keep re-reading one part. This tells me all about sex and how it works. Before this, all I'd heard was from Ann Roberts. She's the eldest daughter of the Roberts family, who live a few doors away on Finchley Avenue. Mrs. Roberts (everyone calls her Jean Roberts) is a Labour Party person and my parents are big supporters of hers. They're also friends with her. I think she's a city councillor. I'm friends with Elizabeth, Ann's sister. She's younger than Ann and about the same age as me. Ann likes to boss us a bit, and one day when we're standing at their front gate, she says she knows how people have sex to make babies.

This sounds really interesting. Together with Elizabeth and some other kids about our age, I get up close around Ann to hear about this. When we're all quiet and listening carefully, she explains: "First, the man puts his thing into the woman and squirts some special stuff, and then she makes a baby that comes out of her from the same place where the man has been. You have to be married before you can do this."

When Ann tells us this, nobody believes her. It sounds daft, so we ignore her, which makes her really cross, and she stomps off. First, though, we have to promise not to tell anyone that she's told us this big secret. Of course, we promise, but I don't think anyone's going to talk about it anyway because what she told us is so stupid.

But now the book shows me that Ann was sort of right. The difference is how the man feels, and how the woman feels, and how the whole thing is supposed to take a whole lot of time. I can even feel some of those same feelings as the man when I read the description, and I think that's why I read it over and over. Of course, I don't speak to my father and mother about any of this, even though they keep saying that I can ask them about anything. I'm too embarrassed. Even so, I think they know I've been reading this book, because the pages in this section start to get worn. When you pick up the book, it sort of opens at this section. But fortunately they never say anything.

Everything about reading changes when my mother and father buy me *The Children's Encyclopaedia* by Arthur Mee. This comes in ten blue volumes. Volume Ten has indexes, and I soon learn how to find things. Each volume also has an index at the front, just for what's in that volume. There are about sixteen sections in each volume. For example, there's a story section, science sections, a history section, a Great Thoughts section, a biography section, a Bible section, a poetry section, an art section and a section on things to do and make. There are lots of pictures, too, some of them in colour. I spend huge amounts of time reading these volumes, and often I come back to the same things again and again. I really like the stories and poems, and I also learn so much. Even my father and mother learn things when they use the indexes to look up stuff they don't know.

Of course, there's plenty of reading at school, but it's not very interesting at all. I prefer what I read in Sunday School. I go to the Sunday School at the Congregational Church on Baddow Road. It's just behind Nana's house. Even though my father doesn't want me to, I still go. That's chiefly because the two old ladies who live opposite us have a big black car that comes to their house every Sunday to take them to church. They offer to take me and my sisters with them. I've hardly ever been in a car, so I say "Yes". My father's disappointed and talks about the claptrap in the church and how I'll soon grow out of it, but he lets me go.

When he's not there, my mother tells me that a long time ago, before I was born, she used to go to church with my father every Sunday. Then something happened, and one day he stood up and yelled out to the minister that what he was talking about was "bloody rot". He and my mother then walked out, right in the middle of the service, and they never went back.

In Sunday School, those of us who can do it get to read out loud the stories that come from the Bible. At the same time, the teacher holds up big pictures that go with the stories. We have Moses in the bulrushes, the Jews escaping from Egypt with the wicked Pharaoh chasing them, and Samson and the Philistines. Of course, there are plenty of stories about Jesus. We do stories about the miracles. I like best the miracle of the loaves and fishes, the one when Jesus heals the leper and the one when he walks on the water. Then, at Christmas, we have the story of the baby Jesus, his father and mother (Joseph and Mary), and the Three Wise Men who are also kings. But I already know this story from school, and there we even do a play about it with me as one of the Wise Men.

At Sunday School, we also read about the Last Supper, the Crucifixion and the Resurrection. The teacher has us draw pictures, and each time we leave to go home, she gives us a small card with a picture about what we've been reading. I collect these, although they're not as interesting to me as some of the cigarette cards that I also collect.

At the end of the year, just before the summer holidays start, the Sunday School has a prize day, and I get a certificate for good attendance. There are no prizes for reading, though. Otherwise, I think I would have got one.

Lastly, there are two other books that I read at home. The first is my dictionary. This is quite small, and you can even put it in your pocket if you want. I'm not sure who gave it to me – perhaps Aunty D. I read it a lot, sometimes to learn about new words that I've never heard about, and sometimes to find the meaning of a word that is in something I'm reading. My dictionary also has other things like abbreviations: A.D., B.A., B.S.A., C.I.D., F.R.A.M., H.M.S., L.C.C. and R.S.P.C.A. And there are weights and measures: ounces, pounds, stones, quarters, hundredweights, tons; and inches, feet, yards, poles, chains, furlongs, and miles. Also there's a list of capital cities: London, Paris, Milan, Madrid, Moscow, Helsinki, Cairo, etc.. When I can't find something in my dictionary, I go to my father and mother's dictionary. This is much bigger than mine and has lots of words mine doesn't have, but it's heavy and hard to hold, so I only use it when I have to. It seems to have every word you can think of, but it doesn't have some of the swear words I know. My father laughs when I tell him this. He says I don't need a dictionary if I already know these words. Still, I think they should be included.

There's also an atlas. This isn't really my book, but I'm the one who looks at it most. Together with my globe, I use it to see where countries are and who owns countries. All the countries that the British Empire owns are coloured red. In school, we learn about other countries in geography lessons. We learn about the different people who live there, what they eat, what their climate is like, what things they make to sell to us, what they wear, what their capital city is, and lots of other things. In the atlas, the main thing is the map of each country. Not only do you learn from it where each country is, but you can see how big each country is, where the chief cities are, and how far away it is from us.

The two countries that interest me most are Canada and Australia. In Canada, there are people that speak English and others that speak French. There are also lots of Indians. They have different languages and were there before white people came from

Europe. The Eskimos were also there before people came from Europe, and they also have their own language. Australia is very big, like Canada. It's south of the Equator, and is on the way to the South Pole. It's sort of the opposite of Canada that goes almost to the North Pole. In Australia there are white people who came from Europe, but there are also aborigines who were there before. Sometimes, I pretend I'm going on a voyage to Australia, and I try out different routes using the maps in the atlas. My favourite route is through the Suez Canal, although you can go another way, through the Panama Canal.

One day, I'm going to have as many books as my mother and father or as many as my Uncle Jack. Already, I have quite a few, and my mother keeps trying to get rid of the ones I got when I was quite young. She says that will give me room for new ones, but I don't want to do that. I want to keep them all, except for the really baby books. I do let her take those. Besides, sometimes I look at some of my old books, though I don't tell her about that. In the books I've read before, I sometimes find things I've forgotten. In this way, the books are like an extra memory that I have. It's like cigarette cards (especially the backs, which often have a lot of stuff to read) or stamps. Even though you've had something a long time, and even though you've looked at it often, when you look at it again, you often see things you hadn't noticed before. That's why I just know that books and reading are always going to be important to me.

CHAPTER THREE

MUSICAL BEGINNINGS

Even more important than books in our house is music. My father is a very good piano player, and my mother sings. That's how they met. Someone asked him to accompany her in a concert. That was before the war. I know that because they got married in 1937. From the time I can remember anything, there has been music in the house, especially at night or at weekends. Whenever I go to bed, there seems to be music. I'm so used to it that it never keeps me awake, whether it's my father on his own, or with someone else. By hearing music all the time, I soon get to know certain pieces and certain composers without even trying.

My father seems to have all of Bach's music, all of Mozart, all of Beethoven, and a lot by other composers. He likes to play Mozart especially, but when he's in a bad mood, there are certain pieces by Beethoven he plays. They can be very loud, and I don't like them very much. If I haven't yet gone to bed, my mother will say, "Just leave your father alone. He's had a bad day. You come out in the kitchen with me and let him get on with it." But when he's in a good mood, I sit on a chair next to him and watch his fingers.

At first I can't read the music, but after I'm seven and start to have piano lessons with Miss Clark, I begin to be able to read music. Then, I can see what he's doing when I look at his music as he's playing. One day he lets me turn the pages for him for a Mozart piece that isn't too hard to follow. After that, I get better and better at following the music, and he lets me turn the pages more and more often until it sort of becomes my job – well, up to my bedtime that is.

If my mother is singing, I prefer to watch her rather than turn pages. She doesn't sing very often, but if she does, it's usually if we have visitors or if she's going to be in a concert and needs to practise. Her favourite songs are by Roger Quilter, such as "Now Sleeps the Crimson Petal" and "The Fair House of Joy". She calls these her 'party pieces'. Every so often, my mother sings something from the *Messiah*, like "O thou that tellest good tidings to Zion," but never anything by Bach. She also does lots of other songs by composers like Schubert, Schumann, and Brahms. But often I don't know the composers of the songs she sings.

The singer she most likes is Kathleen Ferrier, and I've heard her say that they're both about the same age. Whenever this singer is on the wireless, we all go in the sitting room and listen. My mother's voice is not as low as Kathleen Ferrier's, but the two of them sing a lot of the same songs. Of course Kathleen Ferrier is famous. That's why she sings on the wireless, which my mother never does. And, of course, Kathleen Ferrier usually has an orchestra to accompany her. It's not really fair to compare them, but I think I still like my mother's voice best.

My mother also sings in the choir when there's a big concert in

Chelmsford Cathedral. At Christmas there is Handel's *Messiah*, and at Easter there's the *Saint Matthew Passion* by Bach. I don't go to these concerts, but I hear both these pieces at home at a different time on the wireless. They're very long, especially the *Matthew Passion*, but I like listening this way because I can follow along with my mother's copies. My favourite parts are the "Hallelujah" chorus in the *Messiah*. You have to wait a long time for that because it happens near the end. Another favourite is the first chorus in the *Passion*. When I see my mother's copy, I can't believe how complicated that first part is. There are two choirs and two orchestras, and there's also more singers needed to do what the music calls a "Choral". My father explains that in Chelmsford, the boys in the cathedral choir sing this. When I listen on the wireless to different people doing the *Passion*, I can hear that there are also boys singing the Choral.

Sometimes, it's a bit annoying when I listen to something I really like at a concert or on the wireless. I can't stop and listen over again, unlike books, where I can just go back as many times as I like. However, when we have copies of the music at home, I can sit down and read them and sort of hear the music in my head as many times as I want to. It gets really complicated when I try this with music like the *Saint Matthew Passion*, because there's not only the different choirs and orchestras, but there's the words to follow, too. I keep wondering about conductors. How do they manage to conduct every part at the same time?

The other singer in our lives is Aunty D. Her real name is Dorothy Cole, and she's not really an aunty. We just call her that because it's almost as if she's part of our family. She teaches singing and piano and is very well known in Chelmsford as a singer. My father often accompanies her when she's in a concert, and he does this when she is singing in competitions at the Corn Exchange. She's a very good singer and wins lots of certificates. My father practised with her when she was getting ready to try and become a Fellow at her music college in London. For the actual test, though, she paid for someone else to accompany her, someone quite famous, though I can't remember his name. I don't think my father minded. She was so anxious about this that she made him afraid that if he made a mistake, it would be his fault if she didn't pass. Anyway, she did fine. After that, she got the shiny metal notice at the front of her house that shows everyone what she has done. Sometimes she lets us clean the sign with some Brasso, and we like this because not many people we know have letters after their names.

Aunty D is a spiritualist and believes she can heal people just by touching them with her hands. As you would expect, my father thinks this is all rubbish, and he often says rude things about her when she's not there. My mother doesn't agree with him. She thinks there may be something in it. One day, when I have a headache and my father's at work, she invites Aunty D round for tea. Then, she asks her if she can do anything for me. Aunty D takes me upstairs to my mother and father's bedroom and closes the curtains. First she waits until everything is quiet. Then, she puts her hands very gently on my head and mumbles some words. She holds her hands there for quite a long time and then takes them away and asks me how I'm feeling. I'm not so sure there's any difference, and the headache isn't that bad, anyway. I really don't want her to be disappointed, so I say that the headache's nearly gone. When Aunty D and I come downstairs, she and my mother are very pleased, but my mother tells me not to say anything to my father.

It is Aunty D who gives me my first music score, Beethoven's first symphony. I think this is the first book where I write my name at the front. I use green ink. Aunty D uses purple ink, and I want to be different from everyone else, too. Later, I get other Penguin music scores, including Beethoven's Symphony number 2 and the Symphony number 3, the Eroica. It's my sister Celia who gives me the Eroica. I don't have Symphony number 6, the Pastoral, and I'm sorry about that. When the London Philharmonic Orchestra came to Chelmsford, my parents took me to the concert, which was in the Regent, the same place where I saw *Oliver Twist*. The conductor was Sir Adrian Boult, and I really liked watching him. The main piece was the Pastoral Symphony. I'd already heard it before, because I recognized the storm part and the cuckoo calls. Perhaps there'll be a Penguin score one of these days.

Even more than the Pastoral Symphony, I like Symphony number 5. This is more exciting. I have a badge that I wear all the time, and it has the first four notes of the symphony and a big letter "V". I didn't really understand why there was a badge like this, but one of the teachers at school said that the first four notes of the Symphony in Morse code (three short notes and one long note) made the letter "V". In the war, the English wireless programs for people listening in other countries always began with a drum tapping out this letter "V" for victory. That's why I like the badge so much. It's not just about Beethoven, it's about victory in the war. Even though I don't have a score of this symphony by Beethoven, my father does, so I'm not so anxious waiting for it to appear with other Penguin scores in W. H. Smith's.

Each year in the summer at the Promenade Concerts in London, they play all of Beethoven's symphonies, a different one each Friday night. These concerts are on the wireless, and I always listen. I go into the sitting room where the wireless is, and I try and pretend that I am in the Albert Hall with the audience there. The announcer explains what's going on, and I can hear the audience before the concert starts and between each piece. So, because all this is in my head, I get especially cross if someone comes into the sitting room and talks while the music is playing. Once my mother and father did this and I really yelled at them. They just crept away and left me alone. I felt sorry then, but I never said anything to them.

A very bad thing I did also has to do with Beethoven. In our sitting room, the settee faces the fireplace. On the mantelpiece above the fireplace, right in the middle, there's a small statue of Beethoven. My father says it's a bust because it only has the head and shoulders. One day, I'm sitting on the settee playing a favourite game, bouncing a tennis ball off the wall and catching it when it comes back. Well, then I make a mistake, and somehow the ball hits the statue. It crashes down on the hearth and is completely smashed to pieces. I'm so upset, I'm even crying, but my mother's really angry and says, "You'll be for it when your father gets home. He loves that bust of Beethoven. He's had it a long time. And what were you doing anyway with a ball in there?"

All this makes me feel sick and I go to my room and wait for him to come. When he does, he soon comes upstairs, but he doesn't give me a hiding or anything. Instead, he says, "You're a stupid clot, you know. It's time you started growing up. I can't believe some of the things you do. Now you go down there and clear up the mess, and don't ever let me see you with a ball in there again."

A few weeks later, another statue of Beethoven appears. This is not a bust, because it shows all of him. I think this had been packed away, because one of the legs was broken and then was fixed, but you could still tell. They put this on the side of the mantelpiece where there is a small shelf just right for it. The trouble is, I start playing my ball game again when no one else is around to see. Somehow, the same thing happens as before, and the statue gets broken to pieces. I don't dare tell anyone what really happened, so I say I accidentally knocked against it. I promise that I will save up and buy another one, but I can see they don't believe me. But I do save up – no new scores or books, no stamps from the junk store, and no ices from Migliorini's. Just before Christmas, I go to the music shop at the bottom of London Road because there's the exact same statue in the window and I have just enough money to buy it. When I give it to my mother and father on Christmas morning, they're as pleased as can be. I feel pleased too, though I still feel a little bad about not telling the whole truth. They put the statue back in the sitting room, but not where it used to be. Beethoven's new place is much safer, on top of the music cabinet behind the settee. I know it would have been safe on the mantelpiece because I don't play with a ball in there any more.

After the war, Uncle Alf keeps coming on Fridays. He's not really an uncle, just as Aunty D's not really an aunty. My sisters and I, we really like Uncle Alf, but we make jokes about him when he's not there. He has this big adam's apple, and he's the only person we know who wears a bow tie. I think it's because he seems a bit different that he makes us giggle. Although it's not funny, he gets into trouble with my mother because he likes to smoke cigarettes so much. Before he and my father begin a piece, he lights a cigarette and has a few puffs. Then, sometimes, instead of using one of the ashtrays my mother has spread around, he puts the cigarette on the mantelpiece. The end that's alight sticks out over the edge so it won't burn anything. The trouble happens if the piece they're playing goes a long time without stopping. He always smokes a few more puffs at the end of each movement, but it the movement is too long... well, you can guess what happens. The cigarette burns down, drops a whole lot of ash, and burns the wood of the mantelpiece. This happens more than once, and my mother tells him off. I can tell she's quite angry. After that, he tries hard to remember to use ashtrays, but sometimes he just forgets.

My father keeps quiet about all this. He doesn't say a thing. It's almost like he doesn't notice or doesn't care. Grown-ups can be very strange sometimes.

When my father is doing music with Uncle Alf, I always go into the sitting room and listen. I sit next to my father and when I can, I turn the pages. They always start with Handel or Corelli or something like that. Then they do a Mozart sonata, a different one each week. They follow the order in the book, but sometimes they can't agree about which one they did last. Every so often I can remember and tell them, but mostly I keep quiet. After the Mozart comes Beethoven, and they do the same thing, with a different sonata each week. Then, my mother brings in cups of tea, and my father and Uncle Alf talk about what they'll do next. Usually, it's Cesar Franck (there's only one by him) or Brahms. Sometimes, though, Uncle Alf agrees to do the Bach. They both call it that – "the Bach". It's not a sonata but a concerto, and the piano part is what the orchestra would play. From the key signature – I've learned about those from piano lessons – I know this concerto is in E major.

First Uncle Alf does things to make everything special. He moves some of the furniture so there's lots of space where he's going to play. Then he puts the music stand in a corner because he's going to play this whole piece from memory. After that, he spends a long time tuning. Then he starts.

When Uncle Alf does "the Bach", my mother and sisters come into the room to watch and listen. A lot of the time, he has his eyes closed, but he also moves about in time to the music. He seems to get very worked up. At the end we all clap, but he can hardly say anything. It's almost like he's going to cry. After my mother and sisters have left, the furniture gets moved back, and the music stand is put in its usual place. What they play is something quiet, so that Uncle Alf can calm down before he goes home to his wife. Her name is Lib.

Uncle Alf is not only a violinist; he's also an artist. His paintings are watercolours, and we have a big one that hangs in the sitting room. Most of his paintings are of places in Chelmsford or just outside the town. One Christmas, someone gives me a paint set and some brushes, and I try and do a few pictures. Uncle Alf sees this and he invites me to go sketching with him. I have to bring my paint set, a pad of paper, some brushes, a small bottle of water, and a lunch.

Also, he has a really small fold-up stool for me to sit on. We walk just outside the town, and he chooses where we stop. He really surprises me because he walks fast and we have hardly any time to sketch something before he wants to move again.

"Don't worry if you haven't finished. You're only doing sketches. Just get the outlines, and if you don't have time to do a colour, just use your pencil and write what colour you want. That way you'll know for later."

By the middle of the afternoon I'm tired, so we walk home. He seems pleased with my sketches and tells me to take the best one and copy it to make a picture. I try this, but I don't think it's very good. I never go out with Uncle Alf again, but I do something else instead. Uncle Jack, who works in an insurance office, has given me a used bike. I've started to ride this everywhere, usually with my friends, who also have bikes. Because our family always explores any old churches we pass when we're on a walk, I start doing the same thing on bike rides. What's different is that I have a notebook with me. In it I draw a picture of the church, and then I write what I can find out about its history. If I can, I get a copy of a brochure about the church when they have one for visitors. Soon, I start to have quite a collection of pictures and information, and the more churches I have in my collection, the more new ones I want to get. There's Chelmsford Cathedral, of course, but I also have churches like Widford, Galleywood, Danbury, Margaretting, Stock, Fyfield, Great Baddow and West Hanningfield. My favourite is Greensted. It's supposed to be the oldest wooden church in the world. One day I show my church book to Uncle Alf. He says, "There you are now. One sketching trip with me, and you're off on your own. That's how it all starts."

He never says whether he likes the drawings. I don't think they're very good and maybe he thinks the same, but he never says so. He just keeps on encouraging me.

Right after the war, and before I have my bike, my father has someone new to play with. It's a prisoner of war from the camp on Chelmer Road, and his name is Heinz. Before the first time he comes, my mother and father explain to the three of us that not all Germans are bad. Many of them are just ordinary people like us, and some were only just out of school when the war was on. Heinz was a schoolteacher, but Hitler made him go in the German army. My mother says the Red Cross is worried that he might die because he is so sad in the camp. He's been away so long from his wife and little girl. The Red Cross people know he's very musical and plays the cello. They've found one for him, and now they need somewhere for him to go and play. That's why they ask if he can visit us when he is allowed to come out of the camp at the weekend. When my father and mother say yes, the Red Cross leave the cello at our house ready for him.

Somehow my father finds out what sort of music Heinz plays, and he goes to the library and gets a whole pile ready. When Sunday comes, we're all waiting for Heinz to come, and my sisters and I are very excited. Then we see him in his prison clothes coming slowly up the street, looking at the numbers on the houses till he gets to ours, number 27. We all go through the house to the back garden, and my mother and father are very friendly to him. He speaks quite good English and explains that he learned it before the war started. My mother asks him about his family, and she tells him how thin he looks and how he'll have to eat up while he's with us. Then she goes into the kitchen to get lunch ready, and my father takes Heinz into the sitting room to see his cello and to decide what they can play together. I go too, because I want to know what a cello sounds like and I want to know what music they're going to do.

When Heinz takes the cello out of its canvas case, he's very excited and talks a bit to himself as he checks everything. Then we get a chair for him so he can sit and play it. After that, he tunes it. This takes a long time, so we just have to wait. Then he looks at the music my father's got. The first things he picks out are Beethoven sonatas and Brahms sonatas. So they start with the first Beethoven in the book, but before they play anything, my father has to go into the garage for a piece of leftover carpet. He puts that on the floor in front of Heinz right where the spike at the bottom of the cello goes. He knows that my mother would get cross if she saw the spike making a hole in the carpet.

Then they start. It sounds pretty good to me, but after the first movement my father says he's sorry for all the mistakes. He's never played this music before. Then they play the movement again, and my father does much better. The whole morning passes like this, with lots of stops and repeats. Gradually, I begin to get used to how the cello sounds, and I start to hear what a good player Heinz is. My father hears it too, and after we all have lunch, he can't wait to get Heinz back to the sitting room. Heinz wants to play more, too, but pretty soon he gets tired and says his fingers haven't touched the cello for such a long time that they need time to get strong again.

After that, we all go out in the garden again, and my mother brings tea and some biscuits she has made. Heinz is not so nervous any more, and he starts to talk more. He shows everyone a photo of his wife and little girl. My father tries to talk about the war, but my mother shuts him up. "That's enough about the war. Heinz has been through enough. Let it be."

For once my father doesn't argue with her, and for the rest of the time, they talk about other things like music and Uncle Alf, how much longer before Heinz can go home (nobody has any idea), and what the food is like in the camp.

After that first day, Heinz comes every weekend. My sisters and I like him a lot. He plays with us and jokes with us, and sometimes he teaches us German words. He's clever, too. One time, I have a cold sore on my lip. Somehow, he goes off in the woods and makes an ointment from different plants, just a small amount that he wraps up in a piece of brown paper. I put some on the sore, and the next day it's nearly better. No one can believe it, because usually my cold sores last about a week and a half. Everyone, including Mr. Bell, the chemist who lives next door, always says there's nothing that can make cold sores better, but they're wrong.

Each week, I listen to my father and Heinz. During the week before Heinz comes, my father practises the music. I can tell he finds the pieces quite hard, but pretty soon he learns the music. Even then, there's lots of discussion when Heinz is there about how fast or slow to play something, whether my father can imitate just how Heinz plays certain tunes, and how loud or soft to play something. My father's not very good at playing softly, and Uncle Alf doesn't seem to care about that, but Heinz is really fussy, and my father listens to him and tries to do what he wants.

Of course they don't only play Beethoven and Brahms. There's Chopin and Schubert, and a more modern piece by Poulenc. I have to listen to that a few times before I begin to enjoy it. There's also a cello concerto by Elgar. I like this, especially the way it starts with the cello on its own. Then, they play a sonata by Cesar Franck. I already know this piece because it's the same as what Uncle Alf plays. I can't decide whether I like this best with the violin or with the cello.

One day, my father has the idea that he'd like to have Uncle Alf come at the same time as Heinz. That way they can try some trios. Heinz likes this idea, but when my father talks to Uncle Alf on the phone, there seems to be a problem. Uncle Alf doesn't say yes; instead, he says he'll think about it. That's what my father tells my mother when the phone call is over. I can tell my father is quite grumpy about Uncle Alf, but my mother says he has to be more understanding.

"You have to remember that Alf's Jewish. Maybe, he just doesn't want to have anything to do with Germans."

"Rubbish," my father says. "Heinz could never have hurt anyone. He certainly wouldn't have been involved in the business with the Jews. All I'm suggesting is we play some music together. That's the sort of thing the world needs right now. Something to remind us that we're all fellow human beings."

"Well, give him time to think about it," my mother says, "and if it's no, don't push it. Just let it pass."

I can see my father's listening to her, and his grumpiness goes away. I don't really understand it at all. What's "Jewish" mean, and how did the Germans hurt Jews? I know Uncle Alf worked in the

East End of London where there were lots of bombs, but no one said the Germans were just after him. When I ask about all this, both my father and my mother refuse to tell me anything. They say they'll explain when I'm older. I can see they're serious, so I don't ask any more. Then, when Uncle Alf says he will come, everything seems settled and I kind of forget about the mystery.

The big day is here. It's a Sunday morning, but no one seems very happy. Uncle Alf shakes hands with Heinz but he's not smiling. Instead, they all concentrate on getting their instruments ready, and my father sorts out the music. He's got a Beethoven trio that has a name – "Archduke". He's got a Schubert trio, and he's got some Haydn trios. They start with a Haydn because it's shorter and a bit easier, but at the end Heinz says it's not very interesting for the cello because his part is just the same as the left hand notes that my father's playing. So then they try the "Archduke". Heinz is the only one who knows this, so there's lots of mistakes by the other two. They stop quite a few times and go back and repeat things, but I can see they really like the music and they're starting to have a good time.

At lunchtime, my mother does a lot of talking, but Heinz and Uncle Alf do talk a little bit. Heinz asks Uncle Alf about where he works, and Uncle Alf asks Heinz about his family. After lunch, my father wants to do the Schubert, but to my surprise both Uncle Alf and Heinz say they'd rather keep working on the Beethoven. They practise various parts, and then they play the whole thing without stopping. When they're having tea afterwards, my father goes on about how they must do this again, but they never do. I think it must be because of how Uncle Alf feels.

When Christmas comes, it's all very exciting because Heinz is going to sleep in our house. Also, two other men from the camp are coming with him. That's because they don't have a family to go to, so my mother says they can come to us. When they arrive, they have a big surprise for us. They have a huge Christmas tree. They won't say where they got it, and my father says we'd better not ask. He doesn't really like Christmas trees, but he doesn't say anything, and he helps them put it up. At first it's too tall, and my father has to get the saw from the garage so that they can make the tree a bit shorter. Then, they start to decorate it. My sisters and I get to help, and when it's time to put the angel on top, Heinz lifts my baby sister up so that she can do it. After we've had something to eat, we all go into the sitting room, where there's a fire. My father plays the piano for us, and we sing some carols, like "Away in a manger" and "The Holly and the Ivy". But then Heinz and the two others from the camp (one's called Walter) sing some carols to us. One of them I recognize – "Silent Night" – but they use German words. They sing really nicely, even without a piano, and they even make harmonies. After that, my mother sings, and we do roast chestnuts on the fire grate. That night, I sleep in my sisters' room so that Heinz can have my bed. The other two sleep downstairs, but I don't know where.

The next morning, we do presents. The three visitors even have little things for us, even though my mother told them not to bring anything. Later, we have a Christmas dinner. My mother managed to get a chicken, and she's made a Christmas pudding, though she says she couldn't get all the right things to put in it. When it's on our plates, we discover that each piece has a lucky silver sixpence in it. After lunch, Walter and the other man thank my mother and father and say goodbye. Heinz stays a bit longer, and he and my father play some music just like they always do. Later, after Heinz has gone, my mother says she likes Walter, but she won't have that other fellow back.

"He's sullen and not really friendly at all. It's like he's still fighting the war or something. I just don't trust him."

We have about two years with Heinz. It's the same with the Roberts up the street, who have Otto. We get really used to having him, and he's always so nice. Then suddenly he tells us that next week he's going back to Germany. We're all very sorry, and I know my father's going to miss doing music with him. But Heinz is very happy, and my mother keeps reminding us that his family has been waiting for him all this time. We promise to write letters, and my father mumbles about going on a visit one day. Then Heinz is gone. But we do hear from him every year, and we write letters too. He also sends us photos, so that we can see him with his wife and little girl. Most of the time, I forget about him, but every so often I remember, and then I get sad. I know my mother misses him too. When I tell her about it, she says, "I know just how you feel, but we have to think about it all. The war was terrible and did lots of horrible things to people. Heinz was wasting away in that camp before we met him. We helped him, but he was always going to go back to his family. He was very grateful to us, but now he's where he should be. We should be glad we helped someone, and we should be glad that another family is now all together. Try and think about that."

When I'm old enough, my mother and father start taking me to

London for birthday treats. One year, we go to *Peter Pan*. I think it's magic when Peter and Wendy are flying, and I'm nearly crying when Tinkerbell is dying. But even more than *Peter Pan*, I like it when they take me to Sadler's Wells to see my first opera, *Hansel and Gretel*. I didn't know you could have people singing instead of talking. Even if you can't understand the words, there's all the music to listen to. After *Hansel and Gretel*, every so often, I go to see other operas with my father and Uncle Jack. We always go to Sadler's Wells because the other place where they do operas is too expensive. That's what my father says. Usually, we go on a Saturday, and we see two whole operas, one in the afternoon and a different one at night. I can't remember all of them, but I know we see *Il Trovatore*, *Rigoletto*, *The Barber of Seville* and *The Marriage of Figaro*. That last one's by Mozart, and we have to leave before the end because we don't want to miss the last train. I get very tired, and sometimes I fall asleep. My father jokes about that, but he keeps taking me anyway.

One time when we're walking from the underground station to Sadler's Wells, we're in really thick fog. Of course, I've been in fog before, but this is different. It's not white; it's a kind of dirty yellow. Uncle Jack says it's "smog" and we should put our scarves across our faces. It's a good job they know the way, because you can hardly see at all. I keep very close to him and my father so that I don't get lost. After the opera, the smog is still there but not quite so bad. Uncle Jack says the smog comes from all the people burning coal in their fires. But I don't understand that. We have coal fires at home, but we don't have smog in Chelmsford.

When I'm seven, I have my first piano lesson. This is with Miss

Clark. She has a studio in Aunty D's house in the very same downstairs room where Aunty D's father used to be. He was very old and a bit frightening. He had white hair and a white beard. Sometimes Aunty D made us go and say hello to him, but he was very gruff and grumpy and never smiled, so we always got away as soon as we could. No one told us when he died. He just sort of disappeared.

That was when Miss Clark came. She's very nice, and I work hard to learn the music she gives me and to learn to read music. After a year or so, she gets married and moves away. That's when Aunty D becomes my piano teacher. She's much stricter than Miss Clark, so I have to work harder than before.

One time, I know I haven't practised enough. When we get to something I haven't practised at all, I make a big sigh and stop playing. She asks me if I'm all right and if I feel faint. I say I do, even if that isn't true. Then she makes me sit in her armchair, and she brings me a glass of water to drink. When I "feel better", we start the lesson again, and she doesn't say anything when I make mistakes. I suppose my trick worked, but I never do anything like that again. Better to make sure I do my practice every day.

At Moulsham Junior Boys' School, I learn the recorder. My father and mother also learn the recorder when they go away to a music camp at Hindhead. When they come back, my father finds music so that we can all three play together, each of us having a different part to play. Eventually, they seem to give up the recorder, but I keep going, and my father finds me music to play by composers like Handel. My favourite piece is *Jesu Joy of Man's Desiring*, by Bach. We have the piano music of this, and I just play the top line, and my father plays the rest. This becomes my "party piece".

I also start the violin with a teacher that comes to the school once a week and teaches a group of about six of us. The violin is harder than the piano and the recorder, but when you get it right, it can sound very nice, just like when Uncle Alf plays. Adrian Smith, who was at school with me, wrote much later about me and my violin:

"Alan Young brought his violin to school and sawed away at Corelli right under my nose, propping his music in the lunch hour on top of the vaulting horse in the lobby. Having heard Corelli at such close range has given that composer a special place in my scheme of things!"

I don't remember what he describes, but I do remember that piece by Corelli. The notes are fairly easy, so you can concentrate on trying to make everything in tune. I even learn to put in a bit of vibrato, though I find that very hard. When I play it for Uncle Alf, he tells me I'm coming along just fine. I should keep practising, and it might be time for my mother and father to find me a teacher who gives lessons to only one student at a time.

When we're in our last year at Moulsham, we have the 11-plus exam to decide which of us gets to go to the grammar school. I've always been with the top four or five students in the class. They include Adrian Smith (he's nearly always top) and Brian Howard. I'm fairly certain I'll be OK, but I'm still nervous about the exam. Anyway, I pass all right, and so do Adrian and Brian, but my friend Anthony Smith doesn't. This is really bad, not just because he's my friend but because our two mothers have been friends since they were both young. Before we did the exam, the two mothers went to see a kind of fortune teller, and they asked her if Anthony and I would pass the exam.. They were both very upset when they heard that I would pass but Anthony wouldn't. And that's what happens. After that, the two mothers can hardly speak to each other, and I don't think they're able to be friends any more.

Instead of going to the Chelmsford Grammar School (that's where my father and his brothers went), I do something different. Brian Howard and I take another exam and go for interviews to see if we can get into Brentwood School. That's a school in the next town. Usually, you have to pay to go there and you live at the school, but a few boys get to go for free as day boys. Both Brian and I are accepted, and in September we start catching the bus to go to school. The school has classes on Saturday mornings, and for the whole afternoon on Wednesdays and Saturdays there's games, football in the winter and cricket in the summer.

I like the teachers at Brentwood, but the work is very hard, and there's lots of homework. Especially hard are two new subjects, Latin and French. Because this is a boarding school, the boys are divided into different "houses". I'm put with the boys in Dr. Brice's house, even though I don't sleep there. I think I'm in this house because Dr. Brice found out I like music. He's the main music teacher, and he plays the organ every day in the school chapel for morning worship. When he talks to me and I tell him about the recorder, he tells me to bring it to school and play for him. Then, before I can even think about it, he has me play *Jesu Joy* in the chapel in front of the whole school. He plays the organ, just like my father played the piano, but this time the choir is also singing. I've never been so nervous in my life, although once the music starts, I'm concentrating too hard to worry any more about playing in front of so many people. I think maybe I make one mistake, but I get through it OK. Mr. Allison, the headmaster, even speaks to me afterwards and says, "Well done, young man. I'm sure we'll be hearing you again before too long." Sure enough, the next term, Dr. Brice has me do the same piece again. This time, I do much better and don't make any mistakes, though I'm still very nervous right before I play.

During the year, my father meets a clarinetist, so then I want to learn this new instrument. The man lends me a clarinet, but it has a simple fingering system. When we hear what a new up-to-date clarinet costs, my father starts talking about how money doesn't grow on trees. Also, Dr. Brice says I should concentrate on the piano and the violin. I notice he doesn't even mention the recorder. So I agree to give up the clarinet. But later I go to Dr. Brice with another idea. "How about the organ?" But he says no right away. "That's something we can think about when you're a bit older and when your piano work is more advanced. There's also the matter of your height. You have to be tall enough for your feet to reach all the pedals. Wait till you've grown some more, and we'll discuss it again."

He's very kind when he says all this, and I'm nearly crying because I can't do what I really want to do. After a few days, though, I stop thinking about it, and I start practising the piano and violin as much as I can.

One day in the school term before the summer holidays, everything goes wrong. My father tells us we're going to move away from Chelmsford. We're going to live in Maidstone in Kent. I tell him I can't leave Brentwood. He says he's sorry, but I must. Then he tries to make me feel better by saying the grammar school in Maidstone is very good. Because I think he's just saying that, it doesn't have any effect on me. Then I come up with an idea. "Why can't I be a boarder at Brentwood? I could be in Dr. Brice's house." But this doesn't work, because it would be much too expensive. I'm so upset, I don't talk to them any more.

Then they take me to see the headmaster at Brentwood. My mother and father and me, we go into his office, and we all sit down. Mr. Allison then tells me a few things:

"I know this is very hard on you, but you happen to be very lucky. You won't know it, but Maidstone is one of the best grammar schools in the country. Mr. Claydon, the headmaster there, is a good friend of mine, and we see each other all the time at the Headmasters' Conference. I know all about the school, and I've been to see it. What's important for you to know is that there's a very impressive music programme there. I suspect that when you've settled in there, you might find it even better for you than Brentwood. We shall miss you, you know. I was looking forward to seeing how you came along with your music. Dr. Brice has told me all about you. One of these days, you'll have to come back and let us know how you're doing. Perhaps, you'll play for us again."

All this makes me feel a bit better, and at home I start to ask lots of questions about Maidstone. Where is it? And where is our house going to be? My father goes there first to start his job and to find a house for us. Later, he phones us and tells us he's found a very nice one with a big garden, and he tells me that my bedroom is going to be downstairs. I can't quite imagine that, but I like the idea. By the time the rest of us go, we're all very excited. But we're also sad. I hate leaving my friends, although I haven't seen them very much since I went to Brentwood. We're also leaving grandparents and people like Aunty D. I think my father's upset to leave Uncle Alf, but he doesn't say anything, and they both talk about getting together again soon. On the train, my mother cries most of the way, but I start to feel OK. I just know this is going to be new and very different.

CHAPTER FOUR

THE GREAT OUTDOORS

Although the things I like best are books and music, there are other things that are important too. Nearly every week, for example, my father has us all go on a family walk and picnic. He says the fresh air is good for us and the exercise is good for us as well. Uncle Jack usually comes with us. He and my father plan everything before we go, using bus timetables and maps. They decide what bus to take, where to get off it, and where to walk. They try to make sure we'll come to a nice pub at about opening time. There's always a lot of discussion about what kind of beer the pub has. Sometimes they already know, but sometimes they don't. They can be quite grumpy if we get somewhere and find they don't like that kind of beer.

My sisters and I can't go inside pubs, so they also look for pubs that have gardens or special rooms where children can go. While Uncle Jack and my father have a beer (usually it's two), my sisters and I each get a packet of Smith's crisps and a fizzy drink. My mother gets a pineapple juice. Then we have our picnic, or, if we can't have it at the pub, we walk a bit further until they find a place.

After we've eaten, the grown-ups all have naps, and my sisters and I get to play. I like to climb trees if we're in the woods, or we play hide-and-seek. Last of all, we do some more walking so as to be somewhere in time to get a bus home.

My father and Uncle Jack don't like to walk on roads, so they use the map to find footpaths that we can use. That's when they often get into arguments. Sometimes they get lost. Sometimes a footpath on the map isn't there any more or else it's ploughed up. It might even have a fence across it. I like to look over their shoulders when they're looking at the map. Pretty soon, I learn to see how maps work and what the signs on them mean. These aren't maps like those in the atlas; they show a lot more detail, like roads, railways, and footpaths, streams and rivers, churches and pubs, even large farmhouses. My father tells me that one inch on the map equals one mile.

One day when we're lost, I interrupt an argument because I can see a church and a farmhouse that are also on the map. When you line them up, you can see that we're actually on the right path. They look at each other and nod. My father calls me a "smart Alec", but in a nice way. I can see he's quite pleased with me. After that, they always let me look at the map with them, but usually I'm just as lost as they are.

One thing that we do on our walks is visit any church we pass that seems old. My father always checks the organ, and if it's not locked up and no one's around, he'll play it. Sometimes there's no electricity, so someone has to pump by hand. That's always my job. I don't mind too much, but it means that I can't actually watch my father play. If there's electricity, I can stand or sit beside him and watch him pulling out stops and changing hands from one manual to another, and playing with both feet. Every so often, he lets me have a go, but I don't do the pedals, and he changes the stops for me. I only do something really simple, depending on what music's already there in the church. I really like the sounds that the organ can make, which is why I want to learn how to play it properly one day.

We go to all sorts of places, but I especially like it when we walk to Danbury. We start off by walking along the canal on the towpath. Then we follow footpaths through fields. I especially like crossing one big field. My father says this was a fake aerodrome during the war. There were lots of fake planes made of pieces of wood. They hoped the Germans would come and bomb them. That way, they'd use up their bombs and go home without bombing anything else. I keep asking if the Germans ever did bomb the fake aerodrome, but no one seems to know.

After we climb the hill to Danbury, we sometimes go into the church, or we walk to the common and have our picnic. Then sometimes we go to the Griffin, the big pub on the main road at the top of the hill. This pub is run by my Uncle Cecil (he's my mother's brother) and Aunty Chris. It's best if we go in the afternoon after closing time. That way my sisters and I can go into the bar. The pub is very old. Uncle Cecil tells me there's a secret room that you can only get to if you go up the chimney of the big fireplace. Of course, I want to go and see the room, but he won't let me. He says I'd get far too dirty. My mother and father agree with him and tell me to stop bothering Uncle Cecil, so I never do get to look. Years later, when I visit the Griffin on my own, I find he's boarded over the fireplace. Now I wonder if people going to the pub even know about the secret room.

I don't think my mother likes Aunty Chris. She says Aunty Chris doesn't have any children because she doesn't like children. She prefers to work with Uncle Cecil to build their business. I don't understand any of this because Aunty Chris is always nice to us. She lets us watch while she's working in the big kitchen where she makes food for the pub.

Later, when Nana is getting really old, my mother has a big quarrel with her brother and Aunty Chris. They want my mother to have Nana at our house, but my mother says they're the ones who have lots of room. Anyway, we stop seeing them, and my mother stops talking to them. After that, they move away, and we don't see them any more.

Much later, something terrible happens. Uncle Cecil dies, but no one (including Aunty Chris) tells my mother. Instead, someone else reads about it in the paper and sends my mother the page from the paper so that she can read it for herself. That really upsets her, and she sits in the dining room and cries a whole lot. Then she starts to get very, very angry. She says some really nasty things about Aunty Chris and blames her. At the same time, although she never says so, I think my mother feels bad because she never made up the quarrel with Uncle Cecil. After that, I think it's always best to make up after quarrels with people who are good friends and with people in your own family.

The other thing about the family is going away for a two-week holiday every year. This starts right after the war, once the beaches are safe for people to walk on them. At first there are still barriers to stop German boats from landing. The barriers are made of scaffolding like what they use for building, but you can climb through them and get to the water. You have to be careful when you do this. I know because the first time we go on holiday, I see a tall man hit his back on the rusty scaffolding. Because he's bleeding a bit, my mother and father tell him he has to go to the hospital before his back gets infected. When he comes back, he's got a big bandage on his back. He's cross because he had to have an injection and he can't go in the water till everything's better. After seeing that, I'm even more careful when I climb through the barrier.

The first two years, we go to Walton-on-the-Naze, and then we go to Dovercourt. This is not far from Walton. It's across the water near Harwich. We always get very excited when the holiday comes. My father and mother pack all kinds of things, mostly clothes, in a big trunk. When they've finished, my father and Uncle Jack put a rope around it, and Uncle Jack does all kinds of special knots to keep the rope tight. Then a lorry comes to collect the trunk and take it to the railway station, and we don't see it again until we get to our holiday place.

On the day we leave, a man my father knows up the road comes in his car and drives us all the way. It's very crowded in the car, and I always seem to get car-sick, even when my father lets me sit on his lap in the front with the window open. Later, we go to other places much farther away. For that we have to go by train. In different years we go to the Isle of Wight, Dawlish, Hastings and Minehead.

We always stay in a guest house. This is exciting, because everything is so different. My sisters and I share one room. My mother and father have a different room, and Uncle Jack has a room too. We have a big potty in our room, just like at Nana's house, so we don't get lost at night looking for the guest house bathroom. On one holiday, when the three grown-ups go to the pub, they leave the three of us in our room. They tell me I'm in charge. We're supposed to go to sleep, but we stay wide awake. We play a game where you sit on the potty so that when you get up, it makes a farting noise. This makes us laugh a lot. The trouble is that when my youngest sister tries it, the potty breaks and it makes a big cut on her bum. I don't really know what to do, so I make her lie down on a towel on the bed and I try and stop the bleeding with another towel from the washbasin in the room. I'm doing this, and my other sister's helping.

Suddenly, my father and mother come back with Uncle Jack. They don't yell at us because they think we've had an accident. My mother even says it's the fault of the guest house people; the potty must have been cracked. We keep quiet about what really happened, and they even think I've done the right thing with the towels and stuff. Even so, because the bleeding won't stop, my mother and father decide to take my sister to the hospital. They leave me and my other sister with Uncle Jack. When they come back, they say that my sister's cut needed a whole lot of stitches. She won't be able to go in the water for the rest of the holiday. Later, there'll be a scar.

What's really good about each guest house is the food. Every place we go to gives us porridge for breakfast. I like porridge a lot. My mother hardly ever makes it at home because she says it sticks to her saucepans and is such a bother to clean up. Then there's bacon and eggs, and toast and marmalade. My mother always tells us to "eat up" because we're getting only sandwiches for lunch.

After breakfast, we go to the beach. There we have a beach hut where we can get changed when we go in the water. If it rains, we can go in there and play cards. We keep our buckets and spades in the hut, and there are deckchairs for the grown-ups to use on the beach. There's also a spirit stove to heat up water for tea. Uncle Jack is good at doing the stove (it works with methylated spirits), so he's usually the one making the tea. Sometimes, if it's cold, he makes cocoa for everybody. That's the trouble with guest houses; once you leave in the morning, you can't go back till the end of the afternoon, even if the weather's bad. On some days, instead of going to the beach, we go for a long walk, rather like we do at home when it's the weekend. I'd rather be on the beach, though, so I complain a lot when we go on these walks.

After we get back to the guesthouse, we have to get washed. Then we all go out to find something to eat. My favourite is fish and chips, but I'm not allowed to have that every day. There are other activities in the evening. We walk on the promenade where there are amusement arcades. I always try to win something, but usually I don't manage it. My father tells me I shouldn't waste my money because all the machines are "rigged" so you can't win.

There are also shops with souvenirs. These shops often sell postcards with dirty jokes on them. Each year I send one to Nana and Granddad, but I'm not allowed to send one to Gran and my other Granddad. I know Gran would laugh at the joke, but Granddad definitely would not. In those shops, you can also buy candyfloss, ice creams and sticks of rock. In a circle inside the stick of rock, there's always the name of the town where you are. Even if you eat all the way to the bottom, the name is still there. No one can tell me how they do that when they make the rock.

There's also another thing that we do. In each town by the seaside, there's usually a pier that has lots of amusements and even shows. I like those shows where the men put black stuff on their faces. What I like is their singing and their banjo music. The first year, we could only walk a little way on the pier because there was a great big gap. Uncle Jack said that the army had blown up this part of the pier so that the Germans couldn't use it. Because the war is over now, nobody has to worry about this, and next time we come back, we can walk all the way to the end of the pier and pretend we're on a ship out on the sea.

Back in Chelmsford, I learn to get around on my bike. At first, I have a tricycle. It's quite big and has brakes. It's even big enough for me to give my sisters rides, but if I go fast, they start bawling. When that happens, I go even faster. If they tell on me, I get into trouble with my mother.

I often take my trike to Oaklands Park, which is behind the houses across the street. Every winter, the ditch near the big house that's a museum fills up with water. My friends and I call the ditch "the moat", but my mother and father say it's a "ha-ha". This is a joke that I don't get, so I keep on calling it "the moat". My friends always dare me to ride my trike into the water. I do this and use the brakes to stop myself going too far. Because I've got wellington boots, my feet don't get wet. Well, you can guess what happens. At least two different times, the trike goes in right up to the handlebars, the water comes over the tops of my boots and the rest of me gets soaking wet, too.

There are lots of things to do in Oaklands Park. There are swings, a roundabout and a slide. To make the slide really fast, we often grease it with an old candle. After a few runs down, it gets quite fast, but it can mess your clothes up a bit. Some people complain that now the slide's so fast it's dangerous. Close to the place where the swings are, there's tennis courts and greenhouses. We're not interested in those, but one day the police come while we're on the slide and say that someone's been throwing stones. Some glass in the greenhouses has got broken. I know it wasn't us, but one of the policemen just doesn't seem to believe us. Even though we keep telling him we didn't do it, he tells us that if we do it again, we'll be in big trouble. That makes us a bit nervous about going back to the swings. After a few days, we stop worrying about the police and carry on playing there as often as we like.

When you go through some trees near the swings, you pass the place where there used to be Nissen huts. These were for the soldiers who looked after the barrage balloon during the war. Then you come to the football field. Anyone can play on it, and we often bring our football boots and make up teams. I don't think I'm very good at football, and some of the older kids laugh at me because of the way I run with my arms out. They call me "Angel". But I've seen pictures of footballers with their arms out like that, so I try not to take too much notice. Anyway, even if I'm not very good, I really like playing.

In the park, there's also the Monkey Hill where there's a hole with concrete walls where a gun used to be during the war. In the middle, there's a round concrete thing with a shiny spike on top where the gun was. We play there a lot, but sometimes it gets smelly. We think there's a tramp who uses it for a bathroom, but we never see him.

On the other side of the park, there's a big cannon. It was used in the Crimean War, which I read all about in my encyclopaedia. The cannon is fun to climb on, but it's also a bit scary because it's quite high and underneath is all concrete. Once I helped my big sister get up on it, and then for a joke, I ran away. She couldn't get down on her own and she was scared because it was so high. The cannon can't be fired any more because the end of the barrel has wood jammed into it, but we like to pretend we're firing it. My father says that before the war the cannon used to be right in front of the Shire Hall. I'm glad they moved it, because I'm sure they wouldn't let you play on it if it was where it used to be.

The other thing in the park is the big house that's now a museum. I've been in there with Aunty D and with my mother, so I know my way around. My friends and I are not allowed to go in on our own but we do anyway. We have to watch out for the museum keeper. He's a big fat man, and he gets very grumpy if he catches us. We try and make sure he's in his office, and then we creep in. The best part is where there are big glass cases that have stuffed wild animals – tigers and lions, and things like that.

In another room, there are swords and guns and armour. When we go in there, we never see anyone else, and we never touch anything, so I don't see why we're not allowed. If the museum keeper catches us, sometimes he's so grumpy he just throws us out. Sometimes he takes us around and shows us things, but then he throws us out just the same. I think he'd like to be friendly, but he doesn't know how. Maybe he hasn't got any children himself and just doesn't know how to talk to them.

After I grow out of my trike, I learn to ride a two-wheeler. I have a small one at first, but soon I need a bigger one. That's when Uncle Jack gets me a full-size bike. He lowers the saddle and handlebars as far down as they'll go, and then I'm just big enough to ride it. I start going all over the place, and sometimes I go on rides with Uncle Jack. He uses his bike to go to work every day. He tells me stories about the rides he used to do with his friends when he was growing up. They even used to use their bikes to go camping. Going with Uncle Jack is OK. The trouble is, even though he's got three gears (I don't have any gears), he still rides so slowly. But if I go ahead and show how fast I can go, he gets cross and says, "Now, I don't want you doing that. You stay close to me. There's no need to show off. When you're biking with someone else, you stay together."

I know he's right, but I don't like it. Eventually, I stop going on bike rides with him. He never says anything, and he still helps me fix anything that goes wrong with the bike. I learn how to do punctures, how to mend a broken chain, how to put in a new spoke if one's got broken, how to put on new brake blocks when the old ones are worn down, how to put a saddlebag on the back, how to put on a mirror so I can see what's coming behind me, how to put on lights and a dynamo so that I don't need batteries any more at night, and how to put on a milometer to see how far I've biked. The only thing I don't bother with is a speedometer. Then, to make my bike even more special and different from everyone else's, I decide to paint it bright red, almost like a fire engine. I don't tell Uncle Jack about this till it's finished. After the paint's dry, I put on some transfers, and then I show him. He's so surprised he doesn't say anything at first. Then he mumbles something about what a change a paint job can make. I notice he doesn't say anything good about it, but he doesn't say anything bad either. Maybe he's disappointed that I didn't ask him to help.

With my bike, it's much easier to visit friends because I can get to their houses in no time at all. Quite often my mother asks me to do errands. Chiefly, I post letters or go to the shops to get whatever she needs. One day I have a serious errand. Early one morning after my father's gone to work, the phone rings. It's Nana. I can tell my mother's quite annoyed because she's very busy. Nana's always getting upset about something or other and wants my mother to sort it out. It always turns out to be nothing important, and that makes my mother quite cross. This time Nana's on the phone about Granddad. After telling Nana that's she's very busy but will try and stop by later, my mother turns to me and says,

"Just get on your bike and go down there, will you. Your Nana's saying she can't wake Granddad up. Go and see what it's all about. I haven't got time for her shenanigans right now. She seems to want me there all the time. I tell you, this will turn out to be nothing, just another excuse to get my attention."

It's all downhill to Nana's house, so on my bike I get there very quickly. I go inside with her and I go up the narrow creaky stairs with her to their bedroom.

"See, he's sleeping. I can't wake him up, and here it is, nine o'clock already. I'm going down to make some tea. You see if you can get him up."

After she'd gone, I sit on the bed. I try talking to him. I shake him and pull on his arm, but not very hard. I even touch his face, but nothing works. When I come down and tell Nana, she wants me to stay and have some tea, but I say no. Instead, I ride back up the hill and tell my mother about Granddad.

"Well, I don't know. I suppose I'd better go down there and see for myself. You go right away and tell Nana I'm coming."

So off I go, down the hill again. I haven't been there long before my mother arrives on her bike. She can't wake Granddad either, so she tells Nana to fetch a man she knows down the street. When he comes, he goes upstairs with my mother. After a while, he comes down again and asks Nana if he can have the small mirror, the one that's on the wall close to the front door. I don't understand all this. How can a mirror help Granddad wake up?

Then it happens. My mother appears on the stairs, and everything changes. Between sobs and gasps for air, she manages to blurt out:

"He's gone. Mum, he's gone. Why didn't we know? He was so peaceful there. He really did look like he was sleeping. But he's gone, and I wasn't here."

Finally, we all understand. Granddad's dead. Though no one uses that word. But before I can even think about anything, my mother gives me another errand:

"Go back to the house and phone your father. His office number's beside the phone. Tell him what's happened. Tell him I need him here at Nana's. Also, phone Aunty D. The girls are there. Tell her to keep them there, but don't tell Aunty D what's happened."

Glad to be trusted with something so important and still trying to grasp what has happened, I get on my bike and ride up the hill away from Nana's house. This is the first dead person I've ever seen. I'd even been pulling at his arm and touching his face. I know I'm going to be very upset when I start thinking about everything. I've always had such good times with him, making boats and talking about horses. At the same time, I'm quite proud that with my bike I've helped my mother and my Nana. Later, whenever I think about the loss of this gentle and kind man, somehow I always remember, too, pedalling my bike as fast as I can, back and forth, between our house and my Nana's.

I only have one bad memory about my bike. One summer, two friends and I have an idea. We often ride up to Galleywood Common and ride along the various paths up there. We know about a lane that goes down the very steep hill on the other side of the Common. We've been down it a few times and then walked back up because it's too steep to ride up. This time we decide we'll go down as fast as we can. So off we go. I do really well and can't believe how fast I'm going, but right at the bottom where the road turns to the right, I find I'm going too fast to turn. When I put my brakes on, the bike almost stops, but I keep going straight. There's a ditch and a big hedge there, but nothing stops me. I smash over the ditch and go right through the hedge and into the field behind. When I look at myself, I find I've got all kinds of cuts and grazes. The worst is one knee that's bleeding quite a bit and even has pieces of gravel stuck in some of the cuts. How did those get there? Did I hit the road too? I tie a handkerchief around it all and stand up. It all hurts a lot and I'm shaking. I also feel a bit cold, even though the sun's shining. Then the other two push through the hedge, and they tell me I'd better go home right away. I decide that

I can't climb back up the hill; I'll follow the lane that takes you to the main London road that will then take me to the top of Vicarage Road close to home.

The other two leave me, and I start off. My bike is OK once I make the handlebars straight, and I ride it as far as the main road. Then I get off and walk in the grass beside the road because the traffic's so busy and so fast. All the time, I'm feeling very shaky and cold, and it takes me a long time to get home. My mother's there, thank goodness, and she doesn't tell me off for getting in such a mess. Instead, she takes me into the kitchen and washes all the cuts and grazes. She even manages to find more gravel in the cuts on my knee. Then she has me sit in a deckchair in the garden. She puts a blanket round me because I'm still a bit cold, and she brings me some tea and biscuits. Soon, I start to feel a bit better. Besides, I have company. There's a jay bird that's been hanging around our house, and he comes and sits on the fence near me. At first I think he's going to try and steal a biscuit, but he just sits there. In the end I decide he's just being friendly.

Besides the bike, I also have roller skates. I can go to a lot of places with these, like Nana's and Aunty D's, but then you have to take them off before you go inside. It's the same with shops. Some even have notices that say "No Roller Skates". I have plenty of falls with my skates, especially when I'm first learning. It's hard to stop. Sometimes, I crash into something on purpose because it would be too dangerous to keep going, like when I come to the end of a street where it meets a busy road.

When they change Longstomps Avenue from a dirt road to a macadam road, they also make new pavements. As soon as we can, some friends and I walk up to the top of the hill. We put on our skates, and then we come down the hill. We stop in a couple of places so that we don't get up too much speed. The new pavement is perfect for skating, but near the bottom, where there was always some pavement that was too rough for skating, you have to jump over the curb into the road to finish. Here, there's no more hill, and you can slow down and stop before you come to the busy road at the bottom.

One day I go on my own. I come down the last part of the hill really fast and make my jump into the road. I land OK, but there's a huge noise behind me – a loud hooter, screeching brakes, and someone shouting. I'm so surprised that I fall down. When I look up, I see the electric milk van and our milkman. He's stopped just a few feet from me, but he's really angry:

"Are you crazy? What do you think you're doing? I could've killed you, do you realise that? I'm going to talk to your mother about you. You get yourself home right now, and don't you ever let me see you on this street again. You hear?"

He goes on and on like that. His face is bright red, and he's shouting. I can tell he's pretty serious, so I do what he says and start to go home. After I've taken my skates off and walked a little way, I look back. He's fixing the milk crates. Some of them have got shaken about and nearly fallen into the road, but as far as I can tell, nothing's been broken. I don't say anything to my mother when I get home. I keep waiting for him to tell her when he's delivering our milk, but he never does. Eventually, I stop worrying about him. But for some reason I never forget what happened that day. I don't try coming down that hill any more. I think maybe he was right; I could've got killed.

For a time, skating is the rage in Chelmsford, and lots of people go on Saturday to the Corn Exchange. You have to rent special skates with rubber wheels, and you have to skate in this big hall where there's a wooden floor. There's always music playing. Everyone has to skate the same way, round and round in one direction. Then they'll announce that you have to go the opposite way. Then, sometimes it's girls only, or beginners only, or experienced skaters only. They change the music to suit each group of skaters. It's a bit like music at the pictures. Somebody chooses it to fit whatever's happening in the film. I wouldn't mind a job like that – picking out just the right music to go with what's on the screen.

One summer, a kind of dream comes true when my father and mother get us a tent. It's supposed to be for all three of us, but I treat it as though it's mine. We put it up in the garden in the middle of the lawn. Uncle Jack knows how to do it, and I've read what you do in *Scouting for Boys*. Once we've done the poles, then we have to do the guy lines at the corners and along the sides. There's wooden pegs and my father brings us a wooden mallet from the garage to knock them in. Because it's not waterproof, we have to buy a can of special stuff that you put on with a big paintbrush. Also because there's no floor, we have to get a big army groundsheet from the surplus shop.

We play all kinds of games in the tent, but I want to camp in it. In the end my mother and father say I can sleep in it out in the garden if the weather's good. The first night I do it, I hardly sleep at all. It's dark out there, especially after all the street lights are turned off. Also, another reason I can't see anything is because the door of the tent is closed up. There are also all kinds of noises that are a bit frightening. I don't know what's making them, and I don't know where they're coming from. My father and mother have left the back door unlocked so that I can go back to bed indoors if I want. I also have my torch so that I won't bash into anything in the dark. But although I'm a little scared, I stay outside. I know they'd just laugh at me if I went in.

Some time very late, I must have gone to sleep, because the next thing I know is that it's getting light outside, and I can hear birds. There even seem to be birds on the top of the tent. I undo the tapes that keep the front of the tent closed. When I see a light in the house, I put my shoes on and go inside. My father's in the kitchen making tea.

"My, you're up early. How was camping? Did you have a good night out there?"

"Oh yes. I had a really good sleep, and I only woke up when the birds started."

"Well, I'm glad to hear you got some rest. Your mother and I thought you might be too scared to sleep."

"No, I was perfectly OK. I want to do it again."

"Well, not tonight. They're forecasting rain. We'll see about another time later."

I sleep in the garden a few more times, but then I have another idea. One of my friends, John Langton, lives on a farm not far from Galleywood. The farm does not have animals. Instead, they have apple orchards. John asks his father if we can camp in one of the orchards, and he says yes, as long as it's only for one night. We also ask another friend, Brian Howard, who lives on Galleywood Road, if he'll come too. His mother and father are fussy about it, but in the end they say it's OK. On the day, we meet at John's, and I have the tent all rolled up and tied on the back of my bike. I also have the groundsheet and a blanket for sleeping. John's father shows us a place where we can camp, and John's mother gives us piles of food to have for our dinner.

After we are on our own and we've set up the tent, we've got a whole lot of time before it gets dark and it's time to go to sleep. First we eat the food, but then we do other things. In a ditch near the tent, there are some special weeds that I know just what to do with. You cut part of the stem, but not near a joint. Something about three inches long makes a perfect cigarette because the stem is hollow and dry enough to burn. John's father has made us promise not to make any fires because he doesn't want to set the orchard alight. I don't think smoking counts, so we go ahead. The smoke from the weeds doesn't taste very nice, and it burns our throats, but it's still fun.

Just as we're about to give up smoking, John says he's got a surprise. He's nicked three cigarettes – real ones with filter tips – from his mother's bag. These taste much better, but we start to get a bit dizzy before we finish them. So we stub them out carefully and save them for another time.

We also go over to the ditch, and all three of us pee at the same time. We try and see who can pee farther than anyone else. It's hard to tell, but I think probably it's John. I know I pee for the longest time, but they say that doesn't mean anything; it's only because I drank more fizzy stuff than them.

We also compare our things. They're all different from each

other. In the end, we decide that each person likes his own best, and that's that. Then we go in the tent and get ready to go to sleep because it's nearly dark. We get under our blankets, but while we're there talking for a bit, something starts to happen. It's raining. I tell them not to worry because the tent's waterproof. The trouble is, it's not. Even though I painted a whole can of waterproofing stuff on the tent, the rain starts to drip through. There's nothing we can do to stop it. At first we move around to get out of the way of the drips, but then there's rain everywhere in a kind of spray. Just as we're trying to decide what to do, John's father arrives with a huge torch that lights up everything. With him we see Brian's mother and father. They say that Brian has to go home with them immediately, so off he goes, although I think he's really embarrassed. John's father then tells John and me, "This lot's going to be coming down all night. I'm telling you, you can't stay here. Looks like this tent's really leaking, too. You fellas have got a choice. You can come back to the house, or you can finish your camping in another place I'll show you."

We tell him we want to keep on camping, so he takes us to the farm buildings and shows us a barn where we can go. It's nice and dry there, and it smells good from all the apples that are being stored. We soon settle down and John's father leaves. I think we go to sleep very fast, and I don't remember much until we're having breakfast the next morning in John's house. His mother cooks us porridge, and I really like that. I just hope she doesn't find out about the cigarettes.

Although it's not as much fun as camping, I like collecting things. When I was little, I played marbles at school and with my friends. Now I've got a whole lot of them that I've won. I keep them in a cloth bag that my mother gave me. Also when I was little, I collected cigarette cards. I have quite a few different sets. At school when it's break time, groups of us stand around in circles and swap cards. That way, you can often find a card that's missing in a set you're collecting. I try to get complete sets of things like Soldiers' Uniforms, Flags of Different Nations, Cricketers, British Birds, and Kings and Queens.

After a while, I don't bother about marbles and cigarette cards any more. Instead, I start collecting something else: stamps. Unlike the marbles and the cigarette cards, I've still got my stamps even though I don't actually collect them any more.

The stamp collecting begins when people start to give me foreign stamps. Mostly these come from letters that people have sent them. Uncle Jack gets quite a few of these at his office and he brings them home for me. For Christmas, my mother and father get me a stamp album. They also get a big fat envelope full of all kinds of stamps from nearly every place you can think of. My mother says that these stamps are just to get me started. Each page in the stamp album is for a different country, starting with Aden and ending with Zanzibar and Zululand. If you fill up a page, you can buy extra blank pages and put them in the album. This is held together with a big spring clip. At the top of each page, it tells you about the country. Often I get the atlas out to see exactly where the country is, and sometimes I look in the encyclopaedia as well. A lot of stamps have pictures of an English king or queen on them. That's because so many countries are British colonies, or they're in the Commonwealth. These are the countries that are coloured red in the atlas.

I have so many stamps at first that it takes me a long time to sort them out and put them in the album. The stamps on envelopes have to be soaked in water till they peel off, and then they have to be dried on blotting paper. I have tweezers to lift stamps up, and I use stamp hinges to stick them in the album. The oldest stamps I've got have Queen Victoria on them, and I'm especially proud of my one-penny reds and my one twopenny blue English stamp. I just wish I had a penny black, but I've found they're too expensive for me to buy. I also have a blue triangular stamp from South Africa and a red one-penny triangular from the Cape of Good Hope before it became part of South Africa. I think this second one might be really valuable.

At school, there's a stamp club. I get to swap stamps there, and we learn about collecting mint as well as used stamps. We also learn that instead of collecting stamps from everywhere, it's better just to collect stamps from your favourite places. I find this hard, but I do try and get English stamps, and I do get rid of certain other countries such as the United States.

One problem is that when I go to the "Junk Shop", where I buy quite a few stamps, I never know what's going to be there. If something looks good, and if I can afford it, I'll buy it, because otherwise someone else will get it. Often I'll then swap something that I've bought from the Junk Shop for something I really want. Everyone calls this place the Junk Shop, but that's not its proper name. To get there you go down New Street beside the Shire Hall and past the police station and the swimming baths.

The other kind of collecting I do concerns something quite different. At about seven or eight, I become a trainspotter. At first,

I just like to go somewhere and watch trains coming or going. But after a year or so, together with some of my friends, I start to get more serious about it.

There's several things you need for train spotting. The first thing is a watch. I get one for my birthday, so I always know exactly what time it is. Then, with a small railway timetable, I can tell roughly when to expect a train, though of course, the timetable only shows the times when a train stops in a station. A very important thing that each of my friends has, and I do too, is a small book that has lists of all the locomotives of the LNER (the London North Eastern Region). We're not interested in the other regions, especially the Southern Region. This has mostly electric trains, except for some special trains for people going on ferries to France. Our books give the class of each locomotive, its name (if it has one), its number and its wheel layout. Then there's a place to mark down when you've seen an engine. That's very important for us, because we're always comparing each other's books to see who has seen the most engines. Although we write down every engine, we're mainly interested in the engines pulling passenger trains, so we don't care quite so much when we see a tanker pulling a goods train, for example.

With my friends, I go to certain places to do trainspotting. At first, we go mainly to the top of Bridge Road where the Writtle Road crosses over the railway line, but there are other places. Sometimes, for instance, we buy platform tickets and go on the platform at Chelmsford Station. We get a good close-up look at each engine that way, and sometimes the drivers or firemen say hello to us. Another place is across a field from the London Road, right next to the golf course. There's a crossing there for a footpath that goes on towards Galleywood. One day, we're at this place and we're playing around a bit, putting pennies on the line and seeing how they get squashed flat when a train runs over them. One time, I'm putting down a penny, and I forget to watch the train that's coming towards us. I think I have lots of time, but I don't. Somehow I don't even hear it as it gets close. When I look up and see it, it's nearly on top of me, and I only just manage to jump out of the way. The engine driver is shaking his fist at us and is yelling, but we can't hear his words.

I'm pretty shaky afterwards, and I don't even pick up the penny. Instead, we leave as fast as we can. We think that when the train gets to the station, the driver might send the police to get us. After that, we make sure we don't go back there for a few weeks.

Eventually, we find that we're seeing the same engines over and over. That's when we start thinking about other LNER lines, the one that goes north from Liverpool Street Station through Cambridge and Ely to Norwich, and the line that goes from King's Cross to Peterborough and on to Scotland. We could just about reach the first of these on our bikes by going west through Ongar and Epping, but we'd only have a little time there. Then we'd have to start coming home, because it's such a long ride. So what we do instead is go on the train to Liverpool Street Station in London. Then, we get platform tickets and go to the end of the longest platform there. That way we can see every train coming in and out. We see a whole lot of engines that we've never seen before, so we have a pretty exciting day. The first time we do this, my father and mother make a bit of a fuss, but when we get back without any problems, they relax a bit. After that, they stop fussing.

After we've done this a few times, I tell them I want to go to

King's Cross. To get there, you have to get on the underground train. I've never been to King's Cross, but the map of the underground that my father once gave me shows that you have to take the Circle Line. After a bit of fussing, my father says it's OK if I do this, and he gives me all sorts of instructions, like making sure we get a train that's going round the circle towards King's Cross and not away from it. But though it's OK for me to go, a couple of the other boys can't come because their parents say we're all too young. In the end, just two of us go. I'm a bit nervous, but try not to show it.

We find our way to the underground at Liverpool Street, and – big surprise - we find there are plenty of signs, even one that tells you which platform to get on for King's Cross. When we get there, we do the same as we do at Liverpool Street and go to the end of the longest platform. We see a whole lot of engines we've never seen before, so we know this is a good place to be. We also meet a whole lot of other trainspotters, some of them grown-ups who are quite friendly. We show them our books with the engines we've seen, and one of them says we're doing really well and we should keep up the good work.

Not long after this, we start to lose interest a bit, but then we learn that there's a whole class of new engines, and they're going to come through Chelmsford. These engines aren't even in our books, so we have to find a space for them at the back. These are Britannia class engines. Their wheel layout is 4-6-2, and their numbers start with 70000. I'm not the first to see one, but we discover that in the early evening from Monday to Friday, one comes from London. So we all start going to the Writtle Road bridge just to see it. When it comes, we all cheer and wave. It's bright green and has the name over the middle wheel. Though I always thought the LNER streamline engines were the best-looking, I think this is even better. Besides, there aren't any streamline engines on our line. The A4 Pacific Class engines, like the *Mallard*, the world speed record holder, and the *Edinburgh Castle* all run on other lines.

When my mother and father take me to the Festival of Britain in 1951, there's a brand new Britannia engine on show. It is number 70004 with the name *William Shakespeare*. My father says that the engine and lots of other things that we see are meant to show visitors from foreign countries just what Britain can do, even though we just had a war. I notice that the names of other engines are mostly names of famous Englishmen like *Geoffrey Chaucer* (70002), *John Bunyan* (70003), *Alfred the Great* (70009), *Oliver Cromwell* (70013), and *Iron Duke* (70014). The only one I can't understand is *Oliver Cromwell*. Whenever we go into old churches and find statues without heads, or just plain windows without stained glass, my father will say, "Cromwell was here." Why would anyone want to show off the name of someone who was famous for smashing up beautiful things?

In Chelmsford, at first it's just the same Britannia engine we see each day, but then we start to see others with different names and 70000 numbers. If the train is going too fast, the names are hard to read. Instead, you have to concentrate on getting the number that's on the front of the boiler and on the side of the engine cab. Once we've seen all the Britannia engines that they have on our line, we aren't quite so interested in collecting train numbers any more. But

I still keep my book, and if I happen to see an engine I've not seen before, I add it in.

One last thing I do, though it's not collecting, is go to the pictures. There are a lot of cinemas in Chelmsford. As I already explained, I nearly always go to Saturday morning pictures at the Regent. I sit downstairs where it costs 6d. Upstairs it costs 9d, but I don't like it up there because some of the kids are rough. They're always throwing pomegranate seeds and empty sweet wrappers down on those of us who pay 6d. I sometimes go to other cinemas on Saturday afternoon or during the week. Besides the Regent, there's the Odeon on Baddow Road and the Select on New Writtle Street. All three are quite near each other. I don't like the Select very much because it's small and it smells. Also, most of the time, they have films I don't want to see.

My father and mother also go to the pictures quite often. With Uncle Jack, they also go to the Film Club in the Shire Hall. When Laurence Olivier's *Henry V* comes out, they see that. Later, when it comes back again, my father says he's going to take me to see it. The story is by Shakespeare. I know about him because he's in the encyclopaedia. Also, my mother's always talking about seeing his play called *The Merry Wives of Windsor*. The actors were outdoors instead of in a theatre. I think she saw it in Danbury Park. Anyway, it was really funny, especially a character called Falstaff. My father didn't talk much about him. Instead, he talked about *Henry VIII*. This was another play by Shakespeare that was then made into a film. My father liked the bits where Henry VIII belched and when he picked up a whole chicken to eat. If any of us belched or if any of us had bad table manners, he would say, "Now then, who do you think you are, Henry VIII?"

Before he takes me to see *Henry V*, he tells me the story, but he says I might not understand a lot of the words. On the other hand, I'll probably enjoy the big battle where the English beat the French at Agincourt. He's right about that. Afterwards I keep telling my friends about it. How the English don't have as many soldiers as the French, and how they don't have such fancy armour and so many horses. What they have instead are men with bows and arrows. They all shoot together, and there are so many arrows that it's like a dark cloud in the sky before the arrows come down on top of the French. Also, of course, there's Laurence Olivier who's Henry V. He wears silver armour and rides on a big white horse. He makes this amazing speech to his soldiers to get them ready to fight. I can see why Henry V is a famous English hero. I can also see why Shakespeare is such a famous writer. I can't wait until I'm able to read his plays for myself. I already know we've got them all at home. There's a set of three volumes in the Everyman's Library. My father says I'll get to read some of them later on at school.

Usually, the films I see aren't as exciting as *Henry V*. I see *Pinocchio* with Aunty D. That makes me cry a bit. She also takes me to a very serious film, *The Blue Lamp*. It's about an English policeman, P.C. Dixon, who gets shot, and then his murderer is hunted down. She cries when we see this film. Afterwards, she says I must learn that guns are wrong but also we shouldn't hang people, even if they've been bad. I don't agree with her, but I keep quiet so that she doesn't get even more upset. With my friends, I see war films like *Twelve O'Clock High* and *The Desert Fox* (that's about Rommel). But we also see films that have been made from books. My favourites are *King Solomon's Mines*, *Kim*, *The Third Man*, and

Little Women. Then there are religious ones like *Samson and Delilah* and *Quo Vadis*, and all kinds of others like *Scott of the Antarctic* (Captain Scott is one of my heroes), *Winchester '73*, and *The Greatest Show on Earth.*

Of course, all the things I've just talked about aren't the only things I do when I'm not reading or doing music, but they're the main things.

Now it's time to talk about life in Maidstone.

CHAPTER FIVE

MAIDSTONE, GÖTTINGEN, PARIS, BLED

When we arrived in Maidstone in the summer of 1953, I was delighted with the house my father had found. It was bigger than our place on Finchley Avenue. Downstairs were both a bedroom – mine – and the bathroom. Upstairs were three bedrooms, so finally my sisters each had their own rooms, except for when visitors came to stay. What I especially liked about my room was that it had a bay window with a large window sill, big enough for me to put out my small but growing collection of books.

My bed took up a lot of space, but my mother eventually solved that issue by getting me a small settee that was also a pull-out bed. Early on, my mother also got me a small antique wooden desk where I could do my homework. Best of all, my room had its own gas fire, making it the warmest and cosiest room in the house if the weather was cold. Here in this room, not only could I do school work – there was always plenty of that – but I could read and I could be with my friends.

The first time I went to bed in my new room, when I was almost asleep, I was startled to hear a strange and disturbing sound – the distant (perhaps not so distant) roaring of lions. Or that's what I believed I could hear. The next morning when I told my parents, they laughed at me.

"Oh, and did you see that pig fly past the window just now? And you'd better check the garden for snakes. Tonight, don't open your window too wide. That'll keep the lions from making a dinner out of you."

But it wasn't so simple. Whenever I went to bed and it was quiet outside, I kept hearing what I thought were lions. This troubled me greatly. I didn't think I was hallucinating or anything like that. Apart from the roaring, everything else was totally normal – cars passing in the street, the occasional train at the bottom of Grace Avenue, and even the odd aeroplane. I kept quiet about the lions because I didn't want anyone laughing at me, but then something happened. One day, I plucked up courage to speak about the noises to a man who lived across the street, and the mystery was solved.

"Are there animals over there across the river?" I asked.

"Oh, yes, my boy, that's absolutely right. There's a zoo. It's Sir Garrard Tyrwhitt-Drake's pride and joy. He owns it, you know. You should pay a visit."

"And are there lions there?"

"Of course. What's a zoo without lions? Don't you hear them? Usually about eight or nine o'clock at night. I reckon it must be their feeding time, or else they think it's time to go out hunting."

Feeling completely vindicated, I told my parents about my discovery. I really had heard lions. To my surprise and considerable annoyance, they barely seemed interested. "Oh, yes, so you were right after all. Glad we've got that one cleared up."

And that was the end of the matter. Even when I tried bringing the subject up again with my mother, she pretty well ignored what I said and used the opportunity to go off on a topic I'd heard a few times before, about how zoos were cruel. Animals should never be shut up in cages. It just wasn't right. We should leave them alone and let them stay in their natural environments, polar bears in the arctic, camels in North Africa, kangaroos in Australia, and lions and elephants in the African grasslands. She certainly wasn't going to visit the Zoo, not ever.

My encounter with the nocturnal roaring of lions, though it had its comic side, was in other respects quite a learning experience. My own perceptions and intuition in the face of adult scepticism, I discovered, could be right. At the same time, what was of central importance to me might be of only peripheral or passing interest to others. Furthermore, my perception of something (in this instance, lions roaring in the night, a sound to me both magnificent and verging on the frightening) might differ immensely in its focus from someone else's view (my mother's compassion for the lions and for all the animals incarcerated in zoos for profit and entertainment). What's more, there might be merit in both points of view. What then? Now, so much later, having observed lions in their natural habitat, I support my mother's view of zoos. Having heard those same sounds in the wild, I often come back to the memory of my first night in Maidstone and the awe-inspiring and, yes, fearful roaring I had heard.

Of course, once we were settled in our new house, there were plenty of other matters aside from lions to claim our attention. There were, for example, all kinds of new places to see and new walks to take. Uncle Jack still spent a great deal of time with us. Almost every weekend, he would come on the bus from Chelmsford, taking the Tilbury to Gravesend ferry across the Thames, and then more buses to get to our house. With new maps and bus timetables, we began to find our way around our part of the Kentish countryside. Many of our walks took us along segments of the Pilgrims' Way, a walking track along the side of the North Downs. It seemed to go from village to village, so there were always new pubs and churches to explore. Sometimes, rather than going on a walk, we stayed in a single place and explored that. I'm thinking of our visits to Canterbury and its cathedral, Knole Park and the stately home that you could tour, or Rochester, where there was both a cathedral and a castle. As ever, beer was an important factor. Fortunately, the most common local brew in Kent was Fremlins, something my father and Uncle Jack decided was superior to what the Essex pubs served.

Because Maidstone is not too far from Rainham, we sometimes met Uncle Eric, Aunty Kate and my cousins for a picnic. The preferred meeting place was the pub in Boxley, which my father and uncles all said had very good beer. Conveniently, the village of Boxley was about halfway between our two homes. My cousins were Judith, Max, Nick, and Felicity, then, much later, Joanna. They all lived in a small council house in Rainham because Uncle Eric, who was a Labour Party councillor, believed that everyone should live in houses built by the government. He and my father always talked about politics. I suspect that Uncle Eric believed my father wasn't as fervent a Labour Party person as he was. My father may have supported the ideology of socialism, but in reality, as Uncle Eric grumpily pointed out, he sought to live the life of the middle class bourgeoisie. Because my father was happy to accept some of the benefits that Labour had won, like free healthcare, free dental and eye care, publicly-funded education and unemployment and social insurance, it was hypocritical of him, according to Uncle Eric, to own his own house and amass money to better the lifestyle of his family. I think Uncle Eric may have started some of these arguments just because he liked arguing, but I know they made my father uncomfortable and no one else joined in, including Uncle Jack.

At home, my father and mother would sometimes talk about these arguments, and my mother would say how Uncle Eric was the real hypocrite. Council houses were meant for working class people who couldn't afford anything else; Uncle Eric was just taking advantage of the system to get cheap housing for himself and his family.

I liked my Aunty Kate and my cousins very much, and I never understood why we didn't see them more often. Aunty Kate was always lots of fun, and she was always very friendly. She used to ask me a lot of questions, but I didn't mind that because she never seemed in the least bit judgmental. I liked seeing her, and when I learned what buses to take, I would sometimes go to Rainham for a visit on my own. Whenever I did, I had a good time. Judith was my oldest cousin, and she was about the same age as me. I especially liked talking to her, even though sometimes she upset me. For example, she said on one occasion that my family had more money than her family, and that's why they lived in a council house that was so very small. I never knew what the truth was – I suspect she got these ideas from her father – but it was hardly my fault.

Another reason I liked visiting my cousins was that Uncle Eric had a gramophone and a great many records. He knew I liked music, and he would play things for me. Eventually, he showed me how to work the machine and allowed me to listen to records, even when he was not there. Not only did he have records of music by the standard classical composers like Mozart and Beethoven, but he had some more modern music that he urged me to hear, even if I didn't like it at first. That's why it was so good to have a gramophone; one could listen to the same piece of music over and over again and really get to know it.

For me, one of the best features of our house in Maidstone was that it had a large back garden that included an underground air raid shelter. When I explored it, I first had to clear away all kinds of rubbish blocking the concrete steps leading down to the shelter itself. This consisted of a small room, large enough to stand up in and furnished with a small table and a bench. The electric lighting was long gone, so I had to make do with candles or a torch if I was going to spend any time there. This was certainly what I planned, because I realised as soon as I saw it that it would make a perfect den for me and my friends. Not surprisingly, my father was never happy about this, especially after he found I'd put up some pinups on the wall. He and I had constant arguments about my spending too much time there when I could be out in the fresh air.

After a couple of years or so, he seemed to give up arguing with me about the shelter. Instead, without even telling me in advance, he and Uncle Jack got hold of a sledge hammer and a pickaxe. With a lot of swearing and sweating, they managed to smash in the roof and fill in the holes where the steps and room had been. Then they added good soil on top so that the space could become part of the garden. Eventually, my father made a rose bed there.

I was both angry and upset by what my father and uncle had done to the shelter, and for quite a while I shut myself up in my room and wouldn't talk to anyone. But then, about a week later, and maybe as a kind of compensation for what they had done, my father allowed me to create a different kind of den in a far corner of the garden. In this spot, I first dug a large hole, building up walls with the excavated soil but leaving space to cut out steps down into the den. I shaped the interior walls to provide a seat all round, and I made a fireplace. Then, using whatever materials I could find, including some sheets of corrugated iron, I built a roof. A large piece of metal tubing made a perfect chimney for the fireplace. This new den was a great success, and my friends and I spent many hours there. We'd just sit around talking. If we had enough money to buy cigarettes, we'd smoke, something I'd never get away with in the house.

The den belonged to what I might fancifully call the "Huck Finn" part of my adolescence. When Huck felt "cramped up and sivilized", he carved out a measure of freedom from the restraints of life with the Widow Douglas and Miss Watson and the education they sought to give him. Eventually, he "lit out" and drifted down the river on a raft with Jim. No more living in a house, sleeping in a bed, and troubling with itchy new clothes. And no more schooling or lectures about the evils of smoking. I did not read Twain's book until many years later, but when I did, I recognized how well he had captured in Huck something of a boy's desire for a life free from the constraints of society and the adult world. Of course, the den at 19 Maple Avenue was nothing to Huck's raft. Nevertheless, it was something of an escape, even though I never slept in it, and even though I never complained when my mother, in very civilised fashion, used regularly to bring me out cups of tea and biscuits, always announcing well in advance and in a loud voice that she was on her way.

Another step in my bid to be "free" had to do with our annual family holidays. One year, I just refused to go. Somewhat to my surprise, I was allowed to stay behind at home and look after myself. I wasn't supposed to have friends in, but I did anyway. However, I was always very careful to clean up so that there would never be any sign that anyone else had been there.

I quite enjoyed the first week that I was on my own, but then I started to get bored. Everything was so quiet, and making meals was a lot of work. I actually started to look forward to the end of the second week when they'd all be coming home. Of course, when they did get home, I soon got tired of hearing about all the things they had done. I got tired, too, of answering all their questions and telling them that I had got along just fine. I had had plenty to do, I explained, and I hadn't been bored at all.

Soon after this breaking away from the ritual of the two-week family holiday, I had further experiences of time away. In 1956, after two or three years of German at school, our teacher arranged for some of us, together with some students from the Girls' Grammar School, to do an exchange with some German students in Göttingen. Each of us would be paired with a German student in whose home we would stay. Then later, the Germans would come to Maidstone and stay in our homes. I was excited about the venture, but secretly somewhat apprehensive. Would I like my exchange partner? Would he and his family like me? Would they understand my German, and did I know enough German to get by? What would the food be like?

When the time came, we first had to get to Göttingen. Since I'd never been anywhere abroad, this in itself was an adventure. First, under the guidance of my German teacher, we took a train to Dover and then the ferry to Ostend, thereby making Belgium the first foreign country I had visited. Not that we saw much, because, as soon as we left the boat, we got on a train. Soon we were in Germany, but we didn't see much of that country either because in my compartment there were girls to talk to. I was not used to talking to girls because I had been in boys-only schools since I was seven. However, I was starting to think about girls, and here was a good opportunity, so I made sure I was sitting next to one of them.

To my relief, I found it was quite easy to talk to her, but I was interested in something else besides talking. She was well known because she let boys kiss her, or so some of my friends said. Would she let me kiss her? After it got dark and our teacher came round to tell everyone to try and get some sleep, we turned the lights down, and I had my first experience of kissing a girl. She even let me touch her breasts, which was far more than I was expecting. I'd not thought of anything like that, so it was more of a surprise than perhaps it should have been.

During the night, we came to Cologne, where we were briefly able to walk out on the station platform. From the station, I could see the cathedral, which was just like the pictures I'd seen on some of my German stamps, an impressive twin-towered gothic structure. Then it was back on the train and on towards Göttingen. The kissing resumed, but pretty soon we both fell asleep.

When I woke up, it was light. It was time to get ready for Göttingen and for the first meeting with Diethelm and his family.

Diethelm was someone with whom I was very comfortable right away. He was serious about school and things like that, but he was also a lot of fun. His mother was very nice too, and she was always doing things for us. For example, when she found out that I played the piano, she arranged for me to go to the house of someone she knew who had a harpsichord. When I went, she made sure I had some flowers to take with me. I'd never played a harpsichord before, so I was thrilled about that. I played some Bach, and everyone seemed to like it. Later, I was able to go back one more time before coming home, and I've never forgotten it.

In both the house where I played the harpsichord and in Dieter's house, there was no father around, and I soon learned not to ask questions about fathers because if they weren't there, they'd probably been killed in the war. Dieter did, however, have grandparents who lived with him and his mother. They were a very genial couple, and the grandfather seemed to take a liking to me. After every evening meal, he offered me a small glass of schnapps. I always accepted and I always made sure he gave me only a little. I don't think Diethelm's mother approved, and she wouldn't let Diethelm have any. In truth, I would rather have had beer, something I was able to buy at all the cafés I went to, without anyone asking my age as would have happened in England.

Diethelm found a bicycle for me to use, and together we did some exploring. On one trip, he took me to the Wesel river. The trip I most remember, however, was along a country road that ended abruptly at a barrier with a small sign that said "Zoll/Douane". This was the so-called Iron Curtain, marked with a wide strip of ploughed land that went in both directions as far as one could see. There was no one about, but we could see in the distance a tall guard tower. Diethelm said that if we put a foot on the ploughed ground, we could get shot by the East German guards. That was somewhat frightening. While he was explaining all this, everything became more frightening when some guards came along the other side of the ploughed strip. They all had guns, which made me want to leave, but Diethelm said no. We shouldn't let them see we were scared. Then he told me that some of his friends would yell out insults when they saw the border guards, but he thought it was best just to stay where you were and say nothing.

After a while the soldiers continued their patrol, and we got back on our bikes and left. Later, we told Diethelm's mother and grandparents about where we'd been. His mother wasn't too happy about it, and his grandfather used the opportunity to talk about something I hadn't thought about. He blamed the Russians for there being a border, and then he said that lots of families had been divided because of it. He knew people who had family in East Germany but who couldn't visit them. I then understand why many people in West Germany hated the Russians and hated being divided.

Decades later, I remembered all this when I visited West Berlin and then crossed over into East Germany for a short visit. When the Iron Curtain ceased to exist in 1989 and the two halves of Germany were reunited, I wondered about the many families who could now be together again. At the same time I realised that if older people had died, they would often have died without ever having had the chance to see some of the younger members of their family.

Another vivid memory I have of Diethelm concerns the time he dressed up as a girl and we went down to the centre of Göttingen together as though we were a couple. He wore a headscarf that disguised his lack of hair, a calf-length skirt he'd borrowed from his mother and white open-topped shoes, fastened with a thin leather strap. He also used some of his mother's makeup. To complete the effect, he carried a small white handbag. As I tried to point out, his hands were too big for a woman, and his voice was too low, but he insisted on going ahead with his plan.

Once we were in the centre of Göttingen, I took a picture of him sitting on the side of the fountain, and Diethelm took great delight in introducing himself to any of his school friends who happened to pass by. They rarely recognised him at first, much to Diethelm's delight.

While in Göttingen, I was taken to numerous other places, sometimes by Diethelm and his mother and sometimes by our German teacher. The place that most impressed me was Kassel. Although there were brand new buildings and shops in the centre of the city, behind them in many places was a wasteland of bombed buildings. Not just the odd building, but everything. This was the result of an Allied bombing attack in 1943. Even in London, I'd not seen anything quite like this. What if the Germans had done that to Chelmsford? Would I even be here now?

Apparently more than 500 RAF bombers had dropped 1,800 tons of high explosive bombs, together with 460,000 magnesium fire sticks. The idea was to create a fire storm that would cause maximum destruction. Some 10,000 people died as a result, and 150,000 people lost their homes. Decades later, when I returned to Kassel to work for a few weeks in the library, I saw that most of the war damage had been cleaned up. Buildings that had been destroyed had been replaced with new buildings, and some of the more important old buildings, such as the Fridericianum, formerly a library, had been repaired and restored. Even so, if you looked closely, you could find places where the damage was still visible.

Just on the edge of Kassel was Wilhelmshöhe, a huge park on the side of a hill. At the foot of the hill is the Schloss Wilhelmshöhe, a palace that is now an art gallery, and on the side of the hill is an intricate network of water fountains and cascades. For recreation, people in Kassel climb the hill, at the top of which is a statue of Hercules. At certain times the water is turned on and starts its journey down the hill. It's fun to walk down at the same time, visiting all the buildings and waterfalls off to the side. At the bottom is a gigantic fountain where the water shoots up many metres in the air. I had never seen any landscape structure on this scale before. Needless to say, I was glad that the English bombers had not destroyed it all, although, when I saw it the first time, the Schloss Wilhelmshöhe was closed because of war damage.

When I came back to Maidstone, I'm sure I was quite a bore to both family and friends. I felt that I had seen and experienced so much, and I needed to share it all. How else would people know what essentially was my new older self?

A year later, in 1957, I was able to go abroad again, this time to France for a student exchange with Michel, who lived in Paris on the Rue de Sèvres. I enjoyed seeing the sights of Paris, but Michel was not nearly as easy-going as Diethelm. He was often very moody, particularly at first, and we got into some fierce arguments. Usually, he wanted to prove that France was superior to England, and he liked to cite historical things going back to the time of Napoleon. However, he got even more angry if I so much as mentioned Trafalgar or Waterloo. Because I didn't know all that much about this period of European history, I had to let him get the better of me, especially as I didn't really care about the relative prowess of our two countries anyway.

I wasn't the only person who had trouble with Michel. I could see that his parents found him difficult. He was often rude to his mother, but his father wouldn't let him get away with anything. In truth, Michel's father was something of an authoritarian, but he was nonetheless very pleasant about everything, just so long as you did what he wanted. He had a job making maps, something that fascinated me, and he often let me watch him at work. I think he was pleased that someone found his work interesting.

But there was something else. Every night after dinner, which could go on for quite a long time as there were so many courses, we all had to sit down with him and play bridge. Fortunately, I had learned with my friends at school how to play, but really I knew very little. It was as if I was playing chess, knowing how all the pieces on the board moved but not having the least idea about strategy.

It turned out that Michel's father was a member of the French national bridge team, so playing with him was at first very intimidating. When I realised that he seemed to know what cards each person had, I gave up worrying too much and treated the whole thing as a lesson. I even made notes about what he said. First he taught us how to count points during the bidding process, and then as we played, he gave us lessons on what we should be doing. All the time, I could feel my bridge skills getting better and better, and I started looking forward to the time when I could share his lessons with my friends at school.

After a week or two, we all went to the family's summer home in the village of Ouhans in the south east of France near the border with Switzerland. Ouhans seemed very small and remote. As far as I could tell, there was only one bus a week, but no one minded about this. The idea was to have a change from the apartment in Paris.

I had never been anywhere quite like this. At night, I had to keep the windows of my room closed because of the mosquitoes, but when I opened them in the morning, I found I was looking down into the yard of a neighbouring farmer. Right under my window was a big dung heap. The smell was quite strong, but to my surprise I quickly got used to it. To this day, the smell of cow dung doesn't bother me at all.

Every morning, Michel and I had to take turns going to the farmer's dairy for a pail of milk. There was also bread to be collected before breakfast in the morning and before supper in the evening– big round loaves, somewhat coarse in texture but delicious to eat, especially when still warm. In the evenings, the family bridge games continued, except when Michel's father had work to do back in Paris. When he was in Ouhans, he often led us on walks in the neighbouring hills. He liked to collect all manner of mushrooms, and he knew which kinds were safe to eat and which weren't. I'd always thought there was only one kind one could eat, but not so. Back at the house, he would move into the kitchen, make a lot of fuss, but cook the most delicious omelettes for our evening meal.

As in Germany, my hosts knew I played the piano. They themselves did not have an instrument, but in the village, there was an elderly woman who did. She invited me to come and play to her. Unfortunately, it was a terrible piano that was badly out of tune. What's more, she only had a little music, and I wasn't much good unless I had notes in front of me. However, she had a few pieces I could play, including one that really delighted her. This was an arrangement of the 18th variation in Rachmaninov's *Rhapsody on a Theme of Paganini*. This had been reworked as a song, so there were French lyrics above the piano part. The woman would sit beside me as I played and softly sing the words. She wanted to do this over and over. The result was that my playing of the piano part improved immeasurably. Because she had her windows open, I think the whole village could hear us. For days afterwards, people would stop me on the street to say something about it.

Michel had a bicycle, and it was not long before his mother was able to borrow one for me. I think she was delighted every time she could send Michel and me off on bike rides around the neighbouring countryside. Our absence provided a quiet day at home for her.

One day, Michel proposed that we should take a ride into Switzerland. Michel's parents were a bit dubious about this, but that only made Michel even more insistent. After making sure we had all the right documents, they let us go. After all, it wasn't far to the border, and we were only going for a day.

After crossing the border, we soon learned a lesson that no one had anticipated, not even our resident cartographer. Biking in Switzerland is not a good idea. Very soon the road we were on became so steep that we had to get off our bikes and push them. With no end to the climb in sight, we arrived at the foot of a cable lift that went to the summit of the mountain, the slopes of which we had been traversing. After parking our bikes, we hopped on to the lift. The ride took quite a long time, all the while taking us higher and higher.

Now came lesson two. Wearing only shorts and short-sleeve shirts, we were completely unprepared for the frigid temperatures that we encountered. Shivering with cold, and not finding any shelter where we could get warm, we took only a cursory glance at the magnificent view. Then, as soon as we could without too much loss of dignity, we took the lift back down as fast as possible, thinking that perhaps we'd never be warm again.

Once down, we ate the enormous lunch that Michel's mother had made us and gradually began to recover. Before we set off for the return ride, in a rare moment of accord, Michel and I both agreed that neither of us would ever say anything about the negative things that had happened.

Following the family's return to Paris, I was invited to go to Arras and stay with the family of Chantal, a French girl I'd met in Maidstone. She had been on an exchange visit with Ann, who lived in the house immediately behind us. Now, Ann was with Chantal. One day during my visit, Chantal's father, a high-ranking official with the French railways, arranged for his chauffeur to take Chantal, Ann and me on a tour of several mostly First World War cemeteries and memorials. In deference to Ann and me, we first visited a small British cemetery, but then we went on to the French national cemetery at Notre-Dame de Lorette. I was completely awestruck. It was a huge site, laid out to accommodate the graves of some 40,000 French soldiers with a building containing the remains of 22,000 unknown soldiers. I found it quite overwhelming. The sight of so many graves and the need to try and absorb what it meant was an experience that I had neither sought nor expected. As a result, I had difficulty talking to Chantal and Ann once we left. That they had not been affected in any comparable way only made it more difficult to deal with my feelings. What I wanted to do was cry, but that was something unthinkable while in the company of my female friends.

But the tour was not over. From Notre-Dame de Lorette, we went to Vimy Ridge. Again I was taken aback by the scale and immensity of the place. It was not a cemetery but a gigantic memorial on the top of the hill that had been captured by Canadian soldiers towards the end of the war in April 1917. Inscribed around the base of the memorial are the names of over 11,000 Canadians killed in France whose remains have not been found or identified. Close by one can walk through what's left of some of the trenches, a number of which have been reconstructed. In addition, one can go down into the tunnels that permitted soldiers to approach or leave the battle line in comparative safety. Those waiting in the tunnels sometimes made carvings or wrote on the walls. Everything, it appeared, had been left more or less untouched.

Both the memorial itself, with its two pylon towers and its array of sculptural figures, together with the remnants of the war close by, affected me considerably. Memories of them, or more particularly the feelings they evoked, have stayed with me to this day. In part they explain why, a year or so after I returned home to Maidstone, I joined the CND (Campaign for Nuclear Disarmament). At school, I wore a CND badge, in spite of the raised eyebrows of some of the teachers, and I participated in the annual Easter protest marches from Aldermaston to London, Aldermaston being where nuclear weapons were manufactured. Buoyed by the presence of the thousands of other marchers who walked the 83 kilometres (approximately 52 miles), and inspired by the leadership of people like Canon John Collins and philosopher Bertrand Russell, I naively expected changes in government policy to take place as a result of our efforts. Instead, in the years that followed, the government did nothing apart from issuing laughable and idiotic leaflets such as "Advising the Householder on Protection against Nuclear Attack" and "Protect and Survive," this latter containing similar advice on "how to make your home and your family as safe as possible under nuclear attack".

At the time of the marches, I was additionally influenced by the fact that my father, who worked for the Ministry of Agriculture, was sent out to talk to farmers and advise them on the contents of the government leaflet entitled "Home Defence and the Farmer" (1958). I doubt that my father was a very effective choice for this task. He considered he was being made an instrument of bizarre propaganda that had little in common with reality. Assuring farmers that most human beings would be able to protect themselves by taking shelter from fallout, and telling them that bundles of hay at either end of a barn would help keep livestock safe, were to him totally fatuous concepts.

Not only was he angry about such cynical deceptions, he was also disturbed by something else. The government, he had learned, was secretly building a series of secure bunkers where "important" officials (he wasn't one of them) would go in order to be able to maintain governmental control once everything returned to "normal". Certain books – my father had the list – would also be preserved from harm. We laughed together at the choice of some of the titles.

Many years later, memories of my visits to the war cemeteries and memorials in France, and memories of CND and the Aldermaston marches were very much with me when I published what turned out to be a somewhat controversial article on Canadian First World War memorials. I also encountered a certain amount of hostility when I gave an annual guest lecture to the Peace Studies class at Acadia University in the 1990s, and when I presented a lecture on the U.S. Second World War memorial at McMaster University in 2008.

While still at school, I made yet one further venture abroad. In 1958, I joined the Ramblers' Association, an organization that promotes walking and arranges walking holidays. I signed up to take a walking tour in what was then Yugoslavia. As a consequence, I found myself in a hostel in Bled with a group of about a dozen very friendly adults, all older than me and all more experienced walkers than I was. Every morning, there were organized walks close to Bled, and in the afternoons two of the women led informal walks for anyone interested. Alternatively, one could swim in Lake Bled or sunbathe beside it. Much of the walking involved hill climbing, all good preparation for the highlight of the holiday, which was a very strenuous walk to the overnight lodge high on Mount Triglav (2,864 metres or 9396 feet) in the Julian Alps. The scenery was spectacular, but I learned yet another lesson: don't wear shorts when hiking on snow, or you could suffer severe and painful sunburn on the backs of your knees.

The other highlight of the Yugoslav venture was a bus trip via Lubiana to Trieste. Four years earlier, Trieste had become part of Italy after the turmoil of the Second World War and the city's brief period as an independent state. My principal companion on this excursion was George, one of the ramblers with whom I had become quite friendly. He and I wandered about the city for a time before having a magnificent and prolonged lunch at a small restaurant. Food was a constant preoccupation of the slightly overweight George, and as the meal progressed and the wine kept coming, he became more and more relaxed and effusive about his life. He was single and liked it that way, and he had two particular enthusiasms: gambling and walking. On weekends, he would spend much of Saturday at the dog track, and on Sundays he would take a train from one of the main London stations to a not-too-distant place where he could walk. His five-day work week (I never did find out what he did) seems to have been of negligible interest to him, a mere enforced interlude between the enjoyment of what mattered most in his life – the excitements of the dog track and the pleasures of country walks.

As the holiday in Bled progressed, my fellow walkers got used to me and my relatively young age. As a result, I found myself party to all manner of discussions about matters of which I had little or no experience. I found myself getting an education that I had certainly not planned on. In addition, I shared a room at the hostel with George and another man, and they too sometimes had conversations that could be beyond my range of experience. Once or twice, they talked about sex, and I had to ask what something meant. Of course, they found this highly amusing, while for me it was very embarrassing. On the other hand, I felt I had to shove that embarrassment aside and find out everything I could at whatever cost.

After returning from Yugoslavia, I met up with George on a number of occasions to share his Sunday walks. However, it wasn't long before his gambling obsession began to spoil things. On two successive weekends in particular, all he could talk about was how much money he had lost the day before. Gone was his usual cheeriness, and he remained quite glum and morose for the whole of our walk. I found it all very depressing.

As the weeks passed, I came to the conclusion that if the quality of our friendship was going to be dependent upon his luck at the track, I was not willing to carry on. Rather than confront him about this, I'm sorry to say that I took the easy way out and simply stopped meeting him. Often, I have wondered what happened to this man who was capable of being so jovial and friendly and such good company, just so long as he had had a good day at the track.

Financing such things as the trip to Yugoslavia, train fares for weekend walks with George, purchases of books, pellets for my air gun or visits to the cinema was often a problem. I had my weekly pocket money from my father, and both parents were very generous in giving me extra money from time to time, but I always felt financially stretched. A partial solution emerged when a classmate and I jointly took on the task of delivering evening newspapers to the houses in the area in which we both lived. Every day after school, we went to each of two depots (there were two different evening papers) to pick up the newspapers. Often we had to wait while the "stop press" news, horse racing results or football scores were added. Then, carrying our bundles of newspapers, together with our school satchels, which were often full of books, we caught the bus home. After dividing up the papers and dropping off the satchels, we used our bikes to get around our respective routes as fast as possible.

Friday was pay day, and we had to knock on each door to receive our money, part of which had to go to the men from whom we had got the papers. Collecting money was a new learning experience. Each customer was very different. Some, particularly older men living on their own, would want to talk and ask questions. I suppose they were lonely. The only consolation to us was that they often gave the best tips. Others would hardly speak at all. These particular customers would only partially open the door as though to prevent one from seeing inside the house, and they would thrust the money at us, often with the most minimal of tips.

Most difficult for me, however, was going to the house of one of my classmates. His father was a banker, and his mother, though always polite and friendly, often seemed somewhat aloof. Although nothing was ever said, I could tell that she disapproved of a grammar school boy delivering papers. It was very obvious that her son would never have been permitted to do such a demeaning job.

To add to the income we received from our regular customers, we developed a second venture, although it involved carrying even more papers on the bus home. We persuaded the two people who supplied our papers to put up racks next to our home bus stop. The idea was that people coming home from work could then, if they were interested, pick up a paper to read. They were expected to drop the necessary money in a box beside each paper rack. This we would pick up later in the evening, along with any unsold papers. Once a week we would return our unsold papers and be reimbursed for them. This worked surprisingly well, and we found that we acquired a considerable number of customers. However, they weren't all honest, and almost every day there was a small discrepancy between the number of papers taken and the amount of cash deposited. Clearly, some people weren't paying for their papers.

To counteract the dishonesty of some of our customers, we responded with a bit of dishonesty of our own. We persuaded a number of our paper route customers to return their used papers to us when we collected their weekly money. These papers we refolded very carefully and returned for reimbursement with our unsold papers from the bus stop racks. Overall, our total profits were good, but the more customers we acquired, the harder the work. Especially difficult was finding other people to stand in for us when we couldn't manage things, usually because of some event at school or (in the summer holidays) because one of us was away. Eventually, as the end of our school years approached and having learned about some of the demands of running a small business, we passed the whole operation (minus the dishonest bit) on to some other boys.

A major planned use of the money I had earned was for another Ramblers' walking holiday, this time in Spain. But then something happened. Without any prior warning, a girlfriend, about whom I was very serious, announced that she didn't want to see me any more. I was completely stunned and very hurt by this. Furthermore, I'd never before experienced any kind of rejection the like of this. I had nothing to compare it with. Even my totally unexpected failure in British History in the GCE exams hadn't hit me with the pain I now felt. Part of me felt very angry, and quite irrationally I cancelled the visit to Spain and decided to use my savings for something else, a motorbike. But motorbikes were more expensive than I could afford, and my parents were very much against my having one.

The compromise was a used motor scooter which I bought from a friend of Aunty D. It proved to be underpowered and unreliable, but I soon learned to cope with its various limitations. No one I knew had such a thing, and for a time I was able to cheer myself up by giving rides to all and sundry and by surprising the teachers at school when I showed up on it and parked it alongside their cars in the "Teachers' Parking Area".

One place to which I regularly took the scooter was the jazz club on London Road, not far from our home on Maple Avenue. This was partly a means of avoiding the walk home since a year or two earlier I'd been attacked by four men when walking home from the club. They had all gone to prison as a result, but they'd threatened that they or their families would "get" me for this. I took this quite seriously, and at night I took precautions to make sure I didn't walk anywhere alone. When I visited my girlfriend and rode home at night on my bike, I would take a back lane not open to cars. I would switch off the lights on my bike and in the darkness I would ride as fast as I could, knowing that anyone on the path would not see me coming. In case I ran into trouble, I carried a dagger in the form of a sharp-pointed paper knife, and I vowed to myself that if anyone ever messed with me, I'd show no hesitation in killing them. Riding the scooter at night eased some of my worries and in retrospect prevented me from stupidly dashing about with a dagger in my pocket.

However, I still had an important lesson to learn. In my last year at school, when my parents had moved away from Maidstone and I stayed behind in lodgings to finish my school year, I went one Saturday night to the jazz club. As usual, I had a certain amount to drink. Coming home in the rain, I misjudged speed and distance as I approached my lodgings. When I braked, the scooter slid from under me with my foot caught under it. Although bruised and very shaken up, I was able to pick myself up and park the scooter in the driveway of the house.

However, when I got myself indoors, I discovered that my ankle was a mess. It wasn't broken, but it was severely grazed. My landlady was in bed asleep, but her daughter had heard the commotion, and she helped me deal with my ankle. We washed the wound and covered it with a big dressing we found in the bathroom.

Unfortunately, the wound didn't heal as quickly as I had hoped. I was about to say farewell to Maidstone and ride to our new home in Bromley, and I planned to arrive and avoid having to say anything about my ankle. Instead, however, the wound became infected and turned a most unpleasant green colour. It even started to smell a bit.

When I got to Bromley, my mother quickly spotted that something was wrong and sent me off to see a doctor. He was quite annoyed that I hadn't sought a doctor's help earlier, but over the course of a few weeks, the ankle got better, leaving me with an impressive scar.

Did I learn from this episode? In theory, I suppose I did. Don't drink and drive. However, I have to confess that it was a very long time before I developed the maturity to give proper heed to the lesson I'd been given.

Before returning in the next two chapters to my central topics of music and books, two more learning experiences need to be recounted. The first will seem hypocritical, given my involvement in the peace movement. When I arrived at Maidstone Grammar School, conscription had been in place for some time, and everyone understood that once we'd finished school, we could expect to do National Service for two years. On the advice of most of the teachers, many former students had signed up for an extra year as a means of getting a commission. The extra year also permitted one to work on a particular skill, the favourite among ex-Maidstone students being Russian, an obvious choice during the Cold War era.

In preparation for the military experience to come, the school had its own CCF (Combined Cadet Force), membership of which was virtually compulsory. Almost everyone signed up. Most people joined the army cadets, but a few, who planned to go into the Air Force, became Air Force cadets. I chose the Army cadets, and once a week, along with my fellow students, I went to school in my uniform – khaki battledress top with shoulder flashes saying "Maidstone Grammar School", khaki trousers, a very itchy khaki shirt and tie, a black beret with a brass badge, black boots, gaiters, and a belt with brass buckles. The night before was always a hectic business because the webbing of both belt and gaiters had to be cleaned with Blanco, the badge and buckles had to be polished with Brasso and the boots had to be cleaned and shined, preferably so that one could see one's face reflected in the toe caps. All this greatly amused my father, who'd had to go through the same routine during the war. His advice, however, was invaluable when it came to the boots and getting just the right mix of spit and black polish to create the required mirror effect.

Once at school, one could do a little more work on one's uniform between classes, and before the afternoon parade, for which everything had to be perfect. There was also time to go to the school armoury to sign out one's rifle. This, too, had to be cleaned and polished inside and out, together with the webbing sling that came with it. Following the parade, each platoon usually had some drill work, and then there were classroom lessons on such matters as map reading, using a compass, basic military tactics, both attack and defence, the use of a Bren gun (there was one for each platoon), and camouflage. Every so often, we were able to go outside and practise what we had learned, either on the school grounds or in the nearby parkland. We also were taught some basics of hand-to-hand combat, along with how to use bayonets. Our officers, who were teachers who had themselves only a few years earlier been in the war, were knowledgeable and encouraging, but I suspect that what we were doing didn't have much in common with what they had experienced not so very long ago.

Once a year, we went to one of two army training camps: Shorncliffe near Folkestone in Kent or Stanford near Thetford in Norfolk. Other schools sent their cadets there, so some of our training exercises were on a grand scale. With blank ammunition for our rifles and camouflage paint for our faces and hands, along with a special field training outfit to replace what we normally wore, everything started to feel much more realistic. We were taken to our start points in army trucks, and set off to find and attack an enemy, made up from cadet corps from other schools. The whereabouts of our enemy was initially unknown to us. Once we made contact, we started using the tactics we'd learned while training at school, with what effect it was hard to tell since we only had blank ammunition, and our Bren guns, which couldn't fire anything, had to be represented by the sounds of large wooden rattles, one for each gun. In the course of the "battle", thunder flashes were set off among us, and an army officer came around to tag certain cadets as either wounded or dead.

While at camp, we also saw demonstrations of artillery and tank fire power, and we got to ride in armoured personnel carriers. We also went to the army rifle range and were able to fire the few later model Lee Enfield rifles that the school possessed. Although I had always had good scores at the school rifle range (we only used .22 calibre rifles there), I did very well with the regular army .303 weapon on the ranges at camp. One officer/teacher, who was considered an excellent shot, was very surprised. After double-checking that the scores were indeed mine, he sent in a recommendation that I be awarded a marksmanship badge. This rare piece of hardware, two crossed rifles, I then proudly wore on the sleeve of my battle dress for the rest of the time I was in the CCF. It was yet another piece of brass that had to be polished every week, but I didn't mind.

After dark at camp, there were the inevitable fights with cadets from other schools. Such fights usually took place in the NAAFI, and the chief weapons were chairs and our belts with their brass buckles. The trick was to get in a few knocks and then disappear as fast as possible before the MPs arrived with their batons. These fellows were big, brutal and not to be messed with. For daytime amusement, and verging on the same kind of inter-school rivalry, there were the improvised football games, with perhaps a hundred players on each side, all after the same football. These mob events tended to develop into brawls, with the chief culprits being put on jankers.

In 1957, my CCF training came to an abrupt end. One day, when we were all standing on parade in the school yard, the officer in command told us that the government had decided that anyone born after 1 October 1939 would no longer be required to do National Service. A number of parents had been asking whether this meant that anyone born after that date was still required to train with the CCF. The officer then explained that the school had decided that those of us born after the October date could choose to leave if we so wished. Then in his loudest parade-ground voice, he barked out: "All those eligible and wishing to leave take one pace forward."

Like magic, most of those on parade that day, including me, smartly carried out the command. The officer, along with the three or four other officers who were present, appeared to have been completely taken by surprise. Only a small number of senior cadets stayed where they were. The rest of us, many with smirks on our faces, were ready to go. The officers then quickly began walking down each line trying to persuade people to step back. I think they were truly horrified by what had happened. All their voluntary hard work training us, and all the esprit de corps that supposedly characterised the school CCF, were suddenly reduced to nothing.

Recognizing this and beset with second thoughts, a number of cadets did step back, but I held my ground. No more Blanco, Brasso, spit and polish for me. Besides, hadn't I learned most of what there was to learn, and what did I need it for if there was to be no more National Service? What never for a moment crossed my mind, even after my emotional reaction to Notre Dame de Lorette and Vimy Ridge, was that my military training had been completely antithetical to my concerns about peace and my later support of people like Bertrand Russell and the goals of the CND. There was a lesson here, but it would take a year or so before I understood its significance. The training I had had was not about Blanco and Brasso, but about how to survive in combat and how to kill other people. A good marksman was rewarded and singled out with a special badge not because of being able to hit bullseyes but because he would likely be able to kill more people than anyone else.

A quite different lesson came about through sport. One afternoon a week at the Grammar School was set aside either for cricket in the summer or rugby in the winter. Concerning cricket, I was quite hopeless. I knew in theory what one was supposed to do whether batting or fielding, but I never felt the least enthusiasm and never acquired much in the way of skill. In my final years at school, I became increasingly disdainful. When up to bat, I never took the customary defensive stance. Instead I held the bat the way Americans do in baseball. When the ball came at me, I would take a hefty swing at it. If I connected, which happened occasionally, I might get a six or a four, or I might be out if someone caught the ball or the bowler hit my wicket. If I survived the first ball, I'd do the same thing with the next. Usually, I was out before the over was finished, but sometimes with a reasonably good score. Once I was out, I could resume the one thing I did value about cricket, the opportunity to lie on the grass and read while the rest of my team took turns to bat.

Rugby was a different matter. With this sport, there was no chance to do anything but participate. I played outside head in the front row of the scrum, so I had plenty of action. I quite enjoyed it, but I was content to keep my involvement to a minimum. Then one day I noticed that two of the teachers were watching our game and looking at me in particular. They seemed to be having a fairly serious discussion about something. What had I done now, I wondered? Then, during the half-time break, one of them came on the field and said to me:

"OK Young, we've been watching you. We think you might make a good scrum leader. You're going to have to get in there and show your people what's needed. Use your voice, and tell them what you want. What do you think? Can you do this?"

"Yes, sir," I said, without really thinking. There wasn't much time for that. Besides, the second half would soon start.

"Right you are, then. Good luck. I'm sure you'll give it your best."

To this day, I have no idea how my teachers had come up with this idea, but it made a huge difference to me. Rather than hanging back, I was now leading from the front, urging every other scrum player to do whatever I felt was needed. Thereafter, when a game ended, I was dirtier, more bruised and more tired than I had ever been. Also, my voice was often hoarse from all the yelling. However, it's what changed in me that makes me tell this story now. Not only did I begin to really like the game, but above all I liked taking on the extra responsibility. At the same time, of course, I began to play much better, and before long, I was "promoted" to one of the school teams. As a consequence, on Saturdays I found myself playing in games against other schools all over the county. Somehow, amid everything else I was doing, rugby found a place.

Once I left school, it stayed with me for a further seven years. Only then did I hang up my boots. What I did not relinquish, however, were my feelings about responsibility and leadership. I'm not an ambitious person and I'm not at all anxious to take on leadership in anything, but put me in charge, and not only will I do the very best I can, I'll enjoy doing it.

CHAPTER SIX

MUSICAL DEVELOPMENTS

Maidstone Grammar School was at the opposite end of town from us and a bus and trolleybus ride away. Soon after my first term began, I discovered that what Mr. Allison at Brentwood had told me was quite true. The school did indeed have a flourishing music programme. With the behind the scenes encouragement of the headmaster, Mr. Claydon, there were three orchestras, a large Choral Society, a small choir, a chamber music programme, a music club at which established professionals performed and music lessons for a variety of instruments, taught for the most part by peripatetic teachers. For seven years, I was to be immersed in an educational environment where music had the same respect and status as any other classroom subject. It was among the eight O-level subjects that I studied for my General Certificate of Education examinations in 1957, and it was one of my three A-level subjects in 1959 and again in 1960.

Preparing for these examinations involved studying a number of set works, and studying music theory and composition. The toughest challenge, as far as I was concerned, was dictation, an exercise that involved writing down music as it was played. When I approached my final school year, music was one of two possible subjects, the other being English, that I wanted to study at university.

The director of music when I arrived at the Grammar School was Noel Long, an intense, high-energy personality, always in a hurry and, as far as I could tell, imbued with only a minimum of patience. He taught me violin and was very demanding about it. I didn't like him very much, but fear of his disapproval made me practise hard, and I think the discipline he demanded was very beneficial. His wife, Jean, who taught me piano, was by contrast a much warmer personality, with none of her husband's angst. Even so, she expected and got quite a bit from me.

By the end of the year, I had passed my Grade 4 piano examination and was looking forward to continuing my lessons with her. Unfortunately, as the school year came to a close, I lost both teachers when Mr. Long accepted a research fellowship at the University of Leeds. My feelings of disappointment and loss were quickly forgotten, however, when in September I met the man who would teach me both violin and piano for the remainder of my time at the Grammar School.

My new teacher, Jens Boysen, was a soft-spoken, good-humoured man, who was on the staff at the Kent Rural Music School, and so not officially connected with the Grammar School. I worked quite hard for him, getting up early in the mornings to practice before school. By the end of my time with him, I had reached Grade 8 level on the piano and a couple of grades back from that on the violin.

In some ways, he was not the right teacher for me. He never complained when I hadn't practised enough, and he never seemed to worry about technique. This was fine with me, although it shouldn't have been. Without realising it, I did not advance as far as I might have done. What's more, in my final year with him, my piano playing seemed to run into some kind of invisible wall. My technical limitations prevented me from being able to play the more difficult passages in some of the music that theoretically I should have been able to manage. As for the violin, I worked less and less at it, and eventually stopped lessons altogether. With a different teacher, one who from the beginning addressed matters of technique, my piano playing would perhaps have advanced further and there would have been no invisible wall. Perhaps, too, my violin playing would have benefited as well. But there were considerable compensations.

What delighted me about my lessons with Jens Boysen were the conversations we had about music. Often I would share with him things I had picked up in school: the amazing chromaticisms in Mozart's "Jupiter" Symphony; the way Beethoven in the Ninth Symphony held back from revealing whether the work was in the major or minor key until bar seventeen, omitting the all-important third in the opening bars where one hears only the first and fifth notes of a chord which turns out not to be the tonic chord anyway; or the puzzle regarding why Beethoven in the Fifth Symphony used fortissimo bassoons, not horns, in the recapitulation of his second subject group. Invariably, he knew what I was talking about and would recreate the music on the piano. Then he would tell me about other special moments in music, again playing them for me on the piano: magical key changes in Schubert; the extraordinary musical rendering of chaos at the beginning of Haydn's *The Creation*; and the intricacies of some of Bach's fugues.

In time, he told me that he had been a prisoner of war in Russia. Contrary to the experience of many other Germans in the camps, he had not fared too badly. Indeed, his only real complaint was that at the end of the war he had had to wait a long time before he could return to Germany. While in the camp, he and others had formed an orchestra, having obtained instruments from who knows where. The big impediment was the lack of music scores. If I understood him correctly, my teacher had been able to write out a considerable amount of music from memory. If a particular instrument was missing from the improvised orchestra, he would rearrange the orchestration to get around the problem.

I wish now that I had managed to persuade him to tell me more about his experiences as a POW. What music did the orchestra play? Were the Russians more lenient because of the music? Did he have to do manual labour, like most of the prisoners in Russian hands? Did the musicians get better food than other prisoners? Did anyone compose music specially for the camp musicians? And, knowing that there were POWs in Russian camps as late as 1956, when exactly did he get home?

At other times, my teacher would also share his love for particular works of music. I remember him playing me the opening movements of Beethoven's "Hammerklavier" and "Waldstein" sonatas, Schubert's "Wanderer" Fantasy and all manner of works by Chopin. He seemed to have a particular love of Chopin's music, and, since my father did not play Chopin very much, I was introduced to a great deal of music with which I was as yet unfamiliar. Inevitably, I wanted to learn some of it. My teacher acquiesced, even though it meant wandering away from the set pieces required for the London Royal Academy of Music examinations. For a while, Chopin's famous Nocturne in E flat became my party piece, but I also learned a couple of Mazurkas, two Etudes, and some Preludes. Somewhat later, after hearing the "Fantasie Impromptu" beautifully performed at a concert by a young woman I knew, I badgered my teacher into letting me learn it, although it was really just beyond my technical capabilities.

I shall always be grateful to Jens Boysen for sharing his passion for music and for encouraging me to share that passion. Paradoxically, I regret not having had a more disciplined teacher, someone who insisted that I work on improving my technique and on perfecting the examination pieces I was supposed to be learning.

Another teacher, again one not part of the school programme, was David Delarue. He was an exceptional pianist who taught one of my school friends. I got to know him because he started a gramophone club that met regularly at his house. There were about eight of us in the group, some of us from school, together with several adults. It was all very informal, and we were encouraged to talk about the music and musicians that we liked. However, at each meeting, members had to take turns at presenting a programme of recordings for the group to listen to. Each presenter had to introduce the music and say something about who was performing it. On one occasion, for example, when it was my turn, I offered a programme of Chopin played by two English pianists I had come to revere: Solomon (his full name was Solomon Cutner but he was known just as "Solomon") and Benno Moisewitsch. Since LP vinyl records had not yet become available, all our recorded music was on 12-inch 78 rpm discs. These were difficult to keep free of surface noise and scratches and each disc only held a limited amount of music (about 4-5 minutes per side), so that any extended piece of music would periodically be interrupted while one turned the disc over or changed to the next disc in a series.

Inevitably during our meetings, David would play us something. On one occasion, for example, when he had been working on the Grieg Piano Concerto in the hope of getting an engagement to perform it, he surprised and thrilled us by playing the cadenza from the opening movement. So great was his devotion to the piano that when he got married and returned from his honeymoon, he completely unnerved his neighbours by playing the piano all night long. What his wife thought about this we never knew, but the story became something of a legend in Maidstone.

His wife was a delightful and attractive woman who was also an accomplished singer. When she arrived on the scene, she kept out of the way during our meetings, although she did serve us tea and biscuits, something David would never have thought of. She must also have urged her husband to tone down some of his eccentricities of dress. Most notably, David's constant forgetfulness about doing up his zipper, while not completely ending, did somewhat abate.

When I began to have organ lessons with the organist at All Saints, the parish church of Maidstone, David took a great interest in my progress. My organ teacher, Maxwell Menzies, was an austere taskmaster who started me off with some hair-raising exercises. Some involved playing a pedal line that moved in the opposite direction to what the left hand was playing. Other teasers involved the hands playing on different manuals, the left hand playing notes that were higher than those given to the right hand. Fortunately, my frustration in trying to cope with such exercises was balanced by the joy of learning a couple of Bach's Short Preludes and Fugues, and a movement from a Mendelssohn organ sonata.

When David became organist at a church close to Maidstone, he started arranging the occasional concert at which he and his pupils would play. With his encouragement, I played one of my Bach pieces, although I was not officially one of his pupils. Technically, it was relatively easy, but for me the pedal part, particularly in the fugue, was something of a challenge. However, all went well, and thereafter I remained grateful for the confidence David had shown in me and the chance he had given me.

Two other Maidstone organists were also very generous and encouraging. I was a regular Sunday morning attendee at the Methodist church on Tonbridge Road, chiefly, I confess, as a way of meeting girls and of obtaining membership in the church youth club, where one could meet yet more girls. I started singing in the church choir, and I always hung around after services to listen to whatever music the organist played as people left the building. When the organist got to know me and learned that I was taking organ lessons, he invited me to practise on the Methodist church instrument whenever I liked. He even arranged with the minister for me to have my own key to come in and out of the church.

Youth Club in the hall adjoining the church now took on a whole new dimension. Whenever there were activities that didn't interest me, I would slip away and play on the organ. In time, I began to play for church services whenever the regular organist was away for any reason.

The other organist was at the St. Francis Roman Catholic Church. My girlfriend at the time was a Catholic, and somehow she persuaded the organist and the parish priest to let me practise on the organ there. This was of some importance, because the church was closer to the school than the Methodist church. After getting permission to practise the organ during my "free" periods, I was able to go there quite often. I enjoyed playing in this particular church a great deal, chiefly because the organ console was at one end of the building while the organ pipes were at the other.

When playing on one occasion, I had one of life's magical moments. I heard the music wafting down the church towards me, but it was as though it was quite independent of me, for I had lost all consciousness of playing it. I suppose what happened was a shadowy equivalent of the kind of "out-of-body" experience that some mystics have described.

As for my formal lessons with the organist at All Saints, these I eventually gave up. I found my teacher to be cold and unpleasantly demanding. Besides, I rationalised, I had altogether enough to do as far as music was concerned.

When I first came to Maidstone Grammar School, I was introduced to choral singing, which for me was a completely new form of music making. In my first year, Noel Long conducted the school Choral Society in Handel's *Alexander's Feast*. I sang alto, my voice not yet having broken. After months of rigorous rehearsing, we performed the work in the school's "Big Hall", with a full orchestra, a keyboard continuo and first rate soloists, who included Mary Thomas (the Welsh soprano soon to be world famous) and Jack (James) Burke (still a student at the Grammar School, a fine tenor but later renowned as a broadcaster, science historian, author and television producer).

Shortly after *Alexander's Feast*, David Cutforth, of whom I will have much to say below, arrived to take the place of the departing Noel Long. With his leadership, the Choral Society flourished. In successive years, first as an alto and then as a bass, I received a wonderful learning experience when rehearsing and performing such major choral works as Handel's *Samson* and *Messiah*, Haydn's *Creation*, Mozart's *Requiem*, Brahms's *Song of Destiny*, and Constant Lambert's *Rio Grande*. One of David Cutforth's innovations was to expand the chorus to include girls from the Maidstone Girls' Grammar School. This alliance made possible in March 1957 the ambitious and very successful performance of Bach's *St. Matthew Passion*, with its two choirs and two orchestras. The professional soloists included Mary Thomas (see above), Lesley Reid (contralto), and Lindsay Heather (bass). The all-important tenor part of the Evangelist was sung by Ian Stamp, a former student with a remarkable voice. Another bass part was sung by Philip Langridge, a sixth-form student, who was later to become a renowned tenor, famous for his performances of English opera and oratorio and his portrayal of the witch in holiday productions of *Hansel and Gretel* at the Metropolitan Opera. In our *St. Matthew Passion*, he took the roles of Judas, Peter, the High Priest and Pilate.

Quite different in nature was a production of Benjamin Britten's newly composed *Noye's Fludde* (1958), a retelling of the biblical account of Noah's building of the Ark, the great flood, and the eventual joy that greets the return of the dove and the disembarkation from the Ark. This was conducted by David

Cutforth in 1960 and was an amazing organizational feat. Mr. and Mrs. Noye were the only adult participants, while the remainder of those involved came from about 45 different Kent schools. The large orchestra of about 100 players were also all of school age. To make things even more complex, apart from the creation of costumes, a stage set and the Ark that Noah builds, was the fact that performances were given twice in each of three different locations: Rochester Cathedral and the parish churches of both Maidstone and New Romney. There were large audiences for each performance of this venture, and they were expected to participate too in the singing of three well-known hymns. I was cast as an ox, one of the many animals that entered the Ark prior to the coming of the storm and the great flood.

At school I was invited to join the school choir, a small group of singers who rehearsed each morning before assembly at the beginning of every day. The choir led the singing of whatever hymn had been selected for that morning, and once every week or so contributed an anthem. The choirmaster was Nigel Dodd, who came to the school in 1955 to teach both English and Music. He had spent his National Service as a member of the Royal Signals Band. Not only was he a first-rate string player, but he was a fine pianist. As choirmaster, he was very demanding, but he got impressive results. I respected him very much for that and enjoyed the work we did, which sometimes extended beyond our presence at morning assemblies. I recall singing in Christmas concerts, and more than once I believe we sang in All Saints Church, although I do not recall what the occasion was. Once we sang in Detling parish church for a memorial service in honour of a former student, who had recently been killed while in the RAF. His parents very much wanted his school to be represented. It was a very moving event, although none of us were old enough to remember the man who had been killed. I had never been to a funeral or a memorial service before, and I found the intensity of the emotions and the very visible grief of the parents almost overwhelming.

As if managing the School Choir and helping to train sections of the Choral Society were not enough, Nigel Dodd in 1958 founded the Weald Singers, a small group of about twenty voices. This was quite separate from any school group, and the choir met in various people's houses. It included some school-age students (I was one) and a number of fairly experienced adult singers. We worked on a variety of materials, ranging from Elizabethan madrigals to Victorian part songs and some modern works. A great deal of the music was unaccompanied. I enjoyed the Weald Singers a great deal. I liked working with adults in this way, and I liked the challenge of trying to perfect the sound we produced.

My final school experience as a singer occurred in the summer of 1960 during a chamber music concert. This began with a performance of Act 3 of Purcell's *Dido and Aeneas*, conducted by Nigel Dodd. I sang in the chorus with other members of the School Choir, but I also had a short solo role as the Sailor. For this, I'd been trained by Mr. Holyman, who had had over the years enormous success in producing singers, among them James Burke, Ian Stamp, and Philip Langridge. At his suggestion, I had made a deal with him. In return for acting as accompanist during the singing lessons of other students, he would give me lessons too. My role as Purcell's Sailor was my public debut, my coming out as Mr.

Holyman's latest protegé. But things did not go well. Mr. Holyman had fixed me as a tenor, in spite of my always having sung bass. I found the part of the Sailor too high and a strain, especially when I was nervous. There were a series of top Fs and at the climax a top G. Some of these I "missed", and my big moment was clearly something of a disaster. Fortunately, the Sailor appears at the opening of Act 3, and the really good music, including Dido's famous "Lament", comes later. This was all performed so well that I like to think my failing was soon forgotten.

A key figure regarding my musical experiences at school was David Cutforth, the music director who replaced Noel Long at the beginning of my second year. Initially, he took lodgings a few doors away from us on Maple Avenue. The arrival of his grand piano and its very visible presence in the front window of the house was the occasion of a certain amount of good-natured neighbourly gossip. At school, I quickly got to know him. He was, I felt from the start, a very fine teacher, knowledgeable, helpful, but never deviating from the high expectations he had of his students. He was good-humoured, generous and willing to trust certain of his students, including me, with considerable responsibilities. He invited me, for example, to write the programme notes for concerts by the school orchestra and for the Maidstone Symphony Orchestra when he became its conductor. To write those notes, I attended some the rehearsals to get familiar with the music, borrowed the music scores and read whatever books seemed relevant. It was a great deal of work, but I see now that for a music student it was a very effective form of education, as was the writing of reviews of concerts for the local paper that I was sometimes invited me to do.

The Maidstone Symphony Orchestra, which was made up of both amateur and imported professional players, performed each year a season of standard classical works, one of which was usually a concerto with an invited soloist. Some of the works might require a percussionist, and I soon found myself an occasional member of the orchestra, having learned the techniques required to play cymbals, triangle, tambourine, castanets and bass drum. I recall in particular playing in performances of Berlioz's *Roman Carnival* overture, music by Bizet, and most demanding of all, William Walton's *Belshazzar's Feast*. This last stretched me to the limit. I had such difficulty mastering the task that I decided to commit the music to memory so that I would need the music as little as possible. Help came from my Uncle Eric, who loaned me his recording of the work so that I could sit at home and play the work over and over. At the actual performance, a professional timpanist and percussionist arrived to share the work. I have never forgotten how at one point I lost my place and was about to miss a cue. At this point, the "pro" leaned across in front of me and did whatever was needed – a ping on the triangle, I believe. Not only that but he smiled and gave me a quick wink. His name was James Blades. Only later did I learn that "Jimmy", as he was always referred to, was something of a legend. On his death in 1999, *The Independent* published an obituary that began as follows:

> JAMES BLADES *was one of the best loved and most naturally talented musicians to grace the British orchestral scene over the past 60 years. He brought the skills and art of great percussion playing to a wide public not only through his performing ability*

but through his extraordinary talent in communication with people from all walks of life. He was kindly and encouraging to the first efforts of the smallest child and he advised composers like Igor Stravinsky. He was a close friend of Benjamin Britten, who turned to him constantly for advice on percussion techniques and special sounds.

It was only later that I discovered that Jimmy Blades was the creator of the gong sound that preceded every J. Arthur Rank film from 1935 onwards. Furthermore, it was he who had recorded the "V for victory" signal at the start of the BBC radio broadcasts to Europe during the Second World War.

David Cutforth also provided me with other kinds of performance opportunities when he founded an opera group. I made my debut as a timpanist in Mozart's *The Impresario*. Tuning the drums was a completely new skill for me, especially if adjustments were needed during the course of a performance, but I managed. As for playing, I learned that there could be prolonged periods of inaction, so that one needed to count very carefully in order to be ready to play when required.

Twinned with *The Impresario* was Gian Carlo Menotti's *The Telephone*. I was not involved in this, but enjoyed the opportunity of getting to know it during rehearsals and its performance.

On another occasion, I was invited to sing (off stage) in the chorus for Mozart's *Cosi Fan Tutte*. Our small chorus barely had room just off to the side of the stage. As is common in such situations, we could not see the conductor (David Cutforth). A second conductor (I believe it was Nigel Dodd) stood where he could see and could synchronise his beat with that of the main conductor. I found such issues quite intriguing and the whole venture a lot of fun. At the same time, I was getting to know the intricacies of this beautiful opera.

In 1960, knowing of my interest in opera, David Cutforth took both me and my friend Jeremy Hewitt to Glyndebourne, the country house in Sussex, in the grounds of which is an opera house. We left school in the early afternoon with David driving. It was customary to wear dinner dress for Glyndebourne. Neither Jeremy nor I were so equipped, but we made do with suits and ties. We arrived in time to have tea, and, as was customary, we brought with us a picnic supper to have during the so-called "long interval" during the performance, which began in the late afternoon.

It all seemed a bit intimidating at first, but everyone seemed to be having such a good time that we soon relaxed and were able to enjoy the beauties of the place. We had come to see Bellini's *I Puritani*, in which Joan Sutherland was singing the role of Elvira for the first time. It was also the first time Glyndebourne had staged a *bel canto* opera. Her performance earned rave reviews, and I later realised that we had witnessed something of a historic occasion. In retrospect, I wish that somehow I had been able to get to know the music in advance. As it was, it was completely new to me, so I could not fully appreciate her achievement. Now that I have been able to listen to recordings of her *bel canto* work, I appreciate what an extraordinary performer she was and how lucky I was to have been at Glyndebourne that day.

Another way in which David Cutforth influenced me was through the performance of chamber music. During the time I

147

spent at Maidstone Grammar School, those students who played an instrument and those who had trained voices regularly participated in chamber music concerts. I cannot now recall all that I did – there was so much - but I do remember playing violin in the slow movement of the Mozart clarinet quintet. I also know that at other times, I played the Mozart D minor Fantasia for piano (my party piece at the time), I accompanied my friend Jeremy Hewitt in a work by Weber (I believe it was the Clarinet Concertino), and I played piano in the first movement of Beethoven's Clarinet Trio and the slow movement of Mozart's Clarinet Trio. Then, in my final year programme, I played with Richard Clark two movements from Debussy's *Petit Suite* ("En bateau" and "Ballet") for two pianos.

Immediately following the Debussy, the concert concluded with the premier performance of a new composition by Nigel Dodd which he entitled "Toy Overture". The participants in this work were all teachers, except me, perhaps because, like Nigel Dodd, I'd come to the end of my time at the school. Apart from the string quartet players, the remainder of those involved played a highly unusual variety of percussion instruments. These included a bell in G (Mr. Holyman), a hooter (Mr. Page, my French teacher), an Arab drum from Nazareth (Mr. Fawcett, the Art teacher), a squeaker and handbells (David Cutforth) and some seven other equally unfamiliar-sounding instruments. Mine was a cinder shifter, a contrivance (so the dictionary tells me) for sifting dust or ashes from cinders. This tool, a staple in nineteenth-century kitchens before the advent of gas or electric ovens, had somehow come to the attention of the composer. Perhaps I am as a result the only performer in the history of music ever to have played this instrument.

Somewhat similar to the experience of playing in chamber music concerts was that derived from belonging to the various school orchestras. There was the Junior Orchestra for beginners, and then there were the Second Orchestra and the First Orchestra. When I eventually joined the ranks of the First Orchestra, I found myself playing second violin. After a year or so, I was anxious for a "promotion" to a first violin desk. When I asked David Cutforth about this, he said no. He wanted someone reliable to lead the second violins. Was this an excuse that allowed him to avoid telling me that I was not good enough to play first violin? Or did he really mean what he said?

As with the chamber music concerts, I cannot remember all that the First Orchestra played, but I do have vivid memories of the slow movement from Mozart's Symphony No. 34, the first movement from Beethoven's Symphony No. 8, Bizet's *L'Arlesienne Suite No. 1*, Bach's Concerto for Two Violins (Philip Langridge was one of the soloists), and the first movement of Mozart's A major Piano Concerto. In this last, Rodney Smith was the soloist. He was a fellow student but somewhat younger than I. Some time after he finished school, he became a concert pianist and is now particularly associated with the performance of the music of the twentieth-century English Romantics, with Olivier Messiaen's music, and with other European avant-garde composers.

The First Orchestra also played in the Christmas concert each year. In my final year, I made my debut as a conductor at the Christmas concert as part of a segment during which the school choir performed carols composed by school members. Each composer had to conduct his own carol, mine being "Christo Paremus". Composition was part of the music curriculum and the Christmas exercise derived in part from that. However, I had been writing music for some time, mostly songs. Inspired, I believe, by the John Ireland violin sonata, I had also tried my hand at a violin and piano work (on one occasion I got Ray and my father to play it for me).

While I was at the school, there were also concerts given by invited professional musicians. The Music Club had a series of subscription concerts each year. The audience was mostly made up of people from the town and included ardent music lovers such as my parents. Interested students, and I was certainly one of these, had free admission in return for acting as ushers. In retrospect, what was striking about these concerts was the very high calibre of the artists, a number of whom I vividly remember. There was, for example, Alfred Deller, the world's leading countertenor. I was already used to hearing a countertenor voice because one of Mr. Holyman's protégées, John O'Kill, had developed into a fine countertenor. However, Deller, who had pioneered the revival of the countertenor voice in Renaissance and Baroque music, opened my ears to a whole range of music that I knew little about.

There were also concerts by the lute and guitar player Julian Bream; the famous two-piano duo of Cyril Smith and Phyllis Sellick; and the young and quite dazzling piano virtuoso John Ogdon. This last was so vigorous in his playing that many in the audience feared that the school's prized Blüthner concert grand would never be the same.

Most memorable to me were two other artists, whom I later heard whenever I could attend their concerts or acquire their recordings. The first of these was Myra Hess, something of an idol in England on account of the lunchtime concerts she had organized in London during the war, 150 of which she herself performed in. Her signature piece was her own transcription of Bach's "Jesu Joy of Man's Desiring". It was from my father's copy of this that I had played in the chapel at Brentwood School some years earlier. Among my recordings of her that I most prize today are two performances of the Schumann Piano Concerto, one in 1937 with Walter Goehr and one in 1952 with Rudolf Schwarz.

The other artist was Rosalyn Tureck. When for the first time I heard her playing Bach, I was stunned. She had come from the United States to live in England only a short while before, and I had no idea what to expect. Coming from her scholarly studies of Bach and her understanding and experience of the harpsichord, she fashioned a completely new sound and style for presenting Bach on the piano. My clearest memory of her concert was her playing of the *Italian Concerto*, beginning with a "broken" chord in the left hand. Then there was the ornamentation and embellishment she employed in the slow movement, and the incredible clarity she created throughout, so that every musical line was crystal clear. She was a great influence on Glen Gould, whom my mother always raved about, having attended his London debut in 1959, but she had none of his eccentricities. Her performances were all about the music she was playing, rather than the artist's grunts and groans, his bizarre customized chair, and his re-engineered piano, which all seemed to be such a collective self-indulgent distraction when

Gould performed. Much later, I was able to acquire many of Tureck's recordings, my particular favourite being the performance of the *Goldberg Variations*, which she gave as a birthday offering at the home of William F. Buckley Jr. in the early 1980s.

At school, perhaps because of the musical proclivities of the headmaster and his belief in the importance of music, a number of teachers were all too happy to share their love of music. Mr. Holyman and his uncanny knack for identifying potential singers (I must have been one of his few "mistakes") I have already mentioned, but there were others. My German teacher, for example, a rather serious and somewhat doleful figure, always became more enthusiastic and talkative whenever he got the chance to enliven our studies by playing recordings of German Lieder. Our focus was supposed to be on the texts, which he wanted us to read and appreciate. However, we were also taught how the music (invariably by Schubert, Schumann, or Brahms, but sometimes by Hugo Wolf) became an inseparable means of expressing the words of the lyrics, among the poets being Heinrich Heine, Eduard Mörike, Johann Wolfgang von Goethe, Wilhelm Müller, and Friedrich Rückert. While I have today lost much of my German, I still retain a love of German Lieder and vividly remember the classes where we were introduced to "Der Doppelgänger," "Erlkönig," "Gretchen am Spinnrade," and the song cycles "Die schöne Mullerin" and "Winterreise." Sadly, in my final years at school when I was no longer studying German, this teacher, who had brought so much music into the classroom, took his own life.

Another music lover was Vernon Fawcett, who taught art.

When Kathleen Ferrier died in 1953, just after I had arrived in Maidstone, he was deeply affected, and spent our class time eulogizing her and explaining to us what an enormous and premature loss her death represented. I suspect that I was about the only person in the class who knew who he was talking about, having heard some of her broadcasts, but this did not prevent him from sharing his thoughts about her. The passion and fervor that he displayed about so many things always made his classes enjoyable. We may have found his enthusiasms somewhat comical at times, but I believe I at least learned a great deal from him, not just about art but about music too. Every summer, he went to the Bayreuth Festival to experience productions of Wagner's operas in the Festspielhaus, the theatre that Wagner himself had designed for the production of his works.

Always a delightful raconteur, he had me spellbound on more than one occasion when he told the class in vivid detail about the festival and the works he had seen. Especially memorable was his description of going to performances of all four works in the *Ring* cycle over the period of just under a week. His account, together with my own discovery of Wagner, created in me the desire (never fulfilled) to go myself to Bayreuth and, in the footsteps of Vernon Fawcett, experience a complete *Ring* cycle.

The other teacher who clearly loved music was Norman Newcombe (or "Froggy" as he was known). My first classroom teacher at the school, he played the clarinet and taught both English and Latin. Regarding this latter, he and my classmates initially had to put up with my knowing everything on the syllabus since I'd already had a year's Latin at Brentwood. The second year was inevitably a different matter, however, and my initial cockiness soon disappeared, especially when we began to struggle with Caesar's *Gallic Wars*. No longer did I not know everything, but I found it a struggle to keep up. Latin aside, it was "Froggy's" custom to invite three or four of his students to come to his house for tea on Sunday afternoons. When he'd gone through the entire class, he would start down the list again. Whenever I went, the focus of the conversation invariably turned to music. Perhaps he had selected each group according to their interests.

His big love, as far as our group was concerned, appeared to be Mozart operas. He would sit at the piano with a piano/vocal score in front of him and give us a quick run through of an opera, telling us the plot and pointing out key moments of beauty and drama. I particularly remember his renditions of *Cosi fan Tutte* and *The Marriage of Figaro*. He was especially delighted when he was able to buy the newly-published Boosey and Hawkes scores with their lively and fresh translations into English by Edward J. Dent.

Other musical members of staff included Mr. Julier, my irascible French teacher for several years, famous for the accuracy with which he could throw a blackboard eraser at inattentive students, but equally famous for his incomprehensible apologies whenever he did hit someone. He also was a fine pianist. Occasionally, as did I and others, he accompanied whatever hymn was sung by the entire school at morning assembly. I noticed that for the final verse of a hymn he would add octaves to the left hand part to give the music some heft and sense of finality. It was perhaps not much of a musical legacy, but I copied his left hand octaves for the final verse of hymns. No one ever commented on my daring embellishment, but then perhaps no one ever noticed.

Also very prominent was another musical teacher, P. A. Lineham, who joined the school staff during my final years at Maidstone. A semi-professional singer, he was a member of a very well-known choir in London. My chief memory of him is his role as Aeneas in a (to me) best-forgotten performance of *Dido and Aeneas*.

Outside school, there were further musical activities. Some of these involved my father. For fun, I played a great deal of piano music for four hands with him. Some of the music we played, such as the Mozart Sonatas, Fantasias, and Fugue for four hands, or some of Schubert's works, such as the Fantasie in F minor, were composed as music for four hands. However, there was available a vast number of transcriptions of non-piano music. At home, in addition to many of the Mozart and Schubert originals, we had transcriptions of some Haydn Symphonies, Beethoven String Trios, Beethoven's Op. 18 String Quartets, Schubert's "Unfinished" Symphony, and a selection of orchestral Overtures. In addition to these, we often borrowed music from the town library or the Kent County Library. My favourites included the Bach keyboard concertos and the Mozart piano concertos. These, however, were not my father's first choices. Since he always played the upper or primo part, he tended to end up with a disproportionate amount of work. He would complain about this. I understood his point, but this was offset by my getting to know first hand, as it were, some wonderful music.

Equally important was the ongoing learning experience I had listening to my father's new violinist friend, Ray Alexander. A teacher at the same school where my mother taught, Ray was a very fine violinist. He was also a very much more adventurous musician than Uncle Alf had been. Besides playing through a weekly repertoire of Mozart, Beethoven, and Brahms, he liked to explore contemporary works as well, many of which were completely new to my father. I recall in particular the two of them endeavouring to master violin sonatas by Edmund Rubbra, Prokofiev and John Ireland. Ray made special efforts with the Ireland Sonata, the one in D minor, and he persuaded my father to come with him to London for some private coaching. I have forgotten who their teacher was (I believe it was someone who had performed the sonata), but I do remember that my father did a great deal of practising to prepare for this and was uncharacteristically very nervous about the whole venture. Both he and Ray were then delighted by the teaching they received and encouraged by the teacher's praise.

Ray, who played with the Maidstone Symphony Orchestra, on occasion would stand in as soloist when the orchestra was rehearsing a violin concerto. When David Cutforth decided to conduct the Sibelius concerto, it was a very challenging project for Ray, since the concerto is technically very demanding. To help him, Ray asked my father to work on it with him so that he could be ready when the orchestra rehearsals began. I attended as page-turner for my father whenever Ray came to the house, and so was able to add the Sibelius to other works, such as the Ireland Sonata, with which I became familiar.

The music-making of Ray and my father so impressed me that I persuaded the people at the Methodist church to allow me to arrange for them to give a recital in the church itself. The only drawback was the rather beaten-up state of the piano which was carried in from the hall next door where the Youth Club used to meet. After it was tuned in readiness for the concert, it sounded a little better, but it remained incapable of really doing justice to the music. To my great surprise, the concert was very successful, so other concerts followed involving different performers. I enjoyed the organizational work, and the minister seemed delighted to see the church attracting such numbers of people even though they were not there for religious purposes.

Following the Hungarian Revolution in 1956, a great many Hungarian refugees were welcomed to Britain. A number were billeted in some buildings at the disused aerodrome in Detling just outside Maidstone. Hearing about the plight of the group, who had arrived with very little in the way of possessions, and who now had to live in Nissen huts until more permanent housing could be found, my parents offered to put on a concert for them, so one evening our family, along with Ray Alexander, took the bus up to Detling. We were then taken to one of the buildings where about fifty people were waiting, a sad-looking group that included a number of families and their children. There seemed to be a pervading mood of misery, depression and hopelessness. Everyone was very polite, but there were few if any smiles.

Somehow a piano had been procured, so the concert began. My father and Ray played – standard stuff (Mozart and Beethoven) - and my mother sang. Throughout, the audience was very quiet, and there was polite applause at the end of each item. Then, as the last item in the concert, my father and Ray played some Bartok. It was either the *Romanian Dances* or the *Hungarian Dances*. I don't remember which, but what I do remember was the almost instantaneous effect the music had upon the audience. I could see them nudging each other during the opening bars, and suddenly there were smiles on many faces. They knew this music. The Hungary they had left behind was suddenly, if fleetingly, here in Detling. At the end of the performance there was loud and enthusiastic applause, and so my father and Ray played the *Dances* over again, once more eliciting the same energetic and joyful response. I shall always remember this concert and the way those refugees, who must have suffered a great deal, responded so positively to the music of one of their fellow countrymen and to the melodies they knew so well.

At about this time, my father began to organize group excursions to Covent Garden during the opera season. Most of those who went on these trips were people from the Ministry of Agriculture office in Maidstone where he worked. But others came too, including various musical friends of ours. The group ticket prices and the convenience of having transport that dropped one off at the door of the theatre proved to be very attractive, and he rarely had any problems filling the coach.

At some stage, I asked David Cutforth and several other teachers whether they would be interested and got a very positive response. One night, however, it came into my head that I had given the people at school the wrong date. Having already collected their money and purchased the tickets, this looked like a huge and embarrassing disaster. For the first and only time in my life, I went into my parents' bedroom and woke them up to explain what had happened. Imagine the immense relief I felt when they were able to assure me that my concerns were ill-founded.

In contrast to my anxiety about arranging for some of my

teachers to come on the Covent Garden trips, my father always seemed quite calm about everything. However, there was one exception. One night our coach became delayed in traffic, but there was enough extra time built into our schedule to offset this. However, it eventually became plain that this particular coach driver did not know where the theatre was. As a result, he was now completely lost. Once my father realised what was happening, he rushed to the front of the bus and, in a not very friendly or polite manner, started giving the driver directions. We made it to the theatre through a succession of narrow streets with only minutes to spare before curtain time, my father red-faced and in something of a sweat and the driver abject and equally red-faced. What the opera was on that evening I cannot recall. Indeed, for reasons that completely escape me, I do not remember any of the operas I saw at Covent Garden, including one production that I attended quite independently of my father. What I remember of this occasion was that it was snowing outside and I, in total disregard of the customary dress code, was wearing wellington boots in one of the better seats in the stalls.

Whereas my memory of Covent Garden productions remains dim, such is not the case regarding some of the productions I saw at Sadler's Wells, the opera house that my parents had first introduced me to when we lived in Chelmsford. Without any conscious thought of imitating my father's organization of coach trips, I led small groups of friends, boys and girls, on day trips to London. We would travel by train, and in the morning and afternoon we would visit one or two of the major tourist sites – the Science Museum, the Museum of Natural History, the National

Gallery, the Tate Gallery, St. Paul's Cathedral. Then in the evening, either by bus or by underground train, we would either go to one of the Promenade Concerts at the Albert Hall or during the winter we would go to Sadler's Wells. Among the operas we saw there, I especially remember productions of *Tosca, Rigoletto,* and *Don Giovanni.* At various times also, though perhaps not with this same group, I saw productions of Benjamin Britten's *Peter Grimes,* which had received its first performance at Sadler's Wells in 1946, and Igor Stravinsky's *Oedipus Rex.* Operas at Sadler's Wells were customarily sung in English (Oedipus was an exception), but, since one could rarely figure out the singers' words, I never saw the point of it, except perhaps in the comic recitative in Mozart, provided the words were enunciated clearly.

After each opera, with or without a group of friends, there would always be a frantic rush to catch one of the last trains back to Maidstone. *The Marriage of Figaro* was a particular problem, because its length forced one to leave before it was over. Indeed, it was many years later before I was able in another country to see the conclusion for the first time. At Sadler's Wells on a group expedition with friends, no matter what the opera, getting out of the theatre and back in time to the railway station was the one worrying moment for me, and I always felt immensely relieved when everyone was finally settled on the train, and I could feel that my job was done.

Two other experiences helped shape my love of opera. One occurred early on when a friend, David Lambert, who lived a couple of streets away, made me listen to his recording of Puccini's *La Bohème.* David was in many respects broader in his interests and

160

tastes than I was, but his various enthusiasms tended to be catching. He introduced me to jazz, everything from traditional New Orleans to the mainstream of Humphrey Lyttelton, and the more modern Dave Brubeck or the Modern Jazz Quartet. He also persuaded me to go with him to various Big Band concerts by performers such as Ray Ellington and Ted Heath. He was a stalwart fellow member of our local Jazz Club, where people like George Melly, Ken Colyer, Chris Barber, Mick Mulligan, Acker Bilk, Johnny Dankworth and Cleo Laine were regular performers. There was always music at David's house, and when he wasn't playing a record of something, his older sister Ann was. She loved so-called "pop" music, and I still vividly remember the crisis that ensued when her father changed the hinges on the door between the kitchen and the dining room so that it would swing open to the right rather than the left. I was visiting at the time, and when Ann came home from Art School and saw her father's handiwork, she promptly burst into hysterical lamentations:

"That's my jive door! Don't you know that? I need that door for jiving when I have music on! It's the only door in this house that's just right for me. Why didn't you ask me?"

I had never seen her so upset before. Indeed, I'd never even seen her cry. It was all very disturbing, and neither David nor I knew what to do. To everyone's relief, David's father, always the most kindly of men, relented. The door was changed back to its old self and the tearful Ann was quickly reunited with her jive partner.

Just how David came to acquire his recording of *La Bohème* I do not know, but like so many of David's enthusiasms, his feelings for this music were akin to a passionate love affair. For a time he could talk of nothing else, and his friends were expected to be 100% supportive. It didn't take much for me to become caught up in his appreciation, and I suppose that through him and through listening to this opera, I began to fully enjoy romantic opera.

The other experience that helped shape my love of opera was quite different. Regularly, the BBC broadcast performances of opera on Saturday afternoons. If I happened to be at home, I would listen to these. Then there was an announcement that over a period of weeks, the entire Wagner cycle of *Der Ring des Nibelungen* would be broadcast. My father and I agreed that we would listen to all fifteen or sixteen hours together. What's more, we would borrow from the library the piano/vocal scores for all four works. We would also do some preparatory study. We would read about Wagner and his revolutionary vision of music drama. We would read up on German mythology, and we would go through the scores and learn in advance some of the leitmotifs that Wagner used, among them the short musical phrases representing Alberich's Ring, Siegfried's Horn, the Magic Fire, Wotan's Spear, and Valhalla. I know I worked hard preparing for the broadcasts, and I believe my father did too, although he did not have as much free time as I. So, for the four successive performances, we sat together on the living room settee, the relevant music score between us, immersed in what many believe was the crowning achievement of a great musical genius. Later, we saw two more Wagner works at Covent Garden – *Die Meistersinger* and *Parsifal* – but it wasn't until fifty years later that I experienced another complete *Ring* cycle.

The pleasure of listening to the Saturday broadcasts of opera was much enhanced by the fact that a few years earlier the BBC had set up the first radio station in Britain to broadcast in VHF/FM. The station, with its very tall mast, was located a few miles from us on top of the North Downs. Broadcasts began on 2 May 1955, and those who bought a new radio with FM capabilities and who lived within range of the new transmitter were then able to enjoy the almost eerie new experience of zero background noise, zero static interference, and crystal-clear sound.

I was introduced to these wonders very early when the father of my friend Jeremy Hewitt purchased one of the new radio receivers. After listening with Jeremy to some music, I persuaded my father that he should follow the example of Jeremy's father. He did just that and bought the very same model of radio. When we switched it on and tuned it to some music on the Third Programme, I could tell that this was one purchase he would never regret. He was delighted with the "new" sound, and for some time any musical person who entered the house would be given a demonstration of the wonders of VHF/FM radio.

Another technological advance that made a huge improvement to listening to music was the advent of vinyl long-playing records. The twelve-inch discs offered a longer playing time of up to thirty minutes per side, a great step forward from the mere four or five minutes of a 78 rpm disc. Gone was the distracting chore of constantly having to interrupt one's listening to any work longer that a few minutes. Furthermore, the sound quality of the new discs was superior and was shortly to include the advantages of stereophonic sound.

One of my earliest experiences of listening to an LP recording occurred in 1958 when Decca issued as a kind of showpiece a recording of Wagner's *Das Rheingold*, conducted by Georg Solti. Apparently, the recording rapidly became the best-selling opera in history, one of its many attractions being the stunning reproduction of the sound of the eighteen anvils that Wagner used in the interlude between scenes 2 and 3.

David Cutforth, who was now married and lived in the country with his wife and their new baby, bought a copy of the recording. He was so excited about every aspect of it – the high calibre of the singers and orchestra, the quality of the sound, the conducting of Solti – that he couldn't wait to share the unique listening experience. He invited me to come to his house to listen to his new treasure. Having set everything up for me and having shown me how to work his record player, he left me for the day. I was quite terrified by the experience. The recording obviously meant so much to him that I was extremely nervous about making a mistake in handling the records and causing damage. Even so, when I did listen, I understood completely why he was so excited.

At home, and after quite a lot of strenuous negotiation on my part, I persuaded my father to purchase a record player that played LPs and could utilize the speakers in the new radio. Again, we followed in the path of Jeremy's father, who, early on, had bought a record player to take full advantage of the excellent sound system built into the radio.

Slowly I began to acquire LPs. My mother started me off when from somewhere (the origin was always unclear) she brought home for me two LPs, both recorded in the early 1950s. These I played so often that I began to wear them out. They were such fine performances that I have always felt that neither was ever surpassed.

When they were re-recorded in CD format, I was reunited with these two very special friends. Both recordings were of Brahms symphonies: Symphony No. 1, conducted by the young Guido Cantelli, who shortly after in 1956 died in a plane crash, and Symphony No. 4, conducted by Bruno Walter. LPs were somewhat expensive, so buying one was always something of an event.

There was also the special excitement generated when particular artists began recording in the new format. Among my friends, Otto Klemperer's cycle of the Beethoven Symphonies which he recorded between 1955 and 1959 were highly prized. None of us could afford them all, so as they appeared, each work was purchased by a different person and then informally shared. I believe the *Eroica* came out first, to be followed by the 5th, 6th, and 7th Symphonies. Each performance was something of a revelation. There seemed to be such clarity that one felt one learned something new every time one listened. Especially striking in the recordings that came out in stereo was Klemperer's placing of the first and second violins so that one heard the antiphonal effects as perhaps the composer had intended.

During my final four years at school, the main focus was upon academic studies. In the fifth form in 1957, we all took "O" levels, public examinations that were administered by Oxford and Cambridge Universities. My eight subjects included Music, but my chief memory of these examinations is that unaccountably I failed one of the two history subjects. Regardless of having passed English Language, Latin, French, German, Music, Mathematics, and European History, all that seemed to matter to me was the inexplicable failure in English History. The school appealed on my behalf, but to no avail. To this day, the mystery of what happened remains. At the time, however, there were immediate consequences. When the school chose what subjects I could take in the "A" level examinations, History, which I had increasingly come to enjoy, was barred to me. My three subjects were to be Music, English, and French, this last being a subject I always felt insecure about, though my grades always turned out better than I had anticipated.

As I entered the sixth form in 1957, the plan was to prepare for the "A" level examinations in 1959. Then, after a further year of study, I would take the examinations again, hopefully improve the grades, and thus get accepted at one of the universities. My teachers for music throughout these years were David Cutforth and Nigel Dodd. We studied music theory and history, and there were lessons in composition, chiefly involving learning to write something in the style of Palestrina, or Bach, or Mozart.

What I most enjoyed was the study of various set works listed in the examination syllabus. We had to learn how to analyse the form, style and harmonies of these works. What's more, we had to be able to write out from memory key themes and chords. The works that stand out in my memory include Mozart's "Jupiter" Symphony, Britten's *Serenade for Tenor, Horn and Strings*, a Bach Cantata, Debussy's String Quartet No. 1, Mozart's last piano concerto in B flat, and Sibelius's Symphony No. 3. I still have my scores for most of these, marked up with analytical notes, some of which today seem rather simplistic, even naive.

With regard to writing about music, I probably learned most from Nigel Dodd, who was also one of my A-level English teachers. He was a no-nonsense taskmaster who expected precision, clarity and good organization in the essays we wrote for him, whether in discussions of books or music. Unfortunately, the one vivid recollection of working with him concerns a particularly embarrassing matter that I would prefer to have forgotten. It concerned the section of an essay I wrote on an aria in a Bach cantata that we were studying. The problem arose from the language I used when attempting to describe something that induced in me a sense of perfection and spiritual bliss. Mercifully, I have now forgotten the words I employed, because I am sure they were cliché-ridden and quite outside what was appropriate for the kind of essay I was supposed to be writing. Though I hated him for it at the time, Nigel Dodd spilled some red ink on what I had written and wrote some cutting marginal notes about how this kind of rhetoric was an unacceptable substitute for incisive analysis. As both an English and a Music teacher, he was right, of course, but my memory of the episode remains especially painful.

In spite of such minor setbacks, I received a good grade both times I did "A" level music, but the grade remained largely unchanged from one year to the next. However, in 1960, I did receive the Corfe Music Prize. Endowed by a music-loving local pharmacist, the prize was something to be valued, not for its financial rewards, which were modest, but for the recognition it conferred upon its recipient. When I left the school that summer, winning this prize was for me among the proudest of my accomplishments.

As for my struggle to get a university place, that I'll save for the next chapter. After all, music was not the only subject I hoped to study.

CHAPTER SEVEN

ADVENTURES IN LITERATURE

In Maidstone, both at school and at home, not only did my love of music develop further but so did my long-standing love of books. During these years, I came to appreciate Milton's idea that "books are not absolutely dead things, but do contain a potency of life in them to be as active as that soul was whose progeny they are" (*Areopagitica*). A bit pretentious, perhaps, if applied to some of my reading, but none the less expressive of what I felt about many of the books I read at school and at home.

Nowadays, no doubt, I would be embarrassed to speak of books in such a way, but during my teens, I recall having fewer inhibitions about authors or the contents of their works. On one occasion, for example, the minister at the Methodist church invited a small group of us to a meeting. We each had to read a passage from a favourite literary work and talk briefly about it. I do not remember what his purpose was, if indeed he ever explained it. Possibly, he was merely trying to get to know us and to let us feel that our various interests did not have to be left at the church door. My contribution on this occasion was a brief introduction to Keats's

"Ode on a Grecian Urn," followed by a reading. The famous last lines I delivered with maximum drama as though after this statement there was nothing more to be said by anyone about anything:

"Beauty is truth, truth beauty," – that is all
Ye know on earth, and all ye need to know.

The minister, who happened to be the father of a friend at school, was a gentle and kindly man. What he made of my adolescent sententiousness on this occasion I shall never know. I do remember that my reading was followed by a kind of stunned silence in the small meeting room. Then, very quietly, he spoke:

"Well, er, thank you, Alan. Now… who is next?"

Mercifully, that was all the commentary I got. Later, it occurred to me that he may have thought I was challenging him and the faith he represented, although that idea had never crossed my mind. It was simply that the words for me had some kind of mantra-like significance. I had never even pondered what they might actually mean. For whatever reason, the memory of my youthful pomposity remains very vivid, and I am grateful that the minister chose not to engage me in any kind of questioning or discussion. Now, whenever I think about what happened, I see myself through the eyes of I. A. Richards, the literary critic, who talked about how some readers "swallow 'Beauty is truth, truth beauty…,' as the quintessence of an aesthetic philosophy, not as the expression of a certain blend of feelings, and proceed into a complete stalemate of muddle-mindedness as a result of their linguistic naivety" (*Practical Criticism* 1929, 186-7).

Equally embarrassing in retrospect was something that I did in morning assembly at school. It was customary for the whole school to be present in "Big Hall" at the beginning of each day for a short service that included a hymn, prayers, and a reading from the Bible. Those readings were given by senior students according to a pre-established rota. Close to Christmas one year, I was called upon to read the story in Matthew, Chapter 2, of how the three Wise Men came from the east to Bethlehem in search of "he that is born King of the Jews." It was customary to read in a neutral tone. Clarity was what mattered. This I did, but when I came to the final verse of my reading that described the gifts presented to the baby Jesus, I swerved away from the expected tone. As dramatically as I could, I tried to characterize the three gifts: "…and when they had opened their treasures, they presented unto him gifts: gold [voice lifted and a bright tone], frankincense [middle tone], and [dramatic pause before this one] myrrh [lowered tone and as deep a voice as possible]."

No one had ever introduced any kind of drama like this to the morning readings, and I left the lectern feeling quite pleased with myself. After all, wasn't myrrh of great symbolic import? Often used to embalm corpses, it here foreshadowed Jesus's death, even as his birth was being celebrated. My reading was a way of reminding everyone of that very point.

It turned out, of course, that not everyone wanted this kind of reminder. A number of the teachers thought such dramatic mannerisms were inappropriate. Others, however, seemed to have got the point and told me that the readings could benefit from a little "fresh air". However, as I might have expected, the Headmaster's view was decidedly negative. He never spoke directly to me about it, but he let it be known that I was never to be assigned that passage again and that in future I was to stick to reading in the normal manner deemed appropriate for morning assemblies.

My memories of the books we read at school are somewhat scattered. One of the earliest is of struggling line by line through Shakespeare's *A Midsummer Night's Dream* with our form teacher, "Froggy" Newcombe. It was not a good introduction to Shakespeare. Although our teacher kept pointing out moments of delightful comedy, we did not chuckle along with him. Even worse were the classes where we were asked to take turns reading aloud. It was bad enough having to read, but when one didn't necessarily understand what one was reading, the experience was both painful and depressing. Thankfully, we at last got through it all, Puck's concluding words providing a kind of epilogue to our efforts that Shakespeare surely never intended:

> *Think but this, and all is mended,*
> *That you have but slumber'd here*
> *While these visions did appear.*
> *And this weak and idle theme,*
> *No more yielding but a dream…*
> (Act 5, scene 1)

Although my classroom study of *A Midsummer Night's Dream* was something of a disaster, all was not lost with regard to Shakespeare. Rather than reading the plays in the classroom, I got to know a number of them by acting in school productions. I might have had minor roles initially, but through attendance at rehearsals, listening to the director's work with other actors and repeatedly reading the copy of the play in question, I learned to appreciate Shakespeare in ways not dreamed of in "Froggy's" classroom.

My earliest such experience was in the spring of 1955 in a production of *Twelfth Night*. For two exciting nights, I appeared in several scenes as a non-speaking Attendant Lord at the court of Duke Orsino. My scenes, of course, included the opening scene. After all the rehearsals, I had memorised Orsino's lovelorn expositions about music being the food of love and how "Love-thoughts lie rich when canopied with bow'rs" if, that is, one was lying around in "sweet beds of flow'rs." All this, however, was for me only a prelude to my small moment of theatrical triumph. This came in the third act when I stepped on stage to arrest Antonio: "Antonio, I arrest thee at the suit of Count Orsino." Quite a debut. Today, whenever I see a production of this play, I still feel a touch of nervous excitement as the line approaches. After all, for me it was once the most important line in the entire play.

Having acquitted myself satisfactorily in *Twelfth Night*, within eight months I found myself in the cast of *Hamlet*. Though much cut, this was to me an astounding production that included some very fine actors in the major roles, including the female parts of Gertrude and Ophelia that were played by boys whose voices had not yet broken. I was cast as Marcellus and so had some forty lines in the opening scene when the Ghost appears to the men on watch. There followed a few lines in the second scene when Hamlet is told about the Ghost, and then a few more lines when Hamlet himself gets to see the Ghost. Thereafter, I was an extra in some of the scenes, and later one of four coffin bearers. My contribution may have been small, but the intensity of the experience and all I learned in the many rehearsals I attended had an enormous impact upon me. Here, if anywhere, was where I acquired a lasting love of Shakespeare's plays and a fascination with this one play in particular.

The year after *Hamlet*, I played Murellus in *Julius Caesar*, yet another officer-like figure as in my first two plays. Now, however, I was a Roman tribune with a juicy twenty-four line speech close to the opening of the play, a speech extolling the merits, not of Caesar, but of Pompey. What's more, the speech used verse for the first time in the play, Shakespeare's way, perhaps, of giving it maximum impact:

> *You blocks, you stones, you worse than senseless things!*
> *O you hard hearts, you cruel men of Rome,*
> *Knew you not Pompey? Many a time and oft*
> *Have you climb'd up to walls and battlements,*
> *To Tow'rs and windows, yea, to chimney-tops,*
> *Your infants in your arms, and there have sate*
> *The livelong day, with patient expectation,*
> *To see great Pompey pass the streets of Rome. [etc.]*

After the crowd of working men have left, "tongue-tied in their guiltiness," Murellus and Flavius go off to "Disrobe the images" of Caesar that they find "deck'd with ceremonies". Later, as Caesar becomes increasingly powerful, in spite of the state supposedly being a democracy, we hear that Murellus and his fellow tribune

Flavius "for pulling scarfs off Caesar's images, are put to silence" (Act 1, scene 2). So much for freedom of expression and democratic choice in Caesar's Rome.

But my work in the play was far from over, for there were plenty of crowd scenes needing extras. Furthermore, in Act 5, scene 4, I was reborn as the "young" Cato, but, alas, promptly had to die in battle seven lines later. Although the performance of this tiny episode went well, the first rehearsal did not. My opening line was in response to Brutus's "Yet, countrymen! O yet, hold up your heads!" Knowing my lines already and feeling very sure of myself, I began: "What base man doth not?" At which a loud cry came from the back of the hall: "Bastard!"

This was from "Johnny" Johnson and clearly directed at me. The director of most of the plays, "Johnny" was generally enthusiastic and encouraging when we were rehearsing, but if things went wrong, watch out. Things were now as wrong as could be. Why was he calling me that? What had I done?

Having no explanation, I tried the line again: "What base man doth not?" Even louder yells from "Johnny": "Bastard! Bastard!" My third try at the line had him running the full length of the hall towards me. He was red in the face and drooling at the mouth: "Just give me the bloody line!" So I did. At this point, barely able to speak, he demanded to see my text, so I pulled it out of my pocket and showed him. There in black and white: "What base man doth not?" More explosive noises, but gradually subsiding. "All right then, all right, what you've got here, Young, is one of those damned expurgated texts. The whole school's riddled with them. God help me! Just give me what Shakespeare wrote. OK?" He fiercely crossed out "base man" and wrote in "bastard". I never got an apology from "Johnny", and it took me some time to recover from his outburst.

Next came *The Merchant of Venice*, in which I played the exotic Prince of Morocco. Described in Shakespeare's stage directions as "a tawny Moor." With plenty of black makeup to underline the point, I arrive at the opening of Act 2 to woo Portia and attempt the test of choosing the "right" casket from the three that she has prepared. If I fail, then I must agree "Never to speak to lady afterward/In way of marriage." I enjoyed preparing for this role, learning to pitch my voice lower and at the same time bringing out the grandeur and underlying pomposity of my character. Like Shylock, I was an outsider, my chief anxiety being my black skin:

> *Mislike me not for my complexion,*
> *The shadowed livery of the burnish'd sun,*
> *To whom I am a neighbour and near bred.*
> *Bring me the fairest creature northward born,*
> *Where Phoebus' fire scarce thaws the icicles,*
> *And let us make incision for your love,*
> *To prove whose blood is reddest, his or mine.*

When a few scenes later I choose the wrong casket, I'm forced to leave at once and return to Africa. There I must live out my promise never to marry. Fortunately, having left the stage, I'm spared from hearing Portia's dismissive racist comment:

> *A gentle riddance. Draw the curtains, go.*
> *Let all of his complexion choose me so.*
> (Act 2, scene 6)

175

I have few memories about our performances of this play, and I cannot recall how "Johnny" Johnson had us navigate the painful complexities of its anti-Semitism. Instead, I remember what for me was a near disaster, something that today would playfully be called a wardrobe malfunction. To equip me with the exotic grandeur appropriate to an African prince, I had been given a magnificent costume that included a large and impressive scarlet turban. The mishap occurred seconds before I made my first entry at one of the performances. As the musicians were playing the fanfare to announce my imminent arrival, my turban got snagged by a nail in the wooden crossbeam above me. I had to make a split second decision as to whether to try to untangle my turban and so arrive late on stage, or to move forward without it. I chose the latter and stepped out on stage bare-headed. The scene went well, but there was trouble when I left the stage. "Johnny" was there, waiting for me. "Where's your bloody turban?" he hissed. "You ruined that whole damn effect we were aiming for. What did you think you were doing, for God's sake?"

When I explained and we had retrieved the turban, he simmered down a little. "Just make damn sure you duck under that beam for the casket scene. Meanwhile I'll get someone to deal with the nail during the interval."

The following year, I at last was given a leading role: Petruchio in *The Taming of the Shrew*. This was not a play I knew anything about when I was first handed the text, and now, of course, its central idea that women must learn submission and accept their appointed place within the social fabric is unacceptable. Even so, the play still works if we enjoy its farcical elements and if the bluster of Petruchio and the shrewishness of Katherina are perceived as the unconscious means by which the two characters conceal the tenderness and full-blown love that develops between them.

The production received a good review in the local paper, and, as far as I can tell, the reviewer was able to appreciate the nuances that the director had tried to create regarding my role in particular: "As Petruchio, Alan Young revealed talent in a part which demands considerable acting ability. His swaggering insouciance contrasted well with the quiet courtesy he displayed towards his bride, and though outwardly somewhat boisterous, he did show an underlying delicacy when necessary."

I cannot now recall the precise moments to which the reviewer was referring. Perhaps one of them was Petruchio's notorious soliloquy in which he compares his treatment of Katherina with the methods used to train a falcon. "Johnny" had me deliver this very quietly in a tranquil moonlit setting with me sitting down and very still. Everything was in stark contrast to the previous section, in which I had prevented Katherina from eating by complaining loudly to the servants about the food, ultimately throwing it at them, chasing them all over the stage, and overturning the table. This noisy scene I remember very well. Flinging food, yelling at my servants and pursuing them around the table was great fun, but my enjoyment was tempered by a measure of fear that I dared not reveal to the audience. The problem was twofold. First, I was wearing thigh-length leather boots that someone had found for me. They looked splendid but they had very slippery soles. The more running about that I did, the more likely I was to fall. This issue was compounded by a second concern. To help make me look even more formidable, "Johnny" had persuaded a local butcher to lend us a large meat cleaver. This was for me to use as I chased the servants around the table. As far as I could tell, the cleaver had been kept razor sharp, and "Johnny" was unwilling to blunt it to keep us all safe. It was my job to make sure I did not drop it, fall with it, or dismember a fellow actor with it.

Almost as "dangerous" was the earlier scene at the end of Act 3 in which Petruchio prevents Katherina from joining the marriage feast and instead forces her to leave with him to travel to his country estate. Having declared "She is my goods, my chattels," etc, I was supposed to pick her up, throw her over my shoulder and march off the stage with maximum bravado. Fortunately, my Katherina (Gregory Johnson, a boy young enough to have an unbroken voice) did not weigh too much. It was my slippery boots that worried me. To fall would have been disastrous, but without a display of overwhelming bluster and self-confidence the scene would not work. Fortunately for us all, I survived our four performances without any kind of accident and without revealing to the audience my trepidation.

Back in the classroom, between "Froggy's" *A Midsummer Night's Dream* and the two Shakespeare plays set before us in the Sixth Form, my Shakespeare studies were limited to brief anthologised extracts. Often, we had to memorise passages and be able to stand up in class and recite them. There were Henry V's two addresses to his soldiers ("Once more unto the breach, dear friends, once more" and "This day is call'd the feast of Crispian"), Portia's "The quality of mercy is not strain'd," Jaques's "All the world's a stage," Gaunt's

"This royal throne of kings, this sceptred isle," Antony's "Friends, Romans, countrymen, lend me your ears," Macbeth's "Is this a dagger which I see before me?" and Prospero's "Our revels now are ended." There were also a number of Shakespeare's sonnets which we studied and committed to memory, along with many other passages of poetry by a whole range of authors.

In the Sixth Form, the two Shakespeare plays listed in the syllabus for A-level were *King Lear* and *The Tempest*. Study of these was intense, sustained and very detailed. In 1958, to aid my studies of both plays, I bought copies of the (to me) expensive hard-back Arden editions with their copious notes, their information about such things as sources, historical background, and dating and their learned critical introductions by Kenneth Muir and Frank Kermode respectively. I still have both books. Each has a transparent plastic cover, something I used on all my valued books and which made use of a skill acquired in some bookbinding classes I had taken some years earlier. Both books are copiously marked up with my own annotations. They also still show my special markings to indicate what passages should be committed to memory so that they could be used in the A-level examinations. My teachers for the two plays were "Johnny" Johnson and "Bob" Rylands. I remember very little about their classes and the essays we were required to write, but two out-of-school moments remain very vivid in my memory.

When we were about to begin *King Lear*, we were told to take our texts home and give them a preliminary reading so that when we came to class, we could begin our detailed study of the play. Dutifully I sat in my room at home and began the task. It was hard going, but I stuck with it. I was in the middle of reading the early part of Act 5, scene 3, where the virtuous Edgar challenges and defeats the villainous Edmond, when there was a loud knocking on our front door. I heard my mother go to the door, and then I heard my friend David, who lived two streets away and had been my partner selling newspapers. Without even knocking, he came into my room, shutting the door loudly behind him. His face was red and puffy, and he was shaking.

"Dave, whatever's the matter? What's wrong?" In my head, I came up with all manner of terrible possibilities, all involving different members of his family. "What's happened? Just tell me."

Pointing to the text that I'd just been reading, he burst out, "Have you read it? I just can't believe it. Have you? Have you read it?"

"Well no, not quite. I've got a few pages to go."

"OK, I'm just going to stay here until you finish it. I tell you, it's really upset me. I just can't believe what happens."

So I read on, trying to keep my focus on the text, which was hard to do with David standing at the window and intermittently pacing round what was really a very small room. Eventually, I got to the end. I too was profoundly shocked. It was as though Shakespeare had created a giant deception and stabbed us all in the back. Having been reconciled with his virtuous daughter Cordelia, having recognized his errors, and having recovered from his madness, King Lear had seemed on track to enter some kind of venerated state of old age once everything had been set to rights. For her part, having forgiven her father and having demonstrated her virtues, Cordelia seemed about to be rewarded with something equally positive. All was set up for divine justice to assert itself and reinforce the moral order that had been disrupted so severely in the play. But no - Shakespeare took it all away and in the closing section of the play Cordelia is hanged and Lear dies with his murdered daughter in his arms.

When I closed my text, I think I was as upset as David. Indeed, had I finished reading earlier, I would doubtless have run up the road to his house just to be able to share with someone else how I felt about the ending of *King Lear*.

That night, we talked for a long time about the play. No one had warned us about it, and clearly none of the other plays by Shakespeare that we knew contained any kind of parallel to what seemed like a willful distortion of the way one expected the plot to unfold. Why Shakespeare did this has troubled me ever since, and I still have no satisfactory explanation, my only consolation being that others have felt the same way. Even Samuel Johnson, that wonderful commentator on Shakespeare, seems to have shared something of what David and I felt. In his 1765 *Preface to Shakespeare*, he said:

Shakespeare has suffered the virtue of Cordelia to perish in a just cause contrary to the natural ideas of justice, to the hope of the reader, and, what is yet more strange, to the faith of chronicles... I was many years ago so shocked by Cordelia's death, that I know not whether I ever endured to read again the last scenes of the play till I undertook to revise them as an editor.

In 1975, almost two decades after David's knock upon our door, in one of my first publications, I tried to show how Shakespeare's contemporaries must have been equally shocked. For the

Jacobeans, the story of King Lear was well-known from various written accounts and from an earlier play. In addition, there was a group of folktales that employed the same story pattern and formed an oral tradition that was in all likelihood familiar to Shakespeare and his audience. In all of these sources, the Lear and Cordelia figures are reconciled and Lear's kingdom is restored to him. Nothing pointed to the ending that Shakespeare created and the profound shock that succeeding generations of readers and audiences have felt.

Seventeen years after my essay was published and thirty-five years after I had first read *King Lear*, I was pleased to find my essay acknowledged by the editor of The New Cambridge Edition of *King Lear*, Jay Halio. Five years after that, I felt an even greater satisfaction when a further acknowledgement of my essay appeared in the new Arden edition (Arden Series 3) of the play edited by Reginald Foakes.

The other out-of-school memory I have concerning the two A-level plays has to do with *The Tempest*. At the time, I found this work far less engaging than *King Lear*, but, along with everyone else in the class, I worked hard on it. When a production of it at the Old Vic was announced, we all dutifully signed up to go with our teachers. We also signed up to see John Dryden and William Davenant's version of the play – *The Tempest, or the Enchanted Island* (1667). This was performed about a week later so as to provide the opportunity of seeing both works close in time for the sake of comparison.

Not unexpectedly, perhaps, we found the performance of *The Tempest* dull and forgettable, but our return visit to the theatre was a very different matter. The matinee audience of mostly school age students suddenly started to come alive. What we had perceived as staid and dull was now seemingly travestied and, to our delight, suffused with bawdy innuendo such as we had not experienced in our studies before. Caliban was given a twin sister (Sycorax), a woman who appeared to have an insatiable sexual appetite. Miranda, too, was given a sister (Dorinda), a woman, like Miranda, who had never seen a man, and hidden in a cave was another new character, Hippolito, "one that never saw Woman." Finally, the airy spirit Ariel was given a sweetheart (Milcha), another airy spirit. During the play, especially when bawdy jokes were accompanied by the suggestive actions and gestures of the actors, it was inevitable that the largely teenage audience would respond with unrestrained enthusiasm. It was a truly memorable affair, even though on our return to the classroom it was set to one side as we continued our study of Shakespeare's original.

Some of the English works I read prior to the Sixth Form I remember only with difficulty. This is probably because those of us who planned on taking A-level English did not take English Literature at O-level, the idea being to let us read a wider selection of works than those required for O-level examinations. Today, I chiefly recall my first encounters with such poets as Donne, Marvell, Herbert, Jonson and Herrick from the first half of the seventeenth century, Dryden from the Restoration period, Pope and Cowper from the eighteenth century, a number of poets from the Romantic era, including Blake, Wordsworth, Coleridge, Keats and Shelley, and several war poets, chief among whom were Sassoon and Owen. These latter two deeply affected me, and their responses to the horrors of the First World War reinforced the disturbing emotions that I experienced when visiting the French war cemeteries and participating in the Aldermaston marches.

Of particular importance to David and me was the poetry of T. S. Eliot. It was a considerable revelation to discover that *Old Possum's Book of Practical Cats*, which Uncle Jack had read aloud to my sisters and me, was far removed from the world of *The Love Song of J. Alfred Prufrock*, *Preludes*, *The Waste Land* and *Four Quartets*. What appealed so strongly in these works, I suppose, was their rebuttal of romanticism, their portrayal of urban sterility ("The burnt-out ends of smoky days"), their portrayal of the non-heroics of someone like Prufrock ("No! I am not Prince Hamlet, nor was meant to be"), and their general evocation of the post-war malaise that still reverberated in the 1950s after yet another war. I owned the *Collected Poems, 1909-1935*, which I still have in the transparent plastic cover I gave it, and David had a copy of *Four Quartets*. The two of us spent many hours talking about Eliot's poetry and many more hours deciphering his literary allusions. A surprising number of Eliot's lines stuck in our memories, and so our conversations, no matter where, tended to be peppered with brief quotations. We were no doubt insufferably pretentious in the eyes of a good many of our friends, but I mention it here as evidence of the considerable impact of this author.

Important to me (David did not share my enthusiasm) were the works of another writer, the Welsh poet Dylan Thomas. We studied some of his poems at school, among them "Do Not Go Gentle," "And Death Shall Have No Dominion", "Fern Hill" and "The Force that through the Green Fuse Drives the Flower", but what resonated most with me was the experience somewhat earlier of listening to the first performance of *Under Milk Wood*, the "Play for Voices" that Thomas completed just before his death in November 1953. Two months later on January 25, the evening of my birthday, the BBC Third Programme broadcast its now legendary first performance, with Richard Burton as "First Voice". My father, always an avid listener to the Third Programme, made something of an event of it, making sure my mother and I were seated in the sitting room in time for the broadcast. Where my sisters were I do not recollect, but he seems to have sensed that this was for "grown-ups" only. Having that day begun my teenage years, I somehow was deemed to have adult status. From the very first words, I was caught up in the magic and poetry of Thomas's text:

To begin at the beginning: It is spring, moonless night in the small town, starless and bible-black, the cobblestreets silent and the hunched, courters'-and-rabbits' wood limping invisible down to the sloeblack, slow, black, crowblack, fishingboat-bobbing sea.

Gradually, we get to meet the fictional inhabitants of Thomas's small Welsh fishing village and learn their dreams, their innermost thoughts, their feelings and desires. We follow them through an entire day until nightfall and the inhabitants of Llaregyb return to their dreams. Many of the revelations about the characters were very amusing and quite salacious, evoking delighted guffaws from my father, shocked protest (all pretence) from my mother, and delight and giggles from me. At the same time the overriding humanity of Thomas's creations and the lyricism of his text created in one a warm and sympathetic response to the characters and their lives. Some years later, when I had to select a book for a school prize I had been awarded, I chose *Under Milk Wood*, though it was never a work we had discussed in school.

Among other authors we did study in class, alongside Shakespeare, were Chaucer and Dickens. Chaucer's *The Knight's Tale* from *The Canterbury Tales* was a set text for A-level, but I enjoyed far more the General Prologue and the separate Prologues to each of the tales, together with some of the tales themselves, especially the more salacious ones. Another book was Dickens's *Bleak House*, which at the time I found long and dreary, and quite lacking in the kind of appeal that *Oliver Twist* had had for me years earlier. As a result, I avoided reading other works by Dickens, encouraged, I suspect, by discovering that most of my teachers were not fans of his works, though they never said so in class. It was not until some years later, when studying *Little Dorrit* and *Dombey and Son* at university, that I began somewhat grudgingly to appreciate Dickens, but there remain many of his novels that I have not read. Ironically, and almost like a reproach from the grave, I later discovered that when my grandfather, twenty years old at the time, had emigrated to Canada in 1894, he had taken with him a set of Dickens, each volume inscribed by his friends: "Presented to F. Winter by a few Friends on his departure for Canada. 12th April 1894."

During his voyage from Liverpool to Montreal on the *Lake Ontario* and during his train journey from Montreal to Winnipeg, did he read some Dickens? Once in Winnipeg and then upon his return to England, did this young grocer read his friends' gift? Did he come to cherish the imaginative world created by Dickens? Or were the row of red volumes merely a kind of unopened status symbol without any literary interest to him? If he was both a reader and admirer of Dickens, it was something about which I was unaware. Indeed, I'm sure that if I'd ever seen him with any work of fiction in his hands, my view of this seemingly remote and severe shopkeeper, the father of my book-loving father, would have been radically altered.

At school, though I was ambivalent about Dickens, I found Thomas Hardy to be a quite different matter. After reading *Tess of the d'Urbervilles*, which was our one set text, I read at home a great deal of Hardy's other fiction, including *Under the Greenwood Tree*, *Far from the Madding Crowd*, *The Return of the Native*, *The Mayor of Casterbridge*, and *The Woodlanders*. I liked his "Wessex" settings, linking some of them to Dorsetshire where my Grandma grew up; I liked his exploration of those social issues that prevented or punished an individual who might break with the restrictive norms of society in pursuit of love or personal happiness; and I liked his "dark" vision of an all-powerful Fate that at any moment might threaten human aspirations. Ultimately, however, my affection and enthusiasm for Hardy's works were severely tested when I read *Jude the Obscure*. This work, like *King Lear*, seemed to veer into a pessimism that denied all human hopes and dreams. Having bought a copy and then having read the novel for the first time, I have never been able to return to it for a second reading, and my copy is now long gone from my bookshelves. My feelings are perhaps best reflected in what Irving Howe once said of the novel:

It is not the kind of book that can offer the lure of catharsis or the relief of conciliation. It does not pretend to satisfy the classical standard of a composure won through or after suffering: for the quality it communicates most strongly is that of naked pain... the final impact of the book is shattering. Here, in its first stirrings, is the gray poetry of modern loneliness, which Jude brings to apotheosis in the terrible words, "Let the day perish wherein I was born, and the night in which it was said, There is a man child conceived."

Another novelist studied at school was E. M. Forster. Our set text was *Howard's End*, but I so enjoyed this that I soon bought the Penguin editions of *Where Angels Fear to Tread*, *A Room with a View* and *A Passage to India*. Particularly important to me at the time was the scene in *Where Angels Fear to Tread* that depicts a group of three English visitors to Italy who go to the opera in Monteriano to see *Lucia di Lammermoor*. Having brought their English values and prejudices with them, one of the visitors, Harriet Herriton, complains about the theatre's décor with its drop scene sporting "many a lady lightly clad." As the opera begins, Harriet tries to "shush" the talkative and fun-loving Italian audience. She grimly tries to follow the plot, but before the opera is over she leaves, declaring the whole event is "not even respectable". The other two members of the group, Caroline Abbott and Philip Herriton, are affected very differently:

Miss Abbott fell into the spirit of the thing. She, too, chatted and laughed and applauded and encored, and rejoiced in the existence of beauty. As for Philip, he forgot himself as well as his mission. He was not even an enthusiastic visitor. For he had been in this place always. It was his home.

For me, Forster made a telling distinction between the convention-bound, stiff, church-like pretensions of the English

(Harriet Herriton) and the participatory enjoyment of the Italians. Murmuring throughout Lucia's opening aria "like a hive of happy bees", these latter accompany her coloratura with sighs, and drown out its top note with "a shout of universal joy." I knew that I had been brought up as something of a Harriet but was forced to acknowledge the limitations of her over-earnest and joyless response.

Back in the classroom studying *Howard's End*, we of course explored the theme of "only connect" and analysed both the differences between the Wilcox family and the Schlegels (the Germanic name was not accidental) and the differences deriving from the class divide that separates the Basts. Inevitably, I was intrigued by the variety of ways in which the characters respond to a performance of Beethoven's Fifth Symphony that they attend at the Queen's Hall. Their reactions to the music reveal not only something about their individual psyches but about cultural values as well, which also applies to their responses to the other music on the programme, all German (Mendelssohn and Brahms) apart from some contemporary English music by Elgar which is largely disliked.

Of the other authors we studied, Wordsworth and Milton were the most important to me. We studied a number of works by Wordsworth for A-level, but we read many more. Central for me was "Intimations of Immortality," with its concept of the child being "father of the Man," a kind of Platonic idea accompanied by the feeling that "the visionary gleam" of childhood quickly lessens as "Shades of the prison-house begin to close/Upon the growing Boy." I was much affected, too, by Wordsworth's descriptions of encounters with nature, the significance of which the mature Wordsworth talks about in his "Lines on Tintern Abbey":

> For I have learned
> To look on nature, not as in the hour
> Of thoughtless youth; but hearing oftentimes
> The still, sad music of humanity...
>
> A sense sublime
> Of something far more deeply interfused,
> Whose dwelling is the light of setting suns,
> And the round ocean and the living air,
> And the blue sky, and in the mind of man.

Such passages, and many more from various of Wordsworth's works, including selections from *The Prelude* (Books 1 and 2 in particular) were all committed to memory and, in class and privately among ourselves, were avidly discussed. For us, hovering between childhood and adulthood, Wordsworth seems to have had a special resonance.

Milton's poetry was, of course, an altogether different experience, but it was an experience that has stayed with me over the years. I believe our set works for A-level were Books 1, 2, and 4 of *Paradise Lost*, but we also read with equal care a number of other works: *L'Allegro, Il Penseroso, Lycidas, Comus, Paradise Regained* and *Samson Agonistes*. One weekend, a group of us got together and did a marathon reading of all twelve books of *Paradise Lost*. It was this work that most captured our imaginations. In studying it closely, we became immersed in Milton's vision of human history, in his dream of justifying "the ways of God to men," the implications of the Fall and promised redemption, and to us the hugely fascinating and puzzling issue of free will. I still remember how, out of school, some of us had the fiercest of arguments about this last. I know that I was equally captivated by Milton's poetry from the grandeur of the epic invocation at the opening of Book 1 to the pathos and moving sadness of the closing lines of Book 12 when Adam and Eve leave Paradise:

> *Of Man's first disobedience, and the fruit*
> *Of that forbidden tree, whose mortal taste*
> *Brought death into the world, and all our woe, …*
> (Book 1, 1-3)

> *Some natural tears they dropped, but wiped them soon;*
> *The world was all before them, where to choose*
> *Their place of rest, and Providence their guide:*
> *They hand in hand, with wand'ring steps and slow,*
> *Through Eden took their solitary way.*
> (Book 12, 645-9)

Throughout my seven years at the Grammar School, I was constantly introduced not just to literary works in English, but to others in Latin and French. In Latin classes, we began with selections from Caesar's *Commentarii de Bello Gallico* (*Gallic Wars*) and later struggled with bits and pieces from Horace, Cicero, Catullus and Ovid. Selected books from Virgil's *Aeneid* were central. Sadly, our language skills largely prevented us from appreciating the literary qualities of what we read. Our efforts always seemed to be directed at grappling with the meaning of the words in front of us. Achieving an accurate translation seemed to take precedence, and there was rarely time for more. Commonly, students bought very literal translations, and some even memorised key parts to use for tests in class and in the O-level examinations. Although we did not dare bring these "cribs" into class, our teachers, among whom were "Froggy" Newcombe and "Killer" Kemp, knew what was going on and occasionally caught someone who couldn't synchronise his memorised translation with the Latin words in front of him.

In French, by contrast, our language skills were much stronger, and we could better appreciate what we were reading. Because my failure in O-level English History resulted in the school denying me the chance to do A-level History, I instead had to take French at that level. Though I always felt insecure regarding my French language skills, I developed a great love of French literature. Early on, we read some of the stories in Alphonse Daudet's *Lettres de mon Moulin*, and we also read his *Tartarin de Tarascon*, with its amusing account of the swashbuckling Tartarin's adventures, real and invented. Early on, I also read Prosper Mérimée's *Carmen* and became fascinated with how the novella served as a source for Bizet's opera. Also fascinating to me with regard to both the book and Bizet's opera was the complex character of Carmen, her Roma background, and her inner conflict between the bonds of love and the desire for personal independence.

Later I developed a strong interest in French drama. Although

Molière's *Le Misanthrope* was a required text, I read a number of his other major plays as well, including *Les Précieuses Ridicules*, *L'Avare*, *L'École des Femmes*, and above all *Tartuffe*. Corneille's *Le Cid* was another set work, but nothing could compare to Racine. Although *Andromaque* was supposed to be our main classroom text, I became caught up in *Phèdre*. This extraordinary play was like no other I had ever read (I hadn't got to the Greek tragedians as yet) with its portrayal of overwhelming but illicit passions and near madness. Aiding me in my exploration of Racine was a copy of the complete plays which I bought from a friend, three years older than me, who had left school and was about to start his National Service. The two light green volumes, published in Paris, became especial treasures, and I kept them for a long time after leaving school.

I know we read a fair amount of poetry by a number of French writers, who included Alphonse de Lamartine, Alfred de Vigny, Victor Hugo, Alfred de Musset and others, but most I have forgotten, apart from Charles Baudelaire. More than any of the poets we read, Baudelaire had a particular attraction, perhaps because of his seeming modernity expressed in beautiful poetic language. Among all the poets who influenced my own attempts to write poetry, Baudelaire (along with John Donne and T. S. Eliot) was foremost. Now, if I look at what I wrote, I can only smile at my own naïveté while acknowledging the superb artistry of Baudelaire and that of the other two poets.

One other French writer we studied in class has also remained with me – Antoine de Saint-Exupéry. The work we studied was *Terre des Hommes*, in which poetic grandeur and a visionary expression of the beauties of the universe are allied to a series of narrative segments. These recount the adventure and dangers attendant upon aviators who fly over sparsely populated and often inhospitable terrain, in this instance the route from Benghazi to Cairo. Though the author's often highly poetic language was challenging, we persevered. I was particularly enthusiastic about this writer and went off on my own and struggled through *Courrier Sud* and *Vol de Nuit*.

Outside of class, I read a great deal of French fiction in translation. A key aid was the ongoing appearance of the Penguin Classics Series of French works with their distinctive green and white covers. A number of these I bought and a number my father already had. Between us we had a modest collection that included Balzac's *Père Goriot* and *Eugénie Grandet*, Flaubert's *Madame Bovary*, Rabelais's *Gargantua et Pantagruel*, Stendhal's *Le Rouge et le Noir*, Voltaire's *Candide*, Laclos's *Liaisons Dangereuses* and several volumes of Maupassant's short stories. On my father's shelves I also found a copy of Zola's *Germinal* in the Everyman's Library Series, and, following in my father's steps, I read all the Zola in translation that I could find in the Maidstone Public library, including *L'Assommoir*, *Thérèse Raquin*, and *Nana*. I also read Proust's *À la Recherche du Temps Perdu*, one volume of which I managed (with considerable effort) to read in French.

In addition to French literature in translation there was the equally tempting world of Russian literature. Not long after we arrived in Maidstone, I discovered the Everyman's Library translation of *Crime and Punishment* among my father's books. This work I read with some difficulty, but it astonished me with the power of its depiction of Raskolnikov's mental torment and guilt. I had never before experienced in literature anything like the haunting psychological anguish of such a character. I found it totally absorbing, and during the years that followed, I read it more than once. Later in the Penguin series, I read *The Brothers Karamazov*. David had bought this, and after I had borrowed his copy and read it, we had a fierce, stupidly schoolboy argument about which of the two novels – *Crime and Punishment* or *The Brothers Karamazov* – was best. The dispute, of course, was never resolved.

Some time later, David and I had Tolstoy to tussle over. While he read *Anna Karenina*, I doggedly worked through *War and Peace* in a new translation by Rosemary Edmonds. This had been published in two volumes in the Penguin Classics series early in 1957, and that April for fifteen shillings I bought a copy, quickly giving it the plastic cover treatment. As I read my way through this amazing work, I was enthralled and took my copy with me (one volume at a time) wherever I went. As my bookmark moved slowly forward, I was teased to the limit of what I would bear, but I kept going, most notably through several weeks of school cricket. Eventually that summer, I finished and returned the book to my shelves, vowing that I would soon re-read it. That hasn't happened as yet, but I still have my copy with its distinctive red and white paper covers, and I still plan to experience it again, especially now that I know a little more (well, only a very little more) about Russian history. Eventually, I also acquired a copy of *Anna Karenina*. This also greatly impressed me, but it was such a different kind of work, much more like a regular novel and without the philosophical meditations and the extended commentaries on history that are found in *War and Peace*. It was probably the recognition that the two works were so very different from each other that saved David and me from the kind of unproductive dispute we had had regarding the two novels by Dostoyevsky.

At about the same time (perhaps a little later) as I was reading *War and Peace*, David and I, along with some others at school, "discovered" the plays of Ibsen and Strindberg in translation, most of which were published by Penguin. What particularly appealed in Ibsen was the apparent realism of his settings and plots, the very modern-seeming nature of the social issues he dealt with and the ways in which respectable life was often shown to be a façade, behind which all manner of painful things were hidden. Even topics such as venereal disease, euthanasia, incest, all unmentionable in conventional social contexts, were brought on stage. Still studying, as "Johnny" had complained, in an environment riddled with expurgated texts of Shakespeare, we grammar school boys found Ibsen compelling reading, but not a writer to be found on any of our official reading lists.

Sadly, the same strict in-school adherence to Latin, English, and French literary works largely prevented us from exploring further afield. Two areas stand out, though I was aware of only one of them at the time. Because my school (unlike Brentwood School) did not teach Greek, my familiarity with works in that language was limited to works in translation. Important to me were Homer's two epics, the *Iliad* and the *Odyssey*, translations of both of which I purchased, and both of which I read several times. I still have those copies, and occasionally I take down the *Odyssey*. An old and true friend, this work never fails to move me. I also had copies of Sophocles's *Antigone* and *Oedipus Rex*. This latter initially was of great interest to me when I acquired an LP recording of Stravinsky's powerful reworking of the tragedy in Latin with a narration in whatever was the predominant language of the audience. Other Greek authors, however, were for the time being mere names to me: Euripides, Aristophanes, Plato, Aristotle.

More surprising, perhaps, was that the term "English Literature" was interpreted quite literally, as it had been by both the Universities of Oxford and Cambridge. Whereas today "English Literature" tends to signify any "Literature written in English," for a very long time the phrase was interpreted as referring only to works by writers of English nationality. Thus, writers from other English-speaking countries were excluded, most notably American writers. Largely because of this, the writings of Hawthorne, Melville, Poe, Emerson, Thoreau, Whitman, Dickinson, James, Hemingway, Scott Fitzgerald, Miller and others were, for the most part, unknown to me. I believe, too, that my teachers, themselves the products of Oxford or Cambridge, had read little American literature. The blind insularity of being able to look at only writers of English nationality was further perpetuated in the syllabus for the O-level and A-level examinations which was established by the two universities. All that has since changed, but looking back, I feel that the education system of which I was a part had somehow cheated me.

Although my English studies had, I later realised, a limited range, I found them almost overwhelming rich and rewarding. This created a problem for me when thinking about university. I knew I wanted to study Music, but I had an equal desire to study English. Upon the advice of my teachers, I worked out a strategy to guide me when applying for a university place. I would apply to do Music and write the appropriate entrance and scholarship examinations at certain places and apply to do English at other places. In every situation, one of the two subjects would be my principle subject and the other would be, where possible, a second subject. In theory this seemed all very sensible, but in practice it meant that I had to be sufficiently prepared to write the entrance and scholarship examinations in both subjects.

I put my strategy to work at several Cambridge colleges, my big hope being St. John's College, where various boys from Maidstone had gone to study Music in the past. Alas, no success in Cambridge in either subject. As "backups" I had also applied at Nottingham to do English and at Bristol to do Music. Nothing at Nottingham, but at Bristol, after a really intense interview with the Music faculty, who looked at my compositions and had me play a couple of my "party pieces" (the first movement of Bach's *Italian Concerto* and Debussy's F major *Arabesque)*, I was offered something that permitted me to study both Music and English as equals, but there was a price; I had to do French as well. All this because Bristol had what it called a General Honours Degree. One had to take three subjects (four in the first year) in a programme that was graded like other Honours degrees, the ultimate prize being a rarely awarded "First".

I was initially dismayed at this offer, chiefly because I had always felt that French was my weakest subject, despite my marks for A-level having been unexpectedly high and despite having been awarded a school prize for French. Just as earlier I had been forced to do French for A-level, now the same thing was happening at university.

For my fourth subject, which had to be dropped after the first year, I selected a course on Renaissance Art. How all this turned out will be the subject of the following chapter.

Alan with sisters Janet and Celia on the steps of 27 Finchley Avenue, Chelmsford. 1945

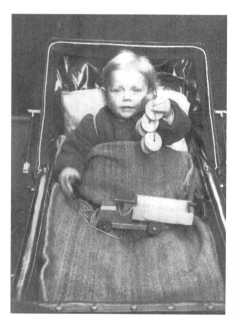

Celia takes possession of
Alan's treasured lorry

Heinz, the German POW and musician
befriended by Alan's parents

Celia, Alan and Janet with recorders

Family holiday (Janet, Mother, Alan, Father, Celia)

Aunty D (Dorothy Cole)

Alan camping at Minehead during a break from studies at Bristol University

Flatmates at Bristol (John Watson, Alan, Peter Standish, David Bowyer)

The *Kenya Castle* in the port of Genoa

Arrival in Mombasa, Kenya. Roland Minor, Richard Tonkin, Alan

View from train approaching Nairobi

Mitchell Hall, Makerere University, Uganda

First safari. Alan, Richard Tonkin, Frank Smith, Robin Pingree

The dam at Jinja

Alan at Murchison Falls in North West Uganda

Road in Karamoja in north-east Uganda

Near Moroto, Karamoja. Roland Minor and Richard Tonkin

Safari camp in Karamoja

Some of the author's students. Kapsabet School, Kenya

Some of the Staff at Kapsabet School

Harry Stein, Kapsabet School

Author coaching rugby at Kapsabet School

Fr. Errity with two nuns. Chepterit Mission, near Kapsabet

The Nandi Store, Kapsabet

Safari to Masai Mara. Teresa Laemmlen and Masai woman and child

Safari to Masai Mara. Frank Laemmlen and his bone collection

Safari to Masai Mara. Anne Laemmlen

Lions, Masai Mara

Alan with Brutus

Children at play in Alan's garden

Mosque on beach near Mombasa

Camping at Hell's Gate. Jackie Heaton, Peter Ryall, Alan

Elephants in Amboseli Game Reserve (now Amboseli National Park)

Mt. Elgon. Frank Laemmlen on crater rim

Mt. Kenya. Jackie Heaton and Peter Ryall

Outward Bound School, Loitokitok, Kenya

Mt. Kilimanjaro near summit

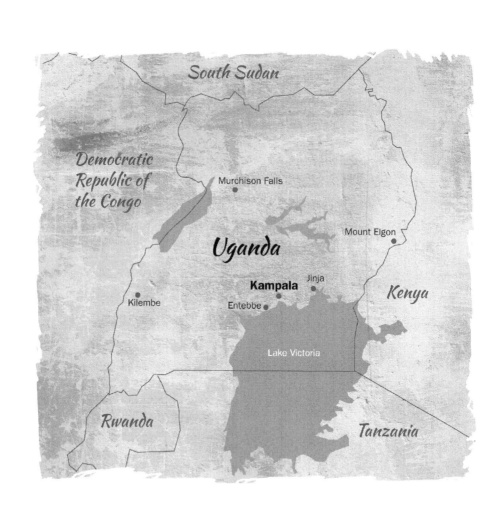

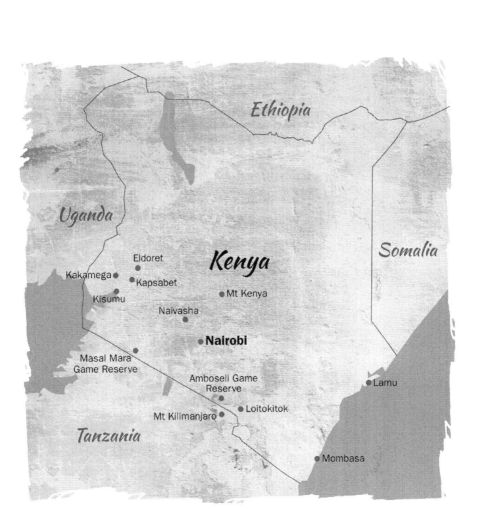

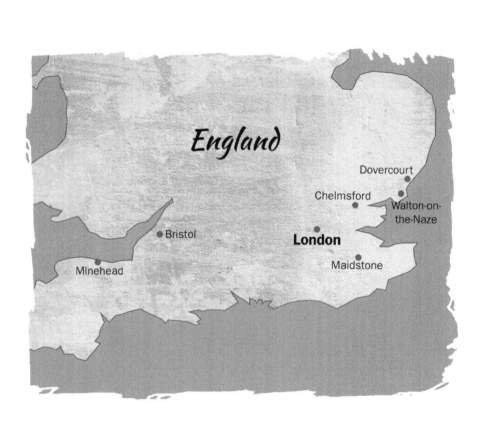

CHAPTER EIGHT

UNDERGRADUATE

The easy part of going off to university in the autumn of 1960 was packing the family trunk, the weary veteran of so many two-week family holidays. Roping it up, I used a poor imitation of Uncle Jack's system of knots and wished that he was around to help. Eventually, after I had successfully thwarted my mother's various attempts to stuff in extra bits and pieces that she was sure I might need, the job was done. A lorry came to the house, and clothes, books, and typewriter were on their way.

Much harder, a week or two later, was getting myself to Bristol, with portable gramophone and large suitcase containing yet more possessions. First a train from Bromley to London, then the underground to Paddington Station, then the long journey to Bristol and then, with suitcase in the luggage area beneath the bus stairs, the ride from Temple Meads Station up to the far side of Clifton Downs, before getting off at Churchill Hall, a student men's residence where it would all begin.

My fellow "freshers" and other older students seemed to be a friendly bunch, and I soon started to get used to the Hall routine. This was largely tied to mealtimes. A hot breakfast in the morning, if one woke up in time, and a formal dinner "in Hall" five days a week. For this dinner, a jacket and tie were mandatory, along with a black gown. This last was a useful protection, since the serving staff, who seemed to be mostly elderly men, tended to be none too steady, so food (chiefly gravy) sometimes got spilled on one.

In what I took to be an imitation of the Oxbridge custom, there was a high table, and no one sat down until the Warden had entered and said grace. Any latecomer had to stand by the door until the Warden deigned to recognize him with the smallest of nods. Only then could he go to a table and sit down. Lunches during the week were at the University, a bus ride away, often in the Refectory. Essentially a cafeteria, the Refectory was run by the University, a convenient place to go between classes. I met all manner of people there, the oddest being a young woman who claimed that a doctor had just diagnosed her with scurvy. Since arriving in Bristol, free from her parents' supervision, she'd lived on a diet of chips. I was greatly intrigued. Did this disease still exist? Did she really have it? Or had her doctor tried to scare her by telling her something that would frighten her into eating properly?

My first week at Bristol was made memorable on account of something that happened to me in Churchill Hall. I had been told that a day or so after my arrival I should expect to receive a cheque in the post. This would be the first instalment of my county grant from Kent. It came as promised, but to my surprise it was for an amount far larger that I had expected. Grateful for the windfall, I deposited it in my account at the Co-operative Bank.

However, the cheque wasn't the only surprise that came in the post. There were several letters addressed to me from people I didn't know, some of them very personal in nature. It was strangely unsettling, even surreal. This continued for a few days until late one afternoon there was a knock on my door. When I opened it, I found myself greeting two charming young women who said they'd like to talk to me. Fortunately, my room was reasonably tidy and I had two chairs they could sit on, although that left me only the bed to sit on. Because the two of them were acting in such a friendly manner, I felt quite relaxed about hosting women in my room. It was something I knew was permitted only during certain hours, but it had not crossed my mind that I would be having any female visitors. Well, not yet.

When we were all seated, we introduced ourselves. When I gave them my name, they turned and looked at each other. What had I done? What did their exchange of glances mean? It didn't take long for them to explain.

"Well, you see, there's been a mix-up. We think you might have got a grant cheque from Kent – bigger than the one you were expecting. And we think you might have got some other letters too."

"Well, yes," I said, "but I've deposited the cheque. I've kept the letters, though. They're right here on my desk, even though I don't know the people who sent them."

"Thank goodness," one of them replied.

"You didn't know," the other one interrupted. "You see, there's another Alan Young. He's also just got here. He's also from Kent, and he's also here in Churchill Hall."

"I can't believe it!" I blurted out. "I'm really sorry. That's an unbelievable coincidence." Then, looking at the two women, "So where is he? Why are you here?"

"Yes, we'd better explain. The thing is, he's blind. We're part of a small group who've volunteered to help him until he can get around on his own. Right now, he's down at the University with some other people, learning his way around."

The other woman then handed me several letters addressed to "Alan Young". They'd all been opened, and I was shocked to see that one was from my girlfriend. The contents of that letter would definitely be extremely personal.

"I'm sorry we opened these," she said. "But that's one of our jobs. We read letters for him." Blushing slightly, she went on apologizing until I stopped her.

"It's OK," I said. "There's no harm done. We just know a bit more about each other than we might normally have done. That's all."

The two of them looked very relieved to hear this, and the smiles returned. Then we talked about various ways to fix the problem. We wouldn't open any hand-written letter that we weren't sure about without checking with the other person, and I would ask my friends and family to start addressing letters to me using my middle initial: "Alan R. Young." As far as the money was concerned, I'd write my namesake a cheque for the overpayment I had received.

Some days later, I met the other Alan Young. He was good-humoured about the whole mix-up. It turned out that he, too, was doing a General Honours degree, but the only subject we shared was English. As might be expected, I saw him frequently, but we never became friends. He was very serious about his studies. Ironically, one of his subjects was History. Was he some kind of alter ego, fulfilling my thwarted desires? As for his support group – all very friendly young women – I regretfully saw very little of them. Were they in the thwarted desires category also?

Very soon after moving into Churchill Hall, I was asked to join the rugby team. This was quite a commitment. There were practices every Wednesday and a game every Saturday. We were not by any means a star team, but we were just at the right level to play against teams from various towns and villages within a short distance of Bristol. Games were usually followed by the customary soak with the opposing team in a large communal bath, a must for any club. If it had been a muddy affair out on the field, inevitably a thin crusting of dirt soon appeared on the surface of the bathwater. No one seemed to mind or even notice. Instead, what we enjoyed were pints of beer lined up around the side of the bath, the singing of bawdy songs and the general male camaraderie.

The only time, as far as I can recall, when these rituals were absent was when we played against a team of prison inmates. The matches against this team took place in the prison yard, a grassy area surrounded by cell blocks. It was an awkward place to play on because it was much smaller than the normal playing area. Players were consequently bunched closer together, and the ball could be thrown more easily from end to end. The inmates knew how to take advantage of these features, but their skills were no match for us once we had got used to the peculiarities of the pitch. One thing, however, that we couldn't match was the aggressive behaviour of the other team. They were determined, I suspect, to show this bunch of privileged students what tough, hardened men they were. After the game, we were able to meet with our opponents, who were friendly enough and clearly enjoying their afternoon, but there was no bath and no beer. Instead there were some minimal washing facilities, followed by some strange-tasting tea. The rumour (something we could never confirm) was that the tea was laced with saltpetre, an anaphrodisiac routinely added to the prisoners' tea. Later, several members of our team, after seeing their girlfriends that evening, claimed that the rumour must be true, but nothing was ever proven.

As I explained earlier, my four subjects at Bristol were Renaissance Art (for one year only), together with French, English, and Music. In signing up for Renaissance Art, I was influenced by two things. First, there were the classes at Maidstone given by Vernon Fawcett. I had always enjoyed his emotional and anecdotal style, his frequent sidestepping into other topics, particularly anything to do with music, and his ways of cajoling us into looking at works of art in ways that we could never have anticipated. He was not very good at retaining class discipline and behind his back, we laughed at him a good deal. Nonetheless, something stayed with me, and I remembered things he had tried to show us when looking at reproductions of works by Leonardo, Raphael, Titian, Tintoretto, Goya and others. Why not do some more of this kind of thing, I thought?

The other trigger for my interest was very different. During my last year or so at school, my friend David had suddenly developed a new enthusiasm which he thought we should both try. He persuaded me to spend some money on oil paints, brushes, canvas boards and the other accoutrements that would allow us to do some painting.

After a few hints from his sister Ann, who was a student at Maidstone College of Art, we got to work. Our studios were the small paved areas that adjoined both our houses below the dining room window. David, always more vocal than I, enthused with great delight about how important it was for us to have the tactile experience of handling the paint, even at times using our fingers instead of our brushes to apply paint to the canvas. All this, he exclaimed, was beneficial to our spirits. Somewhat sceptically, I followed along, but gradually I began to enjoy the venture. We would talk a lot about each other's works. Even though the results of our efforts were unimpressive, to say the least, we kept going. At the same time, I increasingly began to perceive just what those old masters had achieved.

Then, as was typical of David, his newfound enthusiasm began to wane, and our joint backyard studio sessions came to an end. I, however, continued to struggle on my own, and when I set out for Bristol, I took some paints and brushes with me. It was an obvious choice, then, to do the History of Renaissance Art course.

Our teacher was a relatively young man from the Courtauld Institute, a Mr. Steer. He was passionate about his subject, and it often seemed to me that he would forget all about the students sitting in the darkened classroom as he talked eloquently, even poetically, about the art works he showed us. I loved his classes, and towards the end of the year I went to see him. I explained that I was seriously considering the idea of giving up at Bristol. Was there a possibility that I could come to the Courtauld? I knew something about the Institute because a fellow student at Maidstone, Leslie Parris (a fellow Aldermaston marcher), had gone there. My art teacher was clearly embarrassed by my question and strongly urged me to finish at Bristol. Then, if I still wanted to go to the Courtauld, I should apply. I very much respected his advice, so I reluctantly put the idea on hold, then forgot it in the years that followed, and, when my time at Bristol came to an end, I never even thought about it.

Years later, when my own researches required me to work on art and artists from the early modern period, I thought again about that pivotal moment when my life might have taken a quite different course. This "fork in the road" once more came to mind in 2013 when in the *Guardian* for 11 February 2000, I saw an obituary for Leslie Parris, with whom I'd had no contact since the day we had left school. Apparently, following his studies at the Courtauld, he had worked at the Tate Gallery for 35 years and had become a noted art historian. He was particularly well known for his publications and curated exhibitions on Constable, but there was something else that especially struck me. His chief reason for going to the Courtauld, I read, had been the inspiration he had received from his history teacher at Maidstone. Yet another reason for me to wonder, after more than fifty years, what would have happened had I been given the chance to do A-level history. Would I, too, have gone to the Courtauld?

As for my own attempts at painting, these continued at Bristol. One day at a morning English lecture attended by a large number of students, I found myself sitting next to a woman who was quietly crying for the whole hour. Not having a clue about what the social protocol was in such a situation, I asked her if I could help at all and if she'd like to come for a coffee. She took me up on the coffee, and thereafter we became quite good friends.

When she found out that I'd been trying to paint, she told me that I must join the University Art Club. With considerable trepidation, I went along to my first meeting in the Club's room in the Victoria Building. The students I met were a very sociable group and encouraged me to join. They seemed quite unconcerned about my possible complete lack of talent, so I took up their offer.

Each time the Club met, someone organized a different activity. We went sketching outdoors, we visited the Bristol Art Gallery across the street for a guided tour, we painted or drew various subjects inside, sometimes with a model, we went to Prinknash Abbey and watched the monks doing pottery, and we even had a private exhibition of our work. To this last, we invited someone from the Bristol Art School to come and comment on each person's contribution. I was told that I needed to have some drawing lessons, but nothing that I wouldn't be able to manage. I was also told, though, that I had a very good feel for colour, something that showed to great advantage in a still life I had done. I was understandably very pleased by this, but I couldn't help wondering what she would have said about the self-portrait I'd done in my room at Churchill Hall. The angular figure I'd painted had a rather fierce gaze which, together with the full black beard and longish black hair, caused the other students in my building to think of D. H. Lawrence. Thereafter, to my considerable embarrassment, I was for a time nicknamed "Lawrence". What would the teacher from the Art School have said about this?

In my final year at Bristol, I was elected President of the Art Club, an office that I felt was quite inappropriate. However, everyone surely knew my limitations as an artist. I suppose what was needed was someone to organize the Art Club's activities. Nonetheless, the title "President" had some unexpected consequences. The student newspaper had me writing reviews of various art exhibitions, and I received invitations to a number of "openings" at various galleries in the city. Obviously I was supposed to be somewhat knowledgeable about art, a matter that caused me to do what reading and studying I could. In this, my friend (the weeping one) was a great help. She herself was very knowledgeable, and the large Georgian terrace house in Berkeley Square where she boarded with her uncle was full of paintings. Her uncle, evidently a wealthy man, was an avid collector. As one climbed the seemingly endless flights of stairs in his house, one was confronted by an array of the paintings that he had acquired. Every inch of wall space appeared to be taken up with these pictures. I would visit every few weeks, and each time many of the paintings had disappeared, having been replaced by fresh acquisitions. I didn't see much of the uncle, a genial elderly man who always seemed pleased to see me. As my friend explained, he liked to buy works by up-and-coming artists; however, he also owned plenty of works by well-established artists. All these paintings gathered under one roof provided a valuable learning experience for me, my friend being my teacher. Her considerable knowledge had come, I assumed, from her uncle. She herself was a good amateur artist, and I still have a portrait sketch that she did of me on the blank inside of the programme for a concert we went to at the Colston Hall.

But what of my own attempts at painting? Three years after leaving Bristol, I felt it was time to do some house cleaning at my parents' home in Bromley. Among the things I chose to throw out (another "fork in the road" moment?) were all the paintings I had done over the preceding six or seven years. Looking at them, I'd realised how far removed each was from the original concept I'd had in my head. My lack of training and technique meant that not only had I failed to create what I "saw" with my inner eye, but what I had produced was simply bad art. So into the dustbin they all went. Forty years or so later, however, I discovered that my sister Celia had secretly recovered two of the paintings from the dustbin. There they were on display in her house. I was both touched and amused.

So much, then, for my experience of art at Bristol. Mr. Steer's year-long course was central, and its effect on me almost derailed my degree programme. But that formal study of Renaissance art coexisted with a very informal and haphazard education derived from my own attempts to paint, from the activities of the Art Club, and from all that I learned about contemporary art from my friend and her uncle's art collection in that house in Berkeley Square.

Whereas Art History lasted only for a year, my three remaining subjects were with me for the remainder of my time at Bristol. One of these – French – was not something I chose. It was imposed upon me because, ironically, I had received good marks for this subject in both the O-level and A-level examinations. Things began badly with a boring class on French morphology taught by an arrogant teacher who seemed to believe that our frequent failure to comprehend what he scribbled on the blackboard was the result of our lack of attention and our limited intellects. The word from students who had already taken the class was that if one made sure to write down all the terminology and if one learned by rote the definition of each term, all would be well in the exam at the end of the year. The advice proved to be right, and that was thankfully the end of my brief foray into French linguistics.

For all three years, there were ongoing classes in oral and written French. My oral work was a constant worry, especially since my pronunciation was never very polished; however, I muddled along. It was the same story in the case of both translation exercises from French to English and the regular dictation tests.

My big worry was always translating from English into French. In my final year, along with several other students, I was encouraged to do extra exercises to improve my skills in this area. Somehow my efforts were rewarded, and I still remember being in a noisy pub a few days after the exam and meeting my language teacher. Insisting that I tell no one until the results were announced officially, he startled me by explaining that I'd done quite well. In retrospect, I believe he was as surprised and almost as relieved as I was.

My constant anxieties regarding my language skills were mercifully balanced by the delight I derived from the literature classes. Central to our work in the first year was our study of *La Chanson de Roland*. Were our morphology classes supposed to help us read this eleventh century Old French epic? I never figured that out, but I did find the poem (the sections that we studied, that is) very rewarding, a story of heroes and traitors, bloody battles, swords, spears, horses, and Roland's near magical horn. The selection of other set texts was much along the lines of what had been required for A-level, although there was perhaps a greater emphasis on poetry. The essays we were asked to write now had to be in French, a big limitation, I felt, but it was something that no doubt sharpened our language skills.

When we wrote our final exams, time was a problem on account of having to write in French. I remember that I wrote an essay on Naturalism in French literature and opera, bringing together two interests of mine. Apparently, this was received very well, and I believe contributed to the unexpectedly good standing that I achieved in my final year in French. The essay also underscored my belief that there ought to be opportunities within a general Honours degree to explore links between different subjects. Unfortunately, the degree programme was not structured this way, and each subject was studied, for the most part, in isolation from any other subject.

There was one feature of the French programme about which I did feel very positive. At the end of the first year, we were expected to select a course at an institution in France that would offer some intensive language training and a broad study of French culture. I chose the programme offered jointly by the Universities of Bordeaux and Toulouse. This took place in July-August 1962 in the small, picturesque town of Pau in south-west France, famous for its Boulevard des Pyrénées, from which one had spectacular views of the mountains to the south. Not surprisingly, large numbers of local inhabitants, joined by visiting students like me, enjoyed an evening promenade when the view from the cliff top location seemed at its most magnificent.

Getting to Pau was a small adventure, involving a train ride from London to Dover on a "boat train" from Victoria Station, a cross-channel ferry to Calais, a train to Paris, a change of railway terminals and then the long overnight train to Pau. Nowadays, the journey to Paris via the Channel Tunnel and a Eurostar hi-speed train from St. Pancras takes a mere 2¼ hours, very different from the nine hours or so that used to be the norm. From Paris to Pau, there is today a hi-speed (TGV) train that takes five and a half hours, whereas the overnight regular service is eight and a half hours. Imagine, then, my very groggy state on arrival in Pau during the early morning hours with a full day ahead, registering for the course, finding my dormitory, learning where the meals were served, and getting to talk to one or two other students. As it turned out, my dormitory housed about eight students, all from different countries. Among them, and in addition to me, there was a Swede, an Italian, a German, a Spaniard and an American. I believe that this mix of nationalities was deliberate on the part of the course organisers. The goal was to make it easier for us to speak only French, a rule that we broke all the time, particularly when we discovered that we all spoke English far better than we spoke French.

Although our classes were hard work, there were a number of compensations. Food was one of them. Our meals by comparison with university fare in Churchill Hall and the Refectory were impressive affairs with tasty and varied food supervised by a chef who frequently left his kitchen to come and ask us whether we liked what he had cooked for us. Not only was the food a constant delight, but it was accompanied at lunch and dinner by a generous supply of wine. There were bottles on every table, and one just helped oneself to as much as one wanted. This made for some very difficult afternoon classes. After too much wine, it was almost impossible to stay awake, let alone concentrate. In time, we learned to moderate our intake of wine. After all, there would be plenty available at the next meal.

In the evenings, Pau was a delightful place to be. Not only was there the nightly promenade along the Boulevard des Pyrénées but there was music in one of the town squares, and a host of cafes where one could sit, socialise and people-watch. There was one café that students particularly favoured. On two occasions, after an excessive consumption of wine, everything got out of hand, and someone (the proprietor, perhaps, or a nearby resident who wanted to go to sleep) called the police. They arrived in several small vans, batons drawn and whistles blowing. As they came storming through the main door of the café, rather than getting hit with a baton or getting arrested, many of us jumped through the large open windows and took flight back to our dormitories.

At weekends it was relatively easy to hitchhike to the coast, either to Saint-Jean-de-Luz or Bayonne. The former was the most picturesque of places, famous for its narrow winding streets and the Basque church of Saint-Jean-Baptiste. This was where the Treaty of the Pyrénées between France and Spain was signed in 1659, followed in 1660 by the marriage of King Louis XIV and Marie-Thérèse. What most attracted us, however, were the beautiful sandy beaches. The town is only a few kilometres from the Spanish border, and, after the course was over, I stayed there for a few days. On one of these days, a friend and I hitchhiked into Spain along the coastal road to the town of San Sebastian. We were determined to see a bull fight. Having been to Bayonne and experienced the French version of the sport which avoided the slaughter of any of the bulls, I was anxious to see the "real" thing. Because we attended a gala event, we saw some top matadors display their art to a predominantly knowledgeable Spanish crowd. This was not one of those shows put on to please tourists. Appreciation of the finer points of the sport eluded us, but we certainly got to experience the final drama accompanying the death of each bull. It was enough to last a lifetime, since I have never since had the desire to repeat the experience.

With my Certificat d'Assiduité in hand, duly stamped by the Université de Bordeaux and the Université de Toulouse, I returned home, sure that my French had improved and that the remaining years of study would go well. Of course, my fellow students at Bristol all had similar certificates from wherever they had gone, so I soon realised that compared with others in my cohort I was no further ahead.

While attending French classes, I met another student, who quickly became a close friend. He was a few years older than I and had just finished three years of National Service in the army. He did not talk much about this, but he did tell me one thing that has stayed with me. As a lieutenant faced with rioters in Hong Kong, he had had to select one of the rioters and order one of his men to shoot the man. Supposedly, this was a way of keeping the violence to a minimum, while demonstrating to the rioters that one meant business when ordering them to disperse. As far as I could learn, the strategy had worked, but my friend seemed haunted by what he had done.

On a few days each week we would meet in his flat near the university, each taking turns to buy food for lunch. There were shops close by where one could find excellent bread and a great variety of cheeses. We liked to think of this as French fare, a kind of extension of what we had shared in French classes. I always enjoyed our conversations, which ranged widely from the philosophical (my friend), to music (me) and to literature (both of us). We also talked about women, but there my friend was far ahead of me. On one occasion, he gave me a very graphic account of his visit with other soldiers to a brothel in Hong Kong, but was quick to point out that all that kind of thing was well behind him. Now he was engaged and looking forward to getting married. As for me, I had none of his experience and seemed to be drifting from one girl to another, never thinking about such things as marriage.

Very quickly, I realised that my friend was very intelligent and a serious, dedicated student. Week by week, he always managed to get better marks than I, but at the same time, he set a standard that I tried to emulate. Often we studied together. Although I learned a great deal from him, I know that he in turn picked things up from me. Otherwise our friendly and relaxed relationship would surely never have survived.

When we reached the final examination at the end of three years, I felt that I must surely be close on his heels, even if my French language skills were not quite on a par with his. In the end I was awarded an Upper Second, a very acceptable standing with which I was satisfied. My friend, however, was awarded a First. This was a rarity among General Honours students, and that year he was the only one to achieve the distinction, as far as I was aware. As a result, he was almost immediately offered a job in the Foreign Office, but to everyone's surprise, he turned it down, opting instead to study for a diploma in education at the University of London.

When he got married, he lived with his wife in a flat in north London. Some months after I left Bristol, as a kind of wedding present, I sent them a small statuette of an elderly bearded African leaning on a staff. As a thank-you response, my friend's wife sent me an exquisite watercolour she had done. It depicted the African figure standing on the window sill of their flat, deliberately out of harmony with the sunless British winter scene outside and the leafless tree in the background.

Whereas my French studies were a constant source of anxiety – I even had nightmare-like dreams about French – English was a far more comfortable affair. The very first lecture was an experience I shall never forget. Sitting in a large hall filled with students, I watched as a tall, very frail-looking man carefully climbed the steps of the podium. This was L. C. Knights, a man whose essay on "How Many Children Had Lady Macbeth?" I knew very well, along with two of his books, *Drama & Society in the Age of Jonson* and *Some Shakespearian Themes*. Though he was only fifty-four at the time, he seemed very much older. Would this (to us) aged and venerable man have the stamina to last through the hour-long lecture? If his spirit left his body, one wondered, would there be anything much left behind?

For this first lecture, he began by having several of the students at the front distribute a single sheet of paper. On it, to everyone's surprise, was printed a small eight-line poem entitled "The Pasture". I didn't recognize the poem and nor did most of my fellow students, as far as I could tell. Nor did we know anything about Robert Frost, and we certainly didn't know that this was the poem he had placed as a kind of prelude to various editions of his poetry.

After all, Frost was an American, wasn't he? We had only studied British literature. What was Professor Knights, Bristol's most renowned English scholar, famed follower of Leavis and past editor of the journal *Scrutiny*, doing?

For the whole hour, we sat in amazed silence as he talked about just this one poem in ways that made one think, "Yes, this is why I study English". At the same time the last three words of each of the two stanzas ("You come too") seemed like the perfect invitational thought for the start of our English studies at Bristol.

After that initial class and another unforgettable lecture by Knights on Blake's "Tyger, tyger", I sadly had only one further class with him. At some stage during the second or third year, however, when we were studying a Shakespeare play (I've forgotten which), it became known that Knights was lecturing on Shakespeare to the students taking English degrees. The word was spread that one just had to hear him even if one wasn't in his class. Along with numerous others, I went along.

When I arrived, the large steeply-tiered lecture theatre was almost completely full. Before long, more students began to stand at the back and sides, while others began sitting on the steps of the central aisle leading down to the podium. A minute or so before the class was due to begin, there was something of a commotion up by the entry door. Knights had arrived, but this frail, unworldly figure could not without difficulty get through the door. Then, he had to negotiate his way down the steps, most of which were blocked by students. Eventually, he did get to the lectern, and he did give the kind of lecture we'd all hoped for. We interlopers all left, delighted that we had gone. However, there was a problem.

No doubt the packed theatre was something of a fire marshal's nightmare, and there was the issue of the professor's precarious descent. What if he had fallen? Alas, when we returned the following week, at the doors were people with clipboards and lists of those officially in Professor Knights's Shakespeare class. No one else was allowed in. Those of us not listed all complained vociferously, but to no effect.

There were other fine teachers, too, though none had quite the charisma of L. C. Knights. I remember Henry Gifford walking us through the early history of the English novel. I already knew something about that from reading my Penguin edition of Ian Watt's *The Rise of the Novel*. Furthermore, David and I had "discovered" Henry Fielding while at school and had read both *Joseph Andrews* and *Tom Jones*.

I also remember Charles Tomlinson, already a well-known poet but soon to be a *very* well-known poet. He was a constant source of amusement and speculation among the students who came to his classes. Rather than standing at a lectern, he often sat atop the table at the front of the lecture hall, all the better, I suspect, to display the bright red socks he wore or his lack of any socks at all. There was another Tomlinson too, whose first name I have forgotten. Throughout the class, he always stood unmoving behind the lectern. His eyesight was obviously poor, and he wore glasses with very thick lenses. He barely looked at us, but I suppose that was because he couldn't see us. I liked his lectures on Dickens, although I cannot recall with certainty which novel we studied (most likely it was *Dombey and Son*).

Then there was Ronald Gaskell. I still recall his riveting lectures on John Donne. I got to know him a little, because for one year he was my English tutor. A small group of us met with him each week to discuss whatever works he cared to assign us. We also had to write essays for him, and I believe that I learned a great deal from his guidance. A number of years later, I wrote to him to see if he would be willing to write a reference for me. To my surprise I received a friendly reply in which he said that he remembered my work very well. Later still, I met another former student of his. She had become a friend of his family and visited quite often. She became a kind of informal link, passing news of him to me and news of me to him.

Of all the works of English literature I studied at Bristol, one in particular was very much a revelation – Henry James's *The Portrait of a Lady*. James seems to have got onto our reading list because the English claimed him as theirs on account of his domicile. Perhaps, too, James was "allowed" in because the foolish exclusion of American works was also breaking down, as in the case of L. C. Knights having us read Frost's "The Pasture." Although I do not remember who lectured to us on James (one of the Tomlinsons, I believe), I recall being fascinated by the central theme of the young innocent American woman finding herself in the web of old but corrupt and cynical European culture that threatens to destroy her. As soon as I had read it, I wanted more, and soon discovered other shorter works by James, such as *The Europeans* and *Washington Square*. These were relatively early works. Later I went on to *The Bostonians, The Spoils of Poynton, The Ambassadors* and (most challenging to me) *The Golden Bowl*. With *The Wings of a Dove*, however, I met my nemesis and have yet, in spite of a number of determined tries, still not succeeded in reading it all.

Of course, in addition to such hitherto unfamiliar works, there remained the standard texts by authors with whom I was already somewhat familiar. There was Chaucer, for example, taught in an afternoon class by a teacher we considered immensely boring. In her class, the real struggle was to stay awake, especially if the weather was warm and one had just had a big lunch. Then, in addition to the texts I've already mentioned that were taught by Knights, the Tomlinsons, Gaskell, and Gifford, there were, as might be expected, classes on Restoration and eighteenth-century poetry, Coleridge and Wordsworth (this latter's *Prelude* was a set text), the Romantics and some Victorian poets, chiefly Tennyson. Twentieth-century poetry was largely neglected, apart from some brief forays into Gerard Manley Hopkins.

There were, of course, some selected plays of Shakespeare on our list. Particularly enlightening, as far as I was concerned, was the attempt to place Shakespeare within a broader context. The idea was that we should know about medieval drama, about miracle and morality plays, and about the development of the public playhouses, among them Shakespeare's Globe. Lectures on these topics were given by Glynne Wickham in the Department of Drama. Although I was unaware of it at the time, this energetic and passionate scholar had very recently established himself as the foremost authority on these subjects with the publication in 1959 of the first volume of his *Early English Stages*. Little did I realise how much I would later owe to his work when I became involved in theatre studies myself. Nor could I have guessed that I would later meet him when he participated in a seminar I organized in 1981 for the World Shakespeare Congress in Stratford-upon-Avon.

Although English was a demanding subject at Bristol, especially given the demands of weekly tutorials and the essays we were required to write, nothing could compare, as far as I was concerned, to Music and the quite disproportionate amount of my time I spent working on it. The Department of Music was in Royal Fort House, an imposing hilltop mansion built between 1758 and 1761 and approached through a stone gatehouse built in the Victorian era. Professor Willis Grant, the Head of the Department was (in the view of his students) inordinately taken with the location. He loved showing visitors around, and delighted in acquiring paintings of a date appropriate to the age of the house, no matter if the artistic merit of the paintings was questionable.

I still remember him calling us together and introducing us to another kind of acquisition. It was a small fortepiano, rectangular in shape. We were assured that soon we would be able to hear the kind of sound that Mozart or Haydn was used to. However, all we ever heard were some very tinny noises. In spite of Professor Grant's optimism, it would seem that the instrument was past repair. Behind his back, we joked about his proprietary attitude to the house, and what we believed was his misuse of Department funds, though admittedly we never really knew where the money for his purchases had come from.

Professor Grant was a micro-manager who kept a close check on every one of his students. He had an uncanny ability, for example, to notice if anyone was absent from a rehearsal or concert. On one occasion, he and I had a somewhat fierce altercation when he called me to his office and questioned me as to why I had not been at the previous evening's concert – not a University concert but a concert elsewhere, for which music students, as happened all the time, had been given free tickets. He was taken aback when I said that I'd been at a jazz concert, and even more confused, I suspect, when I explained that it had offered a rare opportunity to hear Dave Brubeck, to my mind one of the finest and most musical of modern jazz performers.

On another occasion, it was he who surprised me. Entry to Professor Grant's office was off another large and impressive room. In this antechamber was a very nice grand piano. Music students were permitted to use the room for rehearsals and practice, provided the Professor was not in his office. One day, believing that he was away, a Japanese friend and I took the opportunity to play some music together. My friend was a science student, but he was a good amateur violinist. We had decided that together we would work on the first movement of Beethoven's "Spring" Sonata. With various stops and starts to get things right, we began to stumble our way through the piece.

Everything was going moderately well when to our horror the door to Professor Grant's office suddenly opened. Our playing came to an abrupt halt and, immensely embarrassed, I began to apologise as we quickly gathered up our music and prepared to depart. But no. The usually morose Professor was all smiles. He wanted to know who my friend was. Was he a student? Where was he from? Then he told us that the "Spring" Sonata was a favourite, and, what's more, we should continue practising. Indeed, we should feel free to come and play whenever we liked, even if he was working in his office. With one last beatific smile, he then turned around, closed the door, and went back, we assumed, to his desk.

Needless to say, we ended our playing soon afterwards. It was too anxiety-provoking to go on, knowing who was listening to us mangle his favourite Beethoven violin sonata. Thereafter, we only practised in the antechamber when we were absolutely sure that no one was in the next room.

Because there were only two of us doing Music at the General Degree level, we often attended the same classes as the BMus students. This was particularly the case with music history classes. Many of these were taught by Professor Grant, who was lively and engaging as a teacher and, it seemed to me, particularly enthusiastic and knowledgeable about early English music by composers such as Thomas Tallis, William Byrd, John Dowland, Thomas Morley and Orlando Gibbons. We also learned a certain amount about plain chant. In one of the choirs he conducted, he had us singing plain chant and enjoying the wonderful sound one could create in a large building in which an echo was inescapable. Ideal for this purpose was the interior of the Wills Memorial Tower, a wonderful neo-gothic structure. On either side of the Entrance Hall were ceremonial staircases that led up to a connecting balcony. Above was a vast open space. It was from the balcony that we sang our plain chant and savoured the exquisite sounds resulting from the cathedral-like acoustics of the building.

On a different occasion, the entire Music Department travelled by motor coach to a not-too-distant abbey in a beautiful rural setting. The object was to listen to the monks singing a particular kind of plain chant. Professor Grant attempted, as best he could, to share his enthusiasm about what we would hear. We were urged to recognize that we would be observing an unbroken musical tradition going back hundreds of years. He was quite passionate about all this. Sadly, it seems to me, we students did not fully appreciate the experience he had created for us. Thinking back, I would like to think that I could return to the abbey and hear the same plain chant sung by a new generation of monks. Belatedly, and some several decades after his death, I think I now understand Professor Grant's point; there is something immensely valuable in such a beautiful form of music that has passed down the centuries in this way. It is a direct connection with our forebears, something to be cherished and wondered at. Whereas we may look at ancient works of art, music offers a more direct connection with our past. We can both listen to it where it is still actively a part of the lives of a religious order like the monks we visited, or we ourselves can bring it to life when we ourselves perform it as we did when Professor Grant taught us how to read and sing plainchant.

Besides conducting various choirs, of which I invariably seemed to be a member, Professor Grant also conducted the University Choral Society. All Music students were required to belong, whether they could sing or not. In my first term, I suddenly found myself immersed in Bach's Mass in B minor, a work which simultaneously would be a set score for our studies in music history. The performance would be in Bristol Cathedral at the end of term, so rehearsals by necessity were very intense. Typically, everyone was seated and ready at rehearsals at least five minutes before a rehearsal began. Who would dare to be late for a Willis Grant event? Then, exactly at start time, a door at the front of the tiered auditorium would open and our conductor would march briskly towards his podium, score and baton in hand. On the way, he would call out page number, bar number and the title of the item. The pianist would give us our notes, the Professor would raise his baton, and we were off. I'd never before encountered such energy, such efficiency and such discipline. What's more, he knew exactly what he wanted from us, and, with a mixture of cajolery and very positive encouragement, he got it. I remember especially how he would tell the sopranos and altos how much he liked the youthful lightness and sparkle of their voices. It was just the thing for Bach, he would say. Needless to say, we all worked very hard for him, practising our parts during the week and striving to get the effects he wanted.

The final performance of the B minor Mass was for me an overwhelming experience. Since then, I've never been able to hear the opening four bars of the "Kyrie" without being transported back in time to our performance in the Cathedral. Similarly, whenever I hear the "Gloria", I remember the bright, youthful exhilarating sound of the alto and two soprano parts as I heard them in 1960.

Thereafter, there were performances in subsequent years in the Cathedral (Beethoven's Mass in D in 1961, and Walton's *Belshazzar's Feast* in 1962), and in such places as the Lord Mayor's Chapel (Purcell's, *Lord, How Long Wilt Thou be Angry* and Heinrich Schütz's *The Seven Last Words from the Cross* in 1962), and the University Reception Room (Parry's *The Pied Piper of Hamelin* in 1962). There was a variety of other works, too, such as Handel's *Sixth Chandos Anthem*, two Bach motets (*Be Not Afraid*, and *Komm, Jesu, Komm*), Palestrina's *Misa Aeterna Christi Munera*, Byrd's *Te Deum* and Vaughan Williams's *Lord, Thou Hast Been Our Refuge*. Then, as my final year concluded, there was Vivaldi's *Gloria*.

Alongside the continuous preparations for choral performances were the regular music classes in Royal Fort House. Most of my music history classes were, as I mentioned above, the same as those for the BMus students, a small but friendly group. However, other classes were specifically for us two General students. Week after week, we met with one or other of two members of staff for sessions on other subjects. There were, for example, classes in composition where we presented our weekly assignments, mostly exercises in writing something "in the style of" some well-known composer, such as Palestrina, Bach, Mozart, or Haydn, in an appropriate format, such as a four-part vocal setting of a particular text, a movement (usually a trio) for string quartet, or a movement (perhaps a rondo or even first movement sonata format) for piano.

During our three years of work, we were never permitted to venture beyond the classical era. The Romantics were outlawed, it seemed, and anything later than that was unthinkable. We were deemed not to have sufficient knowledge of harmony to move forward, but, as we kept complaining, that deficit could be remedied if our instructor would only teach us what we needed to know. Composition classes for me thus provided a very effective means of understanding and appreciating the achievements of certain composers, but they did little to make composers of us. Of one thing I am certain, though. Our weekly preparations for each class took up hours of time.

Always anxiety-laden for me were classes in keyboard harmony which more appropriately should have been named "figured bass". Not only was there a weekly assignment to prepare, for which we had the music in advance, but during the class we had to take turns in providing the harmonic underpinnings for a piece we had never seen before. Whether or not we had seen the music in advance, our task was to sit at a keyboard (a harpsichord or a piano) with only the bass line for our contribution to the music score. Below the bass line would be a series of numbers and accidentals indicating what harmonic intervals above the bass notes should be played, and hence what inversions of what chords are to be played. Where the chord is obvious, no numbers are given. The task is made yet more complex when one realises that one is required to play more than the chords themselves. One is expected to improvise an accompaniment that is in keeping with the other instrumental or voice parts. The system was a hallmark of the baroque period, and there were plenty of examples to work with. I never became very proficient, but I did learn to admire the skills of those who could work in this idiom.

To add to our anxieties were our classes in score reading and conducting. Sitting at the piano with a score open, we were expected to be able to play something representative of the music in front of us. This might be relatively straightforward in the case of something like a string trio, but the task could become progressively more challenging in the case of a quartet or an orchestral score. Not only was it vital to include the bass part, but one needed to be able to read the alto clef for viola parts and the tenor clef for some cello parts, and one needed when necessary to be able to transpose the parts of instruments, such as clarinets, horns and trumpets, written in a different key. Preparing something in advance could be challenging and very time-consuming. Sight-reading something in class was always something of a nightmare.

I believe that it was in this same class that my fellow student and I were also taught the rudiments of conducting. I enjoyed this, but it was a far more demanding skill than I had imagined, particularly when our surrogate orchestra (the class teacher) deliberately played wrong notes, or muddled the tempo, or missed a cue. It was all very good-humoured, but we did not develop our skills to a high enough level that we could have tested them with a group of other musicians.

As if our classwork was not sufficient, all music students were required to participate in regular chamber music concerts. These took place in the afternoon in Royal Fort House. Mercifully, what we played was of our own choosing. I know that at different times I played the violin, the harpsichord, and even the recorder, always as part of a larger group. I also sang in items requiring a small choir.

Our audience was made up of the Music faculty and anyone else who cared to come. We students would invite our own friends, and there was always a corps of townspeople who seemed to enjoy the intimacy and informality of these events. The chief pleasure, as far as I was concerned, was working with other students to select and then rehearse items to present.

On one occasion, as Christmas approached, I suggested that three of us should write carols. Each composer would then conduct his/her carol, and the other students would form the choir. This was something that had worked at Maidstone, and it seemed to be very successful in this very different venue. I liked the carol I had written, I enjoyed conducting it, and my small choir gave it a very polished performance.

That I was not alone in finding the Music programme very demanding was to some degree validated some thirty-four years later when the University conferred an honorary doctorate of music upon Jennifer Bate, the world-renowned concert organist. She had come to Bristol as a student in 1963, the year I left. According to Professor Banfield, who read the citation, she came "in a cohort of nine and to a staff-student ratio of about 1 to 5." As the speaker explained, "That the former was, if anything, large and the latter normal will astound today's graduands and my younger academic colleagues." Then follows a general comment on the study programme and a (to me) delightful vignette of Professor Grant:

Staff worked their students hard, and with most tuition on a one-to-one basis there was little chance of slacking. In fact Jennifer had been accepted for Modern Languages but was hi-jacked for Music by Professor Willis Grant, who subsequently wasted no time in exercising upon her the qualities of a martinet for which he was renowned. If this was a toughening-up regime, she was equal to it. At the end of her first year she went to see him. "I'm in the most terrible trouble," she said. He went pale and asked her to sit down. "Of course, I blame the music publisher who got me into this situation." Knowing her London connections, he turned, if possible, paler, with visions of national disgrace to his department's moral reputation. "I mean, if the glockenspiel part doesn't arrive soon I shan't possibly be able to learn it in time for your concert." Visible relief, but he never picked on her again in rehearsal or tutorial. And she was grateful to him and his department for the demanding syllabus.

Later, Jennifer Bate developed a special artistic relationship with the French composer Olivier Messiaen, "recording his (then)

230

complete organ works in Beauvais Cathedral, a series that has won particular acclaim." Apparently, when Messiaen first heard her play, "he was able to analyse the content of her degree programme on the basis of her performance: the intensive study of counterpoint, conducting, score-reading, orchestration, ear-training and keyboard harmony had all rubbed off on it."

http://www.bristol.ac.uk/pace/graduation/honorary-degrees/hondeg07/bate.html

I have only a few regrets about the extraordinary experience of doing Music at Bristol. The first of these concerned my piano playing. I arrived determined to find a good teacher and to improve my skills. When I asked Professor Grant who he could recommend, I received a completely unexpected response:

"My my, you shouldn't be thinking about that. While you're here, you just won't have the time. You'll see. You should just forget about that idea, at least while you're here."

My great regret is that I did what he said. I believe he gave the wrong advice, and I made the wrong decision. It was another of those forks in the road.

My second regret was very different, but one that still haunts me from time to time. One of my teachers was a very kind and gentle man who had a great love for the music of Vaughan Williams. He even had a framed photograph of "Uncle Ralph", as he called him, prominently displayed on his desk. For three years we were constantly invited to share our teacher's enthusiasm. I certainly did, and I still very much admire Vaughan Williams's music. In the final oral examination, however, when each student in turn stood before the entire Music faculty to answer questions,

I was given the chance at one point to talk about Vaughan Williams. I used the opportunity to take some cheap shots at this composer, calling him an English romantic and saying I didn't really care for him. Why did I do that? Was I out to score points with Professor Grant at the expense of his mild and gentle colleague? That same colleague had always been helpful and encouraging.

To this day I still remember how he invited all the Music students to his office on 30 May 1962 for a special event. We were to hear the radio broadcast of the premier performance of Benjamin Britten's *War Requiem*. This was broadcast from the newly-built Coventry Cathedral as part of the celebrations accompanying its reconsecration, the original medieval building having been destroyed in the Second World War. I had no good reason to do what I did in that final examination, and I remain saddened by the fact that I never apologized to someone who had always been kind to me.

Finally, there was another matter; not exactly a regret, but something I've often wondered about, another fork in the road or path not taken. At the end of the final oral examination, Professor Grant said some quite complimentary things about my work before going on to make a suggestion. He'd come to believe that I should seriously continue with my music studies and involve myself in historical research. There was much still to be done on early English composers. If I was interested, he would see what could be done. Wishing that he had said something a few months earlier, I had to tell him that I already had a commitment for the next three years. "Well, think about it," he said. "Perhaps after three years, you'll resume your studies. We'll be here." There at last was my chance to become a historian. It seemed so ironic hearing this in my final days at Bristol.

While at Bristol, and in spite of Professor Grant's attempts to require that every spare moment of time be taken up with music, I did manage to make many friends in addition to those already mentioned (my lunchtime companion, the Japanese violinist, the "weeping woman"). Of all my friends, only one was a fellow music student, a somewhat shy flautist, who quietly used to make sure that I had some kind of role in every chamber music concert. Occasionally, we would go to the cinema together. I remember queuing up with her to see *West Side Story*, but there were other films. Most likely, it was with her that I saw the first two James Bond films and the spectacular *Cleopatra*, starring Elizabeth Taylor and Richard Burton. In the vacations, we met a few times because she lived not far from Bromley. We would play music together, but there was always, to my mind, a small problem. Our mothers were uncomfortably encouraging, overdoing the warm welcome routine and serving us over-elaborate refreshments. My mother would say after these visits what a nice girl she was, hoping, I suppose, that something would develop. However, my mother was wide of the mark. I just wasn't interested in my friend in this way, and, as far as I knew (though I never thought about it), she didn't have any interest of that kind in me.

A number of my other friends were fellow residents in Churchill Hall. Two of them, I now recall with something akin to horror, nearly got me killed. One of these had funds enough to buy a Mini, the small and iconic British car with its revolutionary space-saving front-wheel drive. I believe it was the first I had seen. My friend was very proud of his car and talked endlessly about its ability to negotiate bends at speed. A novel feature in this particular car were the seat belts my friend had installed for the driver and front seat passenger. At the time, only race car drivers and serious rally car drivers had seat belts in their cars. The belts were cumbersome affairs. Bolted to the floor behind one's seat, they extended, harness fashion, over both shoulders and were fastened across the chest and across one's lap. My friend clearly wanted to make a statement: he was a serious driver who could safely drive his car at high speeds. To top it off, he even had special driving gloves, just like those worn by Grand Prix racers.

Churchill Hall provided my friend with the perfect challenge. Close by was a road that encircled part of the Downs. Its primary purpose appeared to be the provision of easy access to one of Bristol's most scenic views. This was at the far end of the circular route, where one could stand at the top of a cliff and look down into the Avon Gorge. When I first came to Churchill Hall, there was already a not-so-secret ongoing challenge to establish the fastest time around the circular route, starting at an agreed-upon point on the side of the Downs closest to Bristol. For my friend, the challenge was irresistible. He had several practice runs to familiarize himself with the route, and then he pronounced himself ready.

With a couple of other friends we went to the starting point. One of the two other friends had a stopwatch and would act as timer. The other fellow's role was that of impartial witness. My role was to sit buckled into the passenger seat as a kind of observer.

When the road appeared to be clear of traffic, we set off, my friend smartly running through the gears as he began to drive as fast as he could. As he entered the bend at the top of the Gorge, we were suddenly in trouble. Rather than adhering to the road surface, the car tyres began screeching and we skidded sideways towards the Gorge.

Two things saved us. The car did not roll, perhaps because of its design and low centre of gravity, and perhaps because of the extra weight I provided. Having seat belts was also a factor, because they anchored us to our seats, something that helped to keep the centre of gravity low.

The other feature that played a major role in saving us from what could have been the worst of outcomes was the substantial stone kerb on the side of the road closest to the Gorge. The car slid into this. There was a loud bang, and we came to a violent halt. White-faced and too shocked to say anything, we got out of the car. Both tyres on the passenger side of the car had burst and the two wheels appeared to be badly buckled.

My memory is somewhat vague as to what then followed. I know that we had to find a phone box as quickly as possible. We needed to have a breakdown lorry come and tow the car before any patrolling policeman found us and started asking awkward questions, and we needed to let our friends with the stopwatch know what had happened.

My friend never again attempted to compete on Churchill Hall's unofficial racing circuit. Once his car had been repaired, he settled down and became an exemplary and very safe driver. If he was driving some of us back from a rugby game, for example, he would even refuse to participate in any kind of post-game drinking. It was years before I met anyone else who cared about such niceties.

Another friend who had a car was an engineering student, on leave from the RAF while he completed his degree. Somewhat older than most of us in Churchill Hall, he always had stories to tell about service life, and was always delighted to play host if one stopped by his room. For a long time, I was puzzled by the way he poured the boiling water into our cups when serving instant coffee. The hand holding the kettle always shook, and it seemed that there was a danger of water being spilled into the saucer, though that never quite happened. How, I kept asking myself, could someone in the RAF get away with having a tremor as bad as that? As far as I know, no one ever asked him about his apparent affliction. Such queries would have been too personal and potentially very embarrassing.

It was only later that I understood. Ever the practical engineer, his method of pouring water was designed as a means of stirring the coffee. Once understood, his circle of Churchill Hall friends adopted the same method of adding water to coffee, often joking among ourselves about our initial misinterpretation of our friend's "tremor", but never telling him about our earlier thoughts.

When he acquired a car, my normally rather dour friend was suddenly and unexpectedly almost childlike in his excitement and enthusiasm. I was among the first to be taken to see it in the parking lot. A shiny light blue Hillman Minx, it had all kinds of special features, and my engineering friend took great delight in pointing them out.

My contribution was to say that blue was the appropriate colour for someone in the RAF. A day or so later, I was invited to go for a drive, the first person, I believe, to receive such an offer. Initially, he wanted to drive the circuit on the Downs, but I said I'd only go along with this if he drove at a moderate speed, just to learn the ins and outs of the course. I didn't want a repeat of my adventure in the Mini. Besides, the Hillman, as was normal, had not been fitted with seat belts.

After we had done the circuit, we drove down to the university. On the way back to Hall, we took a very indirect route, passing through street after street of very ordinary houses. As time passed, I noticed that my friend was becoming impatient and was starting to drive faster. As we passed down one long and straight street, I began to be a little alarmed at our speed, especially when I saw that some way ahead a car was pulling out into the road. My friend didn't seem to notice this, and we continued at the same speed. Then, too late, he realised what was happening. Although our brakes slowed us down, we smashed into the rear side of the turning car and then swung abruptly to the right. Mounting the kerb, we crossed the pavement and went straight through a waist-high stone wall on to the lawn in front of someone's house. We were very shaken but totally unscathed.

When we climbed out of the car, we were amazed to see a scene of some devastation. The car we had hit had spun in a full circle, as far as we could tell, and had then crashed into the side of a parked car, turning it on to its side.

People came running from all directions to check whether my friend and I were all right and to check on the driver of the car we had hit. This turned out to be an elderly, white-haired woman, who was very upset but mercifully unhurt. She was quickly helped from her car and taken into someone's house for that customary British response to such situations – a cup of tea.

When the police arrived and asked what had happened, my

friend explained: "The car you see over there pulled out right in front of us. I put on the brakes, but it wasn't possible to stop in time." When asked about speed, my friend made it very clear that we were driving at a completely normal speed. Once the police had interviewed the elderly woman, who, in her confusion, admitted that she may not have checked with sufficient care for oncoming traffic, the police (and later my friend's insurance company) accepted that it was the woman who was at fault. I knew differently, but no one ever questioned me. My friend had adroitly come up with a neat distortion of the facts which I was never forced to either support or deny. Had anyone been injured and I had been questioned, I suppose I would have been faced with a very difficult moral dilemma.

Once the three damaged cars had been towed away and the police said we were free to go, my friend went off to make arrangements for his car to be repaired, and I went back to my room. Only then did the shock of what had happened really affect me. This had surely been a close call. People often die in crashes like that, and now I knew how. Cars are really very flimsy things that don't offer much protection if driven into other cars or, as in this case, into a stone wall.

By mutual agreement, neither of us ever told anyone about the crash. No one seemed to notice that the Hillman was missing from the parking lot, and no one noticed its sudden reappearance a few weeks later, looking as pristine and shiny as when my friend had first bought it. I would like to think that we both learned something from the experience, but I doubt that either of us did, at least in the immediate aftermath of the event.

Something which invited me to confront my own mortality in a rather different way occurred not many months later. Among my friends were several who were avid rock climbers. They had all the equipment and loved recounting their various adventures on this or that rock face. I recall that two of them, just for fun, even spent an entire night sleeping on a narrow ledge, appropriately anchored in some kind of sleeping harness. At another time, they found a used condom on a different ledge, a sign, they gleefully recounted, of the irrepressible sexual energy of rock climbers at large. Constantly I was urged to go climbing with my friends, but I always turned them down. I had enough things to do. Besides, I was not very comfortable with heights.

One day, however, the whole group (some three or four of them) came to my room. They'd chosen an easy climb for me; they'd all be there to make sure I was all right, and they were sure I'd really enjoy myself. I agreed, but with the proviso that if I didn't like it, they would never ask me again.

A few mornings later, we all drove the short distance to the foot of the Avon Gorge. Two of them had motorbikes and one had a car. There we assembled our equipment – ropes, karabiners, harnesses, pitons and various other bits and pieces, including some borrowed climbing shoes for me. After I had been given a quick lesson on some basic essentials, we walked the few yards to the base of the cliff towering above us to begin the purportedly simple beginner's climb. Two of the others went first and quickly finished the first pitch. Now it was my turn.

To my surprise and relief, the climb was easy. This would surely be OK as long as I didn't look down - this caveat prompted by the fact that the cars on the road below us were already beginning to look rather small and we had barely begun.

For the next part of the climb, I was given careful instructions by the leader on the best holds to use. Some of them required quite a stretch, and my confidence began to fade a little. What if things got harder?

Well, they did. By the time we got to the final stage, I was feeling quite tired, and my inadvertent glances down revealed that the cars on the road below looked very small. Two thirds of the way up this final part of the climb, I was confronted by a frightening challenge in the form of a large protruding boulder. I was supposed to step across on to this and use various holds on it to move up. Aware of the completely exposed vertical drop some 300 feet below the boulder and of the big stretch I was being encouraged to make across its surface, I froze. To make things worse I had an attack of what I believe climbers call "Elvis legs" or "sewing machine legs," involuntary muscle spasms caused by fatigue and nervous contractions. There was a muffled but serious discussion among my fellow climbers about what to do, but in the meantime I pulled myself together and told them I was ready to go on. Loud congratulations and encouraging comments all round, but when I made my transition to the boulder, I made a big mistake. Somehow my feet did not go where they were supposed to go. Then, to get myself to the top of the boulder, I was forced to make a grab at a handhold that was a little beyond my reach. I missed, and found myself falling into the emptiness below the boulder.

People say that as sudden death approaches, memories of your whole past life flash by you, but this was not the case for me. Rather, the realization that I was now somewhere between life and death induced feelings of calm and peace, more a state of bliss than of horror. I also seemed to be floating rather than falling. A sudden and completely unexpected jolt then knocked all such sensations aside, along with all the breath in my lungs, as I slammed into the rock face below and to one side of the boulder. The rope I was attached to and the belay above me had done their job. Having forgotten about their existence, I now realised that perhaps this was not to be my last day after all. Somewhat breathless, but a little more confident than before since I now knew how the belay system worked, I climbed back up, crossed over to the boulder using the correct holds, and then arrived at the top of the cliff. There I was greeted by my fellow climbers with congratulatory slaps on the back, conciliatory admissions that perhaps the climb was a bit harder than they had previously thought, and confessions about their own falls.

In the weeks that followed, the climbing group continued to extend invitations for me to join them, but I knew this was a sport that was not for me. When they began to extend their adventures into spelunking (caving), I was even more sure. Adding mud, water, darkness and claustrophobic crawling spaces to the climbing that was often required when one entered a cave had no appeal for me. I'd stick with rugby as my way of getting covered in mud, of occasionally getting banged up, and of enjoying the camaraderie of like-minded friends.

I never spoke to anyone about the feelings I had experienced as I fell to what I believed was going to be my death. In fiction and in film, those about to die from falling often scream or curse in the interval between the start and end of their all-too-brief final journeys.

Was my experience some kind of aberration? If so, what did it say about me? And, in a broader context, what does it say, if anything, about death? I have wondered about these matters ever since.

For me, it is the poetry of Emily Dickinson that best expresses the human desire to know what happens as a human being makes the transition from life to whatever follows. Nowhere does she come closer to capturing something of what I felt than in her "Because I could not stop for death..." The calm leading to a kind of serenity, the gentleness, the acceptance, and the ultimate ease that comes from letting go and moving towards a new state of being, are all to be found in Dickinson's poem. Not for me Dylan Thomas's "Rage, rage against the dying of the light." Not for me John Donne's negative images of death as falsely arrogant in "Death be not proud." And not for me Irving Layton's depiction of death as an adversary, the thief who took his mother, whose "final mouth was not water but a curse,/A small black hole" that "damned the green earth, stars and trees in its stillness/And the inescapable lousiness of growing old."

Experiences with other male friends were, thankfully, far less dramatic, involving no car crashes or falls from high cliffs. I remember two friends in particular. One was a delightfully good-natured Welshman. He was a science student, and we had very little in common. Having unthinkingly accepted from my mother an irrational bias against the Welsh, I found my friend to be a complete surprise. He was cheerful rather than sullen and dour. He was tall and slender rather than short and stocky, and he never appeared to whine or complain about life's difficulties. My mother's "Cymrophobia" derived no doubt from long-standing English prejudices. Some thirty years or so later, these were encapsulated at their worst in a notoriously racist article in the *Sunday Times* by A. A. Gill. This described the Welsh as "loquacious, dissemblers, immoral liars, stunted, bigoted, dark, ugly, pugnacious little trolls" (BBC News, Saturday, 3 January, 1998).

My Welsh friend and I lived close by in Churchill Hall and we both played in the Hall rugby team. What I most remember were the annual camping trips the two of us made each Whitsun, the extended weekend holiday now replaced in England by the Spring Bank Holiday. On each occasion, we went to Minehead on the north Somerset coast, the site of an earlier family holiday. After arriving the first time at the railway terminal (it closed in 1971 but then reopened as a heritage railway in 1976), we walked a short way out of town close to the shoreline that borders the Bristol Channel, the other side of which was my friend's homeland. Not only did we find the perfect spot to pitch our small tent, but when we found the farmer who owned the land, he turned out to be very friendly, though he became quite stern as he cautioned that we must leave behind no sign that we had ever been there. In addition, we were not to light any fires.

Our little adventure was a wonderful break from the bustle of university living. However, we did bring a modest amount of work with us, since end-of-year exams were not far off. We had a small spirit stove for cooking and boiling water for tea, and there was a shop not too far away where we could buy dietary essentials like bread, cheese, milk and baked beans.

At night, we walked towards the town and found a small pub. Encouraged by some locals, we tried the draught cider, a Somerset speciality known as scrumpy or farmhouse cider. No one – by design, I suspect – warned us how strong this kind of cider could be. By the end of the evening, we two rather naïve students were barely able to navigate our way back to the campsite. My friend, who had a fine voice, sang the whole way back, almost as though he hoped that his family across the water would hear him. Our subsequent queasy stomachs and the violent headaches that greeted us the next morning taught us two valuable lessons. Don't fall prey to the wiles of the locals, who, however good-naturedly, might enjoy deceiving a couple of university students, and don't ever drink more than a pint of scrumpy.

As the end of our trip approached, we decided that we could not camp beside the sea without actually going into the sea. A dip, we further rationalized, would make up for not having any washing facilities in the field that was temporarily our home. Never have I been in water that was so cold. Even the water in the swimming pool at Brentwood School that was forced upon students by the (in my mind) sadistic Scandinavian gym master was never this cold. After immersing our heads in the Minehead water – we had agreed in advance that we would do this - my friend and I ran back shivering to the tent, babbling about how refreshing our bathe had been. Over the following two years, the two of us returned to Minehead, camping in the same place, drinking a modest amount of scrumpy, and, as though it were some deeply significant religious ritual, bathing in the Bristol Channel.

After I left university, I saw my Welsh friend only once more, at a party held in his girlfriend's flat in London. On that occasion, having drunk more wine than I should, I allowed myself to accept a gift from the four girls who lived in the flat. Aware of my piano playing, they offered to give me a piano for free on condition that I paid for its transport. Of course, I gave the instrument a quick tinkle before deciding. The next morning, however, when I woke up in Bromley, I had only the haziest recollection of the previous evening, and I certainly had no idea whether the piano was any good. Now came the hard part. I had to tell my father what I had done. Would he take a second piano into the house without having first checked it himself? And would he pay for its transport? Colouring the whole issue was my painful confession that I might have had too much to drink to be able to make any kind of reliable assessment of the piano.

For reasons I never understood and which were quite out of character, my father took a chance and agreed to take the piano. Against the objections of my mother, he insisted that we would be able to squeeze it into our small dining room where the other piano was already located.

After a day or so, the second piano arrived. To my immense relief, my father, once he had tried it out, said that he felt we had a real bargain. Once it had been tuned, he liked it even more, and in no time began gathering music for two pianos. He and I then had many evening and weekend opportunities to try out this new repertory, most of which was a bit beyond my capabilities. We tried the Mozart Sonata in D major and music by Debussy, Fauré and Grieg, together with a large amount of arranged music, much of which I already knew in versions for four hands on one piano. Indirectly, then, my friend contributed significantly to my musical life. After that summer in 1963, I never saw him again.

The other male friend whose company I particularly enjoyed at Bristol was a member of the Spanish Department. This Department was small, and I got to know a number of its students quite well through my friend. They were a congenial and lively group, and its female members, as everyone often remarked, were especially attractive. Indeed, there was a persistent and notorious rumour that the Professor of Spanish tended to select the female students on the basis of their looks.

Because my friend had a fine voice, he was soon involved in all kinds of music events, chiefly after becoming a member of "The XXXII", Professor Grant's elite choir of carefully selected students. Since he also lived in Churchill Hall, there were numerous opportunities for me to get to know him.

After two years in Churchill Hall, the two of us decided to look elsewhere for somewhere to live, and we found a bedsitting room that seemed to be financially manageable. We soon discovered some of its limitations, however. The woman who let the room to us was a humourless tyrant who never seemed to sleep. At night, we would often hear her prowling around, with prolonged stops outside our door. We never learned what motivated her to creep about in this way, but we had a great deal of fun inventing our own explanations. Our visitors were treated with considerable hostility, and we ourselves felt as though we were barely tolerated. To heat our room, there was a gas fire, and we soon learned to use it sparingly. Beside it was a meter that gobbled coins. We were convinced that the meter had been fixed so as to provide our landlady with a profitable stream of income. Even when cooking on the gas ring, we had to be mindful of the meter. Nothing was worse than running out of gas before food was fully cooked. Next to our room was the bathroom, with a large bathtub and an ancient gas geyser. To generate sufficient hot water for a bath, we always had to ensure that we had enough coins to satisfy the very greedy bathroom meter, a monster that seemed intent on denying us enough hot water for a decent bath.

In spite of the miserable conditions we experienced in our new living situation, my friend and I got along well. I surely had habits that irked him, but I don't recall his ever complaining. He, however, had one habit that I found difficult to tolerate. A fellow music lover, he liked to play records while he worked. This I did not mind in general terms, but from our limited combined collection of recordings, there was one that he liked to play over and over – Beethoven's Ninth Symphony. This was a work I had studied very carefully, and I could never hear it without listening with care and concentration. For me, it could never be casual background music.

Coming home one day and climbing the stairs to our room, I heard the all-too-familiar bars leading into the entry of the chorus in the final movement. Once in the room, I expressed my annoyance, I'm ashamed to say, in quite inappropriate language. The music was abruptly silenced, never to be heard again while I was around. I'd like to think I apologized. That to this day I cannot remember whether I did still troubles me.

It was with this same friend that I experienced an epic winter drive from Bristol to Wimbledon. He had bought a 1929 Austin 7 for something like £25. The chassis, motor and gearbox were all original, but the body had been made out of battens and hardwood and painted light blue. The vehicle had no heating and no means of de-fogging/frosting the windshield. What's more, it had a top speed of less than 40 mph, though since its brakes were cable-operated and very unreliable, its slow speed was undoubtedly a blessing in disguise.

As we left Bristol, the already cold weather seemed to become even colder, and our supposedly warm clothes proved to be totally inadequate. Not only was the weather very cold, but there were periodic snow showers. Constantly we had to try and wipe off the windscreen by reaching out from within the car, or stop completely and clean it off so that we could see the road ahead of us. Throughout our journey, we had to pray that faster-moving traffic coming from behind us on this busy highway would not crash into us. Mercifully, we survived, although I now had a new sense of the true meaning of the cliché "freezing to death". Once we arrived in Wimbledon, my friend took me to the station, and I took the train into London. It took some hours, though, before I warmed up.

Later in 1963, during what was a terrible winter, my friend's car was damaged when a Gas Board van skidded into it while it was parked. My friend claimed damages to the passenger side door, and was paid about £2 for a couple of square feet of hardwood, a box of nails and a tin of paint. If only car repairs were always so cheap. A year or so later, I'm told, my friend's amazing relic from the 1920s failed the MOT. It was given away for 10 shillings, never to be seen again, but I shall not forget it. Whenever I'm outside and feel very cold, the memory of that drive to Wimbledon comes back to remind me that however cold I feel, nothing can compare to my experience in the passenger seat of my friend's Austin 7 as we shivered and struggled for hours along the A4 towards London.

And what about girlfriends? When I went to Bristol, I left behind a girlfriend in London. During the three years that followed, we had a tempestuous, off-on relationship which ultimately self-destructed. The same could be said of my relationship with the Australian woman I met at a dance shortly after arriving at the University. She was a student at a women's teacher-training college just outside the city. When we broke up, my biggest regret was not the break with her, but the loss of access to the building and grounds where she lived. Barrow Court, where the college had been situated since 1949, was originally a Benedictine nunnery dating from 1211. After the Dissolution, it was transformed into a country house and went through various further reworkings. In the nineteenth century, the adjoining church was rebuilt, and Francis Inigo Thomas was commissioned to create an extensive new garden and landscape design.

To get to this enchanted place involved a bus ride from Bristol, followed by a walk down a narrow country lane. The entrance to the college was through an imposing arched gate attached to a three-storey gatehouse, followed by the driveway up to the house itself. Inside was a Great Hall and an impressive Jacobean staircase, a panelled Parlour, a Great Chamber or Solar above the Hall, and a Long Gallery. Close to the house was the stables block, converted into a small dormitory where some of the students, including my girlfriend, lived. Beyond the house were the formal gardens, various terraces, a lily pond, and a copious sprinkling of urns, summerhouses and statuary. Particularly memorable were the twelve sculpted busts flanking the gates on the north-west side of the garden, each representing a different month. No visit was complete without a stroll in the gardens, ideal for couples looking for the privacy provided by strategically planted tall shrubs and hedges.

Memories of this magical and, to me, very romantic place came back to me years later when I made a study of sixteenth and seventeenth-century English architecture. Later still, I sketched out plans for a novel (since abandoned) in which a fictional version of me returned from Canada with his family to live as a house-sitter at a now empty and renamed version of Barrow Court. Past would meet present, romantic fantasy and nostalgia would meet reality, and somehow, as the novel unfolded, the disparate threads of memory would be integrated within the consciousness of the protagonist who now symbolically passed once more through the arched gate at the end of the driveway leading up to the house.

Among other Bristol girls was someone I visited a couple of times during the summer vacations. She was an earnest and studious student taking French. I liked her because she seemed to be very intelligent, and because, lurking beneath her serious demeanour, was a sense of humour that occasionally flashed to the fore, surprising her friends and, I suspect, her. She lived with her mother in south London, two long bus rides away from Bromley. Her mother, who seemed to have a similar personality, was French and insisted that we speak only French during my visits. This was fine for the daughter, who had grown up speaking only French at home, but it was a bit of a drag for me. Needless to say, whenever her mother left the room, we would revert to whispering in English.

Then there was a tall, somewhat athletic girl whom I met in French classes. She lived in Oxford, and I was invited during one vacation to go and stay with her family for a few days. While there, I got to see the city and its colleges for the first time. It was a marvel to me, and I could not totally suppress the small degree of envy I felt regarding the students, including some of my Maidstone classmates, who could call this place home during the three years they were there.

When not wandering from college to college or browsing in bookshops, my friend and I had some fierce drawn-out battles on the tennis courts. She was far more skilled than I, so I had to compensate with extra effort and stamina to try and redress the balance. Even so, she won most of our matches, while I did my best to be the most gallant of losers.

Although it was an enjoyable visit, the chances of any kind of developing relationship were undercut by my friend's mother. To me, this somewhat imperious matron seemed to be something of a snob, and I sensed from the day I met her that she disapproved of me. I was too rough a fellow, not sufficiently genteel to suit her daughter. Perhaps I was wrong about her; perhaps her behaviour was the nervous reaction to having a young man visit a daughter for whom she wanted only the best. But at the time, it did not occur to me to give the mother any benefit of the doubt, and when I noticed back in Bristol a certain waning of interest on the part of the daughter, I left off trying to take things any further. Remarkably, however, we remained good friends, although once we both left Bristol, we were never again in touch.

A decade or so later, I returned to Oxford on my own terms. While working at the Bodleian and various college libraries, I spent a year as a Visitor at one of the colleges writing a book on the

English renaissance writer Henry Peacham. For many years thereafter, I returned to Oxford almost every summer to do further research, most of it on emblem literature.

During my final months at Bristol, I met the woman I would marry some three years later. One of my flatmates had organized a weekend expedition for a small group of outdoor enthusiasts, and he invited me to join them. Our destination was Steep Holm, a small uninhabited island in the Bristol Channel about five miles (8 km) offshore from Weston-Super-Mare. In the 1860s, it had been fortified. Updates to its nineteenth-century defences had been made during both world wars and included a small group of brick barrack buildings, one of which we had permission to use. Our leader had made arrangements with a local fisherman to ferry us to the island in his boat. This he did on a rather misty day which kept us from seeing the island until we were fairly close to the landing place at the foot of some cliffs. As he left us, he promised to come and pick us up in a couple of days at an agreed time, but he warned us that if there was heavy fog, he would not be able to come until it lifted.

Once he and his boat had disappeared into the mist, we gathered our gear together and climbed the 256 feet (78 metres) up to the deserted barracks buildings. The building assigned to us had a bare concrete floor and a number of very beaten-up iron bedsteads. Although we all had sleeping bags, these had to be rolled out either on the concrete floor or atop one of the dilapidated bedsteads, a choice, it turned out, between competing versions of discomfort.

After eating a very rudimentary supper and sorting out who

would sleep where, I invited the woman in the next bed to me, someone with whom I had already been talking, to explore the island with me. Since the island was only about half a mile long (800 metres) and a quarter mile wide (400 metres), this was no great task. All one had to remember was that there were steep cliffs on every side. However, the heavy mist, the coming darkness, and the noisy presence of huge numbers of seabirds and their nests that covered the ground in all directions turned our evening stroll into an unexpectedly eerie experience.

Equally unexpected was the trick played on us the next morning by the other group members. Having observed my new friend and me, they had concluded that something was up. Before either of us was fully awake, they picked up our beds and carried us outside. Unlike my friend in the other bed, I was not wearing much of anything and so was effectively marooned until someone could be persuaded to bring me some clothes. After an embarrassing delay, during which I was the object of a great deal of predictably risqué banter, my friend was allowed to bring me my trousers.

Later, as the time for the group's rendezvous with the boatman approached, we all assembled at the landing place ready to leave. It was then that another facet of the weekend adventure became apparent. The island was cloaked in thick fog, and most of us had come to the conclusion that we were not going to get back to Bristol that day. This was something of a crisis, since there was very little food left for such an emergency. Immersed in discussions of how to deal with this situation, we were suddenly startled when the boat burst through the fog exactly on time. How our rescuer managed to find us with just a compass with which to navigate has always been a mystery to me. Today he would have had a GPS device to guide him, and we would all have had cellphones to check whether or not he was coming, but this lone mariner must have had an almost instinctive understanding of distances, winds, currents and directions that guided him when visibility was denied him. He clearly had skills that none of this group of university students would ever acquire.

The expedition to Steep Holm was hardly propitious for the start of any kind of romantic relationship. On the island, the fog prevented us from seeing much of our location at all, and certainly it denied us any view of the Channel, of Wales to the north and the Somerset Shore to the south. Outside, everything was very wet, and inside physical comforts were largely non-existent. However, the irrepressible spirits of youth prevailed within the group, and, to the mild amusement of many, one romantic relationship did begin.

The dominant concern of my last year at Bristol was the approach of "Finals", that array of multiple examination papers and oral tests designed to evaluate how well one now knew one's chosen subjects. But alongside this growing anxiety was another. Parchment in hand, what then? This was a question my parents raised whenever they could. Their preferred future for me was teaching. My father, a civil servant in Whitehall, was particularly in favour of this, placing special emphasis on the extended holidays that teachers enjoyed, far different from the meagre breaks he was allotted. I was not averse to this choice of career. It would mean a year's training in a teaching college, but that might be done in Bristol at Redland Teacher Training College. Plenty of other graduates had done this, all sharing the delight of being able to stay in Bristol for yet one more year. But two other possibilities had emerged which I deliberately avoided telling my parents about. Sounding as though I was in favour of teaching quieted them and gave me scope to think about these.

The first was one that involved teaching, but not, I suspected, in a form my parents would approve of. One afternoon I paid a visit to the Careers Officer, a cheerful and persuasive woman who described in glowing terms a project named "Teachers for East Africa". Participants would go to Makerere University in Uganda and study for one year to earn a Diploma in Education. Because this was a scheme jointly sponsored by the British and United States governments, it was guaranteed that the Diploma would be recognized in both countries. Furthermore, travel and tuition expenses would all be paid for, and there would even be a living allowance while one was studying at Makerere. In return, one had to agree to being posted for two years to a school in one of the three East African countries – Uganda, Kenya, or Tanganyika (soon to be Tanzania). At the end of the three years, there would be free transport home and a monetary payment of an amount representing half of the fairly generous government salary one had earned while teaching.

The second possibility the same Careers Officer told me about was one that immediately leapt to the top of my list. Was I interested, she asked, in applying to the BBC as a trainee studio manager? Here was an exciting chance, I thought, to make use of my knowledge and love of music, not as a performer but as a programme manager. I knew this was a job I would like and one that I would be good at, so I applied.

Now I had three possible next steps and was thus fully prepared with a response when my parents next demanded to know what I was doing about my future. When, rather coldly and without much sensitivity, I told them of the three possibilities, they were somewhat relieved. Both approved of my trying to go to Redland. In addition, my father, an avid Third Programme listener, was intrigued by the BBC opportunity. Neither of them, however, liked the thought of my spending three years in East Africa. As far as I was concerned, Fate was going to decide this one.

Early on, and greatly to my annoyance, Redland rejected me, something that necessitated applications to teacher training programmes at other places. Then it was the turn of the BBC. There were various stages in the competition to obtain a place, each separated by a few weeks. At first it was fun - having a voice test, reading aloud in whatever other languages one claimed to know (French and German in my case) and answering questions about one's interests.

When I reached the final round, however, I was too anxious to enjoy the process any more. On arrival at the BBC building in London, I found myself sitting in a waiting room with only one other candidate. Surely there were more, but she was the sole competitor I met that day. She was a fellow student from Bristol, someone I already knew, an attractive, vivacious woman, but not someone, I believed, who could match what I had to offer.

When my name was called, I was shown into a high-ceilinged room, devoid of any furniture apart from a wooden chair and a small table. Somewhat nonplussed, I sat down, whereupon a disembodied voice addressed me, telling me to study the sheet of paper on the table. I had six minutes to do this. Hastily, I pulled my chair up to the table and began to read. There were passages in English, French, and German, many of them containing names of people and places which would be difficult to pronounce if one did not already know them. The voice then returned, and I stumbled through my reading. Then I was invited to make my way to another room for an interview. Another shock awaited me. The room I entered was quite large, and around the large table that took up most of the available space were more than a dozen men, including the directors of the various BBC regional services.

Everyone had the opportunity to question me. How would I feel about working below ground or in studios without windows? How would I feel about working night shifts? Whenever I had the opportunity, I tried to talk about my interests in music, making it very clear, by exaggerating what I really felt, that light music didn't interest me and that pop music was something I very much disliked. Stupidly, I contrived my own downfall, giving myself the appearance of a cultural snob with very narrow interests, whereas my interviewers were looking for someone with broader interests. Having a particular enthusiasm and knowledge in one area was fine, but breadth and versatility were also desirable. If only I had had advice and a little advance coaching, I could perhaps have avoided losing out. As it was, I was told that I had done very well and should consider reapplying in a year's time. I should also bear in mind that serious music was a very small segment of what the BBC did and involved only a small staff. I should keep up the interest in the music I favoured, but at the same time I should expand my knowledge and interests and demonstrate that I could be more versatile.

Being turned down was a huge disappointment, to be ranked

alongside my History examination failure and the ensuing consequences and my failure to get a place at Cambridge. Having so recently been rejected by Redland, another rejection would be hard to live with. Hearing that my fellow Bristol student had been accepted by the BBC only added to my bewilderment and sense that perhaps I was not who I thought I was. I had no one to talk to about the doubts and questions that now were beginning to gnaw at my store of self-confidence. Not surprisingly, I began to develop increased concerns about the East African venture.

I needn't have worried. When I went for my interview at the newly-named Commonwealth Office (formerly the Colonial Office), I was treated as though my acceptance was already assured. The interview was conducted by a version of Colonel Blimp, who asked the hackneyed questions about what school I'd gone to and what my father's job was, all veiled means of establishing matters of social class and whether I was a member of the "Club". A genial chat developed as we sipped our tea, and I noticed that the "Colonel" kept consulting his watch. When our conversation turned to sports and cricket in particular, I began to see what was preoccupying my interviewer's thoughts. He was thinking about the ongoing test match. When I turned the conversation to that very topic, all was revealed.

"Actually, after we're finished here, I'm going to be dropping in at Lord's to catch the rest of today's match," he said.

Egging him on, I told him what a splendid idea that was. Needing no further encouragement, he closed the file folder in front of him, shook my hand, and reached for his coat. As we passed through the door, he said,

"No need to worry about all this. You'll hear from us officially some time next week, I should think. I'm sure you're going to really enjoy Africa. You know, even though they're going independent, they'll need our help for a long time yet."

With that, we walked out to the street. His back to me, he stepped up to the kerb. He seemed oblivious to my presence, his mind no doubt focused entirely upon his favourite sport. Then, with what seemed like a very practised gesture, he waved down a taxi and was off to Lord's.

Within a week, as he had promised, I had a letter offering me a place in the Teachers for East Africa (TEA) programme. If I accepted, I would be required to attend an orientation day, when I would meet all the other successful British applicants. With two out of three doors having closed in my face, I wrote the required acceptance letter and went to the orientation meeting.

My memories of the talks we were given are somewhat vague, with two exceptions. The first was a presentation on "Servants and how to manage them". This was given by a large woman with a plummy voice and grating counties accent. It was a shock to learn that it was somehow assumed that we would have servants. Indeed, we were told that once we were assigned in the second year to the schools where we would be teaching, each of us should expect to take on at least two servants, one to cook and look after the housework and another to do the gardening. Not hiring servants would be a blow to the local economy, depriving experienced and well-trained men of their livelihood and the means to pay for their children's education. What's more, not having servants would lower our status in the eyes of Africans. Listening to this woman and others who spoke to us, it was hard to believe that the newly independent Tanganyika (9 December 1961) and Uganda (9 October 1962), and the soon-to-be independent Kenya (12 December 1963) would want to retain such vestiges of a social structure so prevalent in their recent colonial pasts.

The other talk I remember was by a doctor. He had valuable advice about what inoculations we were required to have before we went. We also learned all about the perils of malaria and the need to be disciplined about taking our daily anti-malaria pill even if we were living in a malaria-free area. We were given, too, warnings about the possibly dire consequences of contracting bilharzia (schistosomiasis). We must avoid swimming or washing in lake or river water. Even touching a wet fishing line could be dangerous. Then there were warnings about drinking local African-made brews of various kinds, and admonitions about drinking on one's own. We should take a tip from the Catholic missionaries, who can only have a drink when entertaining a visitor. Finally, using almost unintelligibly euphuistic language, he spoke to the men in his audience about the temptations and perils of involvement with African women, particularly the fun-loving and attractive women we were sure to meet in bars in cities like Kampala and Nairobi.

So it was that one afternoon a few weeks later, having already sent off the family trunk on its longest journey yet, I found myself in Liverpool Street Station. There, together with my family and my girlfriend, I boarded the grimy steam train that would take us to the King George V Dock in east London. Upon seeing the boat, the *Kenya Castle*, I was for the first time struck by the immensity of what was about to happen. Why was I leaving my family like this, stifling and overbearing though they may at times have seemed?

Why was I leaving my girlfriend like this, trusting that our relationship would survive three years of separation? And why was I turning my back on so much that I valued – friends like David, who had taken me in his newly-acquired car to some of our old haunts on the south coast and had been on the verge of tears when we said goodbye? Why was I leaving places like Bristol, London and Maidstone, which had been so important to me in becoming who I now was? And what about the entire cultural web that had grown around me, the music, the theatre, and the art, all taken for granted but now largely to be left behind?

Such qualms were quickly replaced by my feelings on seeing the ship itself, a relatively new Union Castle liner built in 1952 which carried both passengers and cargo between London and Cape Town. I had never seen an ocean liner up close before and was amazed by the height of this lavender and white vessel with its distinctive red funnel. This would be home for the next few weeks, and I was eager to get on board.

But first, the goodbyes. These were difficult. Tears and a long-drawn-out embrace with my mother, a serious handshake with my father, accompanied by a few jocular paternal admonitions, a playful farewell from the one sister who was able to come, and a final hug with my girlfriend, who did her best to keep the tears at bay.

Once upon the ship, I joined numerous fellow passengers waving down to those below. Because we were not leaving for some hours, those on shore would not be able to see us depart. There'd be no opportunity, thank goodness, for that ritual with the paper streamers that I'd seen in Hollywood films. Instead, my father, ever the organizer, after a suitable interval of time had elapsed, called an end to the waving. Tapping his watch, he indicated to me that it was time for them to leave, and with that, along with some final backward glances as they disappeared into the building beside the dock, they were gone.

Looking around me, I noticed several of the people I had met at the orientation meeting, including some I knew to be from Bristol. Close to me and leaning over the rail above the dock were two men, Richard and Roland, who, like me, were on their way to Uganda. Richard was with the TEA group, but Roland, who was a little older, had a different mission. A newly-qualified veterinary surgeon, he had a government contract to work in a remote area in north-eastern Uganda. The three of us seemed to get along very well, and that night a friendship began that was to last for the next three years.

After finding our respective cabins and eating our first shipboard meal, we all came back on deck. As the sun disappeared and the ship moved slowly eastwards into the darkness, the three of us, as if by common consent, became increasingly reflective, and there were long interludes when not a word was spoken as we stared out into the night. I had as yet not read Conrad's novels, apart from *Nostromo*, but later I recognized with what artistry he had elsewhere depicted the experience of a small group of friends about to sail down the Thames as night fell:

"The sea-reach of the Thames stretched before us like the beginning of an interminable waterway. In the offing the sea and the sky were welded together without a joint... A haze rested on the low shores that ran out to sea in vanishing flatness. The air was dark above Gravesend, and farther back still seemed condensed into a mournful gloom, brooding motionless over the biggest, and the greatest, town on earth."

As we peered into the darkness, broken only by the distant lights on the Kentish shore to the south and the Essex shore to the north, the three of us shared, I believe, the unspoken recognition that, as Conrad put it, "the old river" had for ages not only served "the race that peopled its banks," but for centuries had served as "a waterway leading to the uttermost ends of the earth". Many had made this journey before. No doubt my "Colonel Blimp" had been one of them. A good servant of colonialism, he and his like had now passed the torch to us. We were supposed to be the youthful face of a new order, servants rather than masters, invited to help out with a temporary need, and destined to become redundant as soon as the newly-independent countries could replace us with their own. As my brief encounter with those at the Commonwealth Office had revealed, no one really seemed to have grasped what we were supposed to be doing, let alone how we were supposed to do it. This was indeed going to be a voyage into the unknown, though mercifully not into the darkness that Conrad's Marlow endeavoured to describe.

CHAPTER NINE

JOURNEY TO AFRICA

The voyage south took three weeks. It wasn't much fun at first; no sun, and the sea too choppy for comfort. It seemed that the experienced old-timer I'd met while still at the dock in London might have been wiser than he had at first seemed. "I always bed down when we leave London," said Frank, "and I stay there, asleep if I can, till we get round the corner at Gib."

Sure enough, after leaving the English Channel and crossing the Bay of Biscay, everything changed as he had predicted. To welcome us to the port of Gibraltar, the sea calmed down, the sun came out and up on deck came Frank, genial, friendly and, not surprisingly, very hungry. He owned a small business in Nairobi that made glass bottles, and, as I will explain later, he and his wife Molly were in time to become good friends.

Because the *Kenya Castle* was both a passenger and a cargo ship, each port involved a stop of a day or so for loading and unloading cargo. While in port, we passengers were free to disembark and explore. Like tourists on modern-day cruise ships, we headed for the obvious attractions, took plenty of photographs, and helped out the local economy by purchasing overpriced knick-knacks and souvenirs. But there were invariably surprises. In Gibraltar I took a taxi drive up the rock to see the famous apes, took some photographs, and bought some postcards. But what I most remember about the place were three other matters. My first surprise was the "more British than the British" atmosphere of Gibraltar – Union Jacks at every turn, red pillar boxes, fish-and-chip shops, English-style pubs with English beer, and countless other overstated reminders that this place was *not* part of Spain. After all, Gibraltar had been British since before the founding of the United States. Furthermore, it was a place where Britannia still ruled, however fiercely the Spanish might contest the point.

Equally unexpected was the sight of the airport. Great ingenuity must have been involved in building it in such a confined place; yet, there it was, a single runway built out into the water very close to the border with Spain. Indeed, for a long time, the single road from Spain has crossed the runway, necessitating traffic lights and barriers to hold up traffic whenever a plane takes off or lands.

Finally, there were the elaborate systems for capturing and holding rainwater, water always having been a scarce commodity on "The Rock". Much later in 1993, the use of the catchments and cisterns that had so intrigued me was discontinued in favour of more effective and cost-efficient desalination plants. Nowadays the potable water produced by these plants is stored in reservoirs inside the Rock, while a quite separate system supplies salt water for Gibraltar's sewage system.

From Gibraltar, the *Kenya Castle* moved on to Genoa, Italy's largest sea port and the birthplace of Christopher Columbus. Though I was impressed by the architecture and grandeur of some of the buildings, my memories are chiefly of wandering the narrow streets of the old town at night. My cabin steward had cautioned some of us about this area: "Stay together. Better not wander around on your own." Then, with a sly grin, "And watch out for the ladies. Best to stay away from them, I can tell you."

Nothing could have encouraged us more, so a small group of us made a return trip ashore after dark to see for ourselves. Innocent that I was, I'd never seen anything like the spectacle we encountered. Everywhere we went, whether in the bars or on the streets, there were women of all ages and degrees of attractiveness, their dress and gestures all proclaiming their availability. Very different from the occasional wary, humourless working women I had observed in London, the women of Genoa appeared free from interference by the police. They were completely open about what they had to offer, laughing and joking among themselves and, of course, promising would-be clients the very best of times.

We quickly realised, however, that we were of little interest to them. They'd encountered groups of tourists like us before. They didn't seem to mind that we were mere voyeurs, good for no more than a little passing repartee. As long as we didn't get in the way of business, namely the steady flow of men, mostly sailors, who clearly intended to enjoy and pay for the delights on offer, we were cheerfully tolerated.

Freed from the temptations of Genoa, we next sailed down the west coast of Italy, eventually coming to a place long familiar to me from Homer's *Odyssey*. In Book 12, having (like us) survived the temptation of the Sirens, Odysseus arrived with his crew at the Strait of Messina, the narrow (3.1 kilometre or 1.9 mile) channel between what we now know as Italy and Sicily. On the Italian side lived a six-headed monster named Scylla, and on the Sicilian side was a dangerous whirlpool named Charybdis. Odysseus had been warned by Circe to sail as close to Scylla as he could to escape the whirlpool, but he must recognize that Scylla would devour any men she could capture. As Homer tells it, the intrepid navigator brought his boat through the passage but lost six of his best men, one to each of Scylla's six heads. Thankfully, the captain of the *Kenya Castle* conducted us safely through the Strait without any loss of life. To add to our blessings, nature provided a sunny day and a fine view of Europe's highest active volcano, Mount Etna. Now we headed for the coast of North Africa and our next port of call, Port Said, at the head of the Suez Canal.

Before we arrived, however, something both unanticipated and, for me, momentous occurred. Early on at university, I had continued my somewhat turbulent relationship with my Maidstone girlfriend. She was a Roman Catholic, much to my parents' horror, but this made no difference to me. I became increasingly attracted to the gentle understated faith of her parents and four siblings. At university I mentioned these feelings to a Catholic girl in one of my classes, and she suggested that I go and discuss them with a priest she knew. I did, and finding him easy to talk to, I began a series of weekly meetings with him. I learned a great deal and slowly became convinced that I should become a Catholic.

One day I asked him how he thought we were doing and whether I was ready. "Oh," he said, "if you're certain, then come next week. I have someone who can be your witness, and it will all be settled." True to his word, he met me the following week along with an older woman to witness my baptism. The event was over in a few minutes. I then shook hands with the priest and left. I rarely saw him again. From then on, it seemed, I was on my own.

During the weeks that followed, I went every Sunday to mass, and even went to confession, although I was quite lost as to what one was supposed to say. However, that didn't seem to matter to the near-invisible man behind the screen in the confessional box. Soon after this, I discovered that at a particular hour each Sunday, there was a mass attended largely by Poles. Unlike their English fellow Catholics, who were somewhat solemn in demeanour and tended to mutter and mumble their contributions to the service, the Poles sang full voice and with great fervour. Surely this joyous and very musical expression of faith was how things should be. Though I couldn't join in, I found great satisfaction in being there and participating, if only on the fringe, in this weekly outpouring of religious worship.

By the end of my time at university I had finally broken off my relationship with my Catholic girlfriend, but my new-found faith remained intact. Early in the morning on the day after we had left the Straits of Messina, I went on deck to walk a few pre-breakfast laps around the ship. Close to the bow, I looked down at an empty deck area close to the bow. There, with their backs to me and facing forward into the sun were three black-suited figures standing side by side. From their gestures it was clear that they were priests celebrating mass. It was an almost visionary spectacle, their hands and arms acting in concert like some mythical dance. But I found no pleasurable spark of recognition. As if I'd received some heavy and completely unanticipated blow, I could only gasp at how alien they appeared, how removed from the beauty of the seascape surrounding us, and how irrelevant (or so it seemed to me) to the world towards which the ship was pointed. In an instant, my relatively new-found faith left me never to return.

Since that moment, a kind of reverse "Road to Damascus" revelation, I've been an atheist. Though I never discussed any of this with him, my father would no doubt have been delighted. The poor man was then, however, confronted by something else. In March 1963, just before I left for Africa, the older of my two sisters became a Roman Catholic. Then in March 1974, she married a Catholic, thereafter remaining a Catholic and comfortable with her faith to this day. Though upset at first, my father eventually came around. Apparently, he and the priest who had performed the marriage ceremony developed a friendship based on their common love of music. When my father was given permission to play the organ in the church, he was able to set aside his misgivings and accept what had happened.

Not too long after my early morning experience at the ship's prow, we had our first sight of the continent to which we were bound. To our surprise it was not the view of a distant shoreline. Rather, Africa announced itself with a change in the colour of the sea itself. The blue Mediterranean water turned a dirty brownish-green, as a result, we were told, of the outflow of the waters from the Nile delta. It was far from the romance of any welcome to Africa that we might have expected, but such thoughts soon dissipated when somewhat later we arrived in Port Said, the busy assembly point for convoys of ships moving through the Suez Canal.

As we reached our berth, the ship was besieged by bum boats, large colourfully-decorated scows packed with trinkets which their vociferous owners hoped to sell. At the time it all seemed quite exotic. Prospective purchases were placed in canvas bags and pulled up on a long line to the ship's rail where they could be inspected by an interested customer. Then came some fierce and noisy bargaining to establish a price. If the transaction was successful, money was lowered in the bag down to the bum boat owner. By this means, some of the passengers acquired fezzes, embroidered prayer mats, brassware, and leatherwear items. I noticed that the older, experienced passengers, who'd seen it all before on previous visits, bought nothing. They were there to watch the show and smirk at the gullible ingénues having their first taste of Africa. I don't recall buying anything. On the other hand, where did my small stone model of a pyramid come from? And what about my leather camel stick with its concealed sword, and my small but lethal-looking leather club?

Turning away from the ship's rail and the loud sounds of frenetic commerce emanating from the bum boats and passengers high above, we were confronted by another exotic local phenomenon, the hully-gully man. With quite extraordinary sleight-of-hand, he appeared to pull baby chicks from the pockets and sleeves of onlookers, all the time repeating his magical incantation, "hully-gully", until he had a whole flock of baby birds running about on the deck at his feet. I noticed that even the old timers applauded the performance and contributed generously when it was time to tip him.

While the ship passed through the canal, Roland, Richard and

I, along with others, joined an overnight excursion to Cairo. Walking from the ship to the bus, we realised how intensely hot it was. As if in answer to some unspoken prayer, we passed a child vendor of cold Coca Cola. Then, remembering warnings about street vendors that we'd been given on the ship, we reluctantly passed on. But any regret about the moment vanished when, a little further on, we came across another child who seemed to be filling a Coca Cola bottle with a measure of syrup of some kind and water that appeared to be coming from a puddle.

Our bus journey was a long one, and darkness fell several hours before we reached Cairo. The closer we got, the more crowded the road became, not so much with other vehicles as with streams of people on both sides of the road, all going in the same direction as us and all carrying baskets and bundles of goods. What we were seeing was part of some huge commercial machine whereby the great city's insatiable appetite for food and other goods was, at least in part, catered to by rural folk who carried the products of their labour into the city to be sold. Had it always been like this, I wondered? Had the highways into European cities like London and Paris once seen similar night traffic?

Once in Cairo, we were taken to our hotel, where we ate a modest meal before taking a short stroll on the streets outside. I was totally unprepared for the experience that followed. I had never encountered such a density of people, so many beggars, so many people sleeping on the sidewalks and so much poverty. Back in the faded grandeur of our hotel, the heat was oppressive, and it was nearly impossible to sleep. With windows closed to keep out bugs, a slowly-turning and squeaky fan was supposed to keep us cool, but all it seemed to do was move the hot heavy air around. Lying on the bed, half asleep and half awake, I started wondering whether this was a prelude of things to come. Was the heat a dirty secret carefully kept from us by those at the Commonwealth Office who were sending us off to live close to the Equator?

Early next morning, such gloomy thoughts were quickly forgotten in the excitement of a visit to the pyramids at Giza. Once we had climbed off the bus a short distance from the site, we were immediately pestered by various camel owners to ride – for a fee, of course – the last part of the way. Roland, Richard and I, fresh from having watched Peter O'Toole in *Lawrence of Arabia*, couldn't resist this gimmick to extract a bit of money from gullible tourists. Entering into the fun of the venture, we all three bargained hard (or so we told ourselves) with our chosen camel men to establish a price, adding a little to have our pictures taken once perched on our camels' backs in our best imitation of T. E. Lawrence.

Before approaching the largest of the pyramids, the Pyramid of Cheops, we paid our obligatory respects to the Sphinx, a monument both old (c. 4,500 years) and very large (73.5 metres long, 19 metres wide and 20 metres high, or 241 x 63 x 66 feet). Set it down on a football field in the United States and there wouldn't be much playing space left. I knew about this mythical beast from browsing my childhood encyclopedia, but my first face-to-face encounter was oddly disappointing. I found none of the mystery I expected to feel, nor was I assailed by any of the mythical fear that some claimed the monument was supposed to engender.

That said, my encounter with the Great Pyramid of Cheops was an altogether different matter. As we walked towards the Pyramid,

I was shocked and very moved, as I later discovered many others have been, by the sheer "rightness" of its combined size, shape, form and proportions. This was an aesthetic experience the like of which was completely new to me. With a height of 146.6 metres (481 feet) and a base of 230.4 metres (756 feet) on each of its four sides, its massive size is almost overwhelming. But I believe it is the magical interrelationship of all its features that leads to its unforgettable emotional impact, something I am lost to adequately describe. No wonder this was one of the Seven Wonders of the ancient world, sadly the only one to survive today.

Once at the base of the Pyramid, we joined the line of those interested in taking the staircase inside to the now empty chambers. This was not a task for those with claustrophobic tendencies. The passage was steep, dusty, poorly lit, and very narrow, wide enough for only one person at a time. Once having begun, retreat was impossible as a steady stream of other people followed close behind. In addition, the interior was hot and very humid. I found it difficult to keep calm and suppress any traces of claustrophobia, and I was very relieved when the ordeal was over and I was outside once more. Climbing up a short way, I was able to get away from the crowds and recover some peace of mind. It was a good spot, too, from which to observe some of my more energetic shipmates who had the stamina to climb to the top of the Pyramid. Once a popular activity for visitors, such impromptu climbs, which over time resulted in the untimely deaths of several tourists, are no longer permitted, having been officially forbidden since the 1980s.

After leaving Giza, we had two more places to visit. First we went to the Egyptian Museum of Antiquities at Tahrir Square. The museum is famous for its immense collection of pharaonic artefacts, the royal mummies and the treasures of Tutankhamun. On arrival at the entrance to the gallery containing these last, the guide announced that the gallery was temporarily closed. We were very disappointed about this, but not as much as one man in the group, who was virtually reduced to tears. Begging to be let in, he was firmly rebuffed. Talk of waiting his whole life for the chance to see the golden wonders was of no avail. Did he ever return, I sometimes wonder? Or did he ever see selections of the treasures that were on various occasions exhibited abroad?

The other place we visited during our very brief visit to Cairo was the nineteenth-century Muhammad Ali Mosque at the Citadel of Salah el-Din. This stands atop a limestone hill with impressive views of Cairo and the distant Pyramids. Often referred to as the Alabaster Mosque, the very grand and impressive building is characterized by its use of alabaster from Upper Egypt (Beni Suef) for its columns and for the tiles which cover the walls of the lower storey up to thirteen meters high.

Finally it was back onto a bus and the ride down to Port Suez, where our ship was waiting to take us through the Red Sea to our next port of call – Aden. While Cairo had seemed unbearably hot, it did nothing to prepare us for the heat we now experienced. At night, it proved impossible to sleep in the small airless cabins assigned to us down below deck. There were four of us to a cabin, in each of which there were bunk beds and little room to move around. To add to our discomfort, there was no air conditioning. Indeed, up to that time, I'd never experienced an air-conditioned environment. What did it do? Did it really cool things down?

I soon found out. Having heard a rumour that first-class

passengers had an air-conditioned lounge, several of us on our first day out from Suez climbed the external stairway that led up to quarters reserved exclusively for such passengers and stepped inside. So this was what it was all about. What bliss! Here was a different world, delightfully cool and comfortable. Standing just inside the door, we surveyed a scene of tranquillity – people in armchairs reading books, some playing cards in groups of four and others just snoozing. No one looked at us or acknowledged the existence of us sweaty underlings come up from below to gape at our betters. Who knew that this world existed just a few feet away from what the rest of us were experiencing? Not sure what to do, we stood and stared, relishing the change of temperature and feeling the sweat drying on our bodies.

But not for long. Within minutes, various white-jacketed ship's personnel appeared and pronounced sentence on us: "You're going to have to leave. This area is strictly for the use of first-class passengers only. You're not supposed to be here at all. Didn't you see the notice outside?"

We knew all that, of course, and we had seen the notice. So, acknowledging defeat and muttering time-worn British epithets about toffs and the inequities deriving from differences in wealth and social class, we backed out through the door into the stifling heat.

That night, rather than attempt to sleep in the confines of our hot and airless cabin, most of us took the pillows from our bunks and went up on deck. There, with the encouragement of a slight breeze, most people managed a few hours of fitful sleep. It may have been earlier on that night that Richard and I had a long discussion with Roland. Passionate in many of his interests, he talked eloquently to us about his fascination with astronomy. As we stood leaning on the rail of the ship, he pointed out a number of constellations, far more than the two or three that I had learned to identify. As we travelled further and further south, he had become increasingly excited about the number of different constellations that would become visible. Above all, he explained, he wanted to see Crux (the Southern Cross), something not visible from most latitudes in the northern hemisphere.

"Here we are," he exclaimed, "south of latitude 30 degrees. We should start to be able to see it very soon." We didn't find it in the sky that night, but ever since I've carried with me the memory of Roland's talking about the heavens in near veneration. Some fifty years later, when I read his account of working in Africa, I wondered if he would say something about any of this. I was not disappointed. Describing "the sheer pleasure of nights in camp," he said at one point:

Above, the great sweep of the stars moved majestically from east to west, returning back to the same place the following night. Like aliens among these natural phenomena, one or two man-made satellites glided serenely from horizon to horizon most nights; satellites which within a few years of the flight of the first sputnik in 1957 the Karamojong had learned to distinguish from other celestial objects and named. In the stillness of the bush the magnificence of the cosmos above quite overwhelmed me, in much the same way as a Mozart concerto can. It was easy to understand how early men in their attempts to explain the awesome reality of the universe invented whole pantheons of gods to give meaning to it. (Roland Minor, *A Lot of Loose Ends* [Cirencester, 2013], 89)

Long after nightfall we arrived in Aden, a seaport city in Yemen which was at the time still a British crown colony. While the ship refuelled, passengers were permitted to go ashore. A tax-free zone where prices could be very attractive after even a modest amount of bargaining, Aden was eagerly anticipated by many passengers, some of whom had elaborate shopping lists. I was determined to buy a camera. Not knowing much about cameras, I bought for very little a 35mm device that served me well enough during the years that followed. Not being an SLR affair and hence not supportive of telephoto or wide-angle lenses, my newly-acquired camera often proved to have severe limitations when it came to photographing birds, animals and panoramic views. Only very recently, when I digitally scanned and edited my Africa slides, was I able to make up for its shortcomings and my lack of understanding in 1963 of Pentaxes and Canons, the interpretation of specs for various add-on lenses and a whole language of related technical bibble-babble.

Equally naïve, perhaps, was my choice of two other purchases, both also significantly influenced by their "bargain" prices. The first was a carpet. Knowing nothing about carpets, though aware that those from the Middle East were often prized and valuable possessions, I looked for something cheap and, of course, completely missed anything akin to what I should really have purchased. Nevertheless, what I did buy, with its awkwardly-configured image of a leopard, gave me pleasure and service as a conversation piece for many years before I passed it on to my son a few years ago.

The other purchase was a watch. There were plenty of small stores selling jewellery and watches, but I didn't bother with any of these. My "bargain" came from a trader on a quiet, poorly-lit street who pulled up first one loose sleeve and then the other, each time revealing a whole array of wrist watches strapped one above the other the length of each arm. These had to have fallen off the proverbial truck. Stolen goods that had to be disposed of out of sight of the regular retailers ought to go for bargain prices, I thought, so I chose a good-looking watch with a Swiss label and plenty of jewels in its mechanism. In the years that followed, it served me very well. However, when I took it into a high-end jeweller's back in London and asked its value, the person I was dealing with, after apologizing very politely for being the purveyor of bad news, explained that what I had was a cheap knockoff, hardly worth the cost of a good cleaning. Lesson learned, the watch I bought shortly thereafter was a self-winding Tissot which I've worn every day since and which now appears to be worth more than I originally paid for it.

Four days after our adventures in Aden and after sailing down the coast of Somalia (no pirates to concern us in those days) and crossing the Equator (we were all Shellbacks now), we arrived in Kenya and docked in Kilindi, Mombasa's deep-water harbour. While waiting to board the train that would take us inland to Nairobi and on to Kampala, our final destination in Uganda, we spent one more night on the *Kenya Castle*. This gave us a full day to step onto East African soil for the first time and explore, however briefly, this intriguing city, with its long history and mix of cultures – Arab, African, Indian, and European (chiefly Portuguese and then British). Although I was to return a number of times, I retained several vivid memories of this initial visit. There was the moment of coming up on deck that first morning to discover the ship had arrived in Kalindi. Using my camera, someone took a picture of Roland, Richard, and me, the three of us leaning, as so often, on the ship's rail. We look very pleased with ourselves and ready for this new world: Roland, intense, unsmiling and slightly formal in dark grey pants; Richard, arms folded in a characteristically nonchalant pose, smiling, and in khaki pants; and me, new watch on wrist, the only one in shorts and a non-white shirt.

On shore, we visited Fort Jesus, built by the Portuguese in 1593 and strategically situated at the mouth of the Old Harbour. Subsequently, it was fought over by rival interests for almost two centuries, changing hands nine times before 1875. The Old Harbour, too shallow to accommodate large ships, was still frequented to our amazement by wooden lateen-sailed dhows purportedly from the Red Sea, the Arabian Gulf and further east as far as India. Their sails filled by the north eastern monsoon winds, they had traditionally brought such items as carpets and elaborately-carved wooden chests to trade for ivory, timber, and rhino horn. When we visited, we saw none of these exotic wares, only large sealed sacks of some unidentifiable product (perhaps flour or grain) being loaded under the watchful eye of the boat's captain, who stood in the stern, missing nothing.

Walking in the more modern part of Mombasa, we experienced what for me was the final highlight of this first visit to Kenya's second largest city. On a busy street, we came upon a small confectionery store. In the lower corner of the store window, unobtrusive and all-too-easily missed, was a small card with the near magical announcement: "This Shop is Air-Conditioned". Stepping inside from the fierce heat of the street outside, I had my second encounter with this wonder of modern science. What I bought to justify my presence in the store I no longer remember – just the delight of the cool air that temporarily eradicated all memory of the heat outside.

The next day we left the ship, no doubt to the great relief of those travelling on towards South Africa. To them, we must have seemed a raucous group, ignorant of "the way things are done," a threat to quiet afternoons of bridge and an annoyance at evening games and quizzes, most of which we won. When we boarded the train in the late afternoon, ignoring in our excitement the sticky tropical heat, we were following the path of countless others who had made this journey inland ever since the railway had been completed in 1901 as a means of providing land-locked Uganda with access to the sea. To my delight, the train was hauled by a large and magnificent steam engine of considerable vintage, I suspect. The carriages were probably of equal age but still offered a kind of faded grandeur which was matched by the smartly-uniformed attendants, especially in the dining car where we were served a fine dinner.

As we climbed away from the coast, the heat and humidity began to abate, allowing for a comfortable sleep in the bunks that our attendant had set up for us in the compartment. During the night we crossed the Tsavo National Park, notorious as the area where in 1898 two lions had killed (according to some estimates) as many as 135 workers while the railway was being built. The stuffed carcasses of the lions, both shot by Lt. Col. John Henry Patterson, can be seen to this day in the Field Museum in Chicago. Today, Tsavo, one of the world's largest game sanctuaries, is famous for its elephants, lions, rhinos, hippos, buffalos, giraffes, zebras, and many other species. But, alas, it has become a notorious hunting ground for ivory poachers. Where the elephant population was more than 30,000 in the early 1960s, today it has been reduced to about 12,000 by gangs of ever more ruthless and violent poachers armed with automatic weapons. The problem would receive worldwide attention early in 2013 when a gang of some ten to twenty poachers massacred an entire family of eleven elephants.

In the dark, we saw nothing of Tsavo. Instead, our introduction to Kenyan wildlife occurred when we opened our eyes the next morning. As the train huffed and puffed its way across the Athi River plains, we saw from the window a grassy landscape dotted with zebra, Thompson's gazelles, wildebeest, and even the odd ostrich. This continued while we ate breakfast in the dining car. All too soon, we arrived in Nairobi, but then it was on towards Uganda after a picturesque descent into the Rift Valley, and an amazing climb to recross the Equator at about 9,000 feet. Another night followed, during which we crossed into Uganda. Early the next morning we crossed over the Nile, reaching Kampala a little later. There, Roland was met by his contact, and we were taken to Makerere University, our assigned home for the next year. Women went off to Mary Stuart Hall, the women's residence, and we men were taken to Mitchell Hall, a newly-built residence named after a former Governor of the Uganda Protectorate. Our long journey now was over, and it was time to begin the work ahead of us.

CHAPTER TEN

MAKERERE

Hardly had we had time to get used to our new situation than we British had yet another cultural shock to absorb – the arrival of the Americans, and the reminder that the Teachers for East Africa project was a joint Anglo-American affair. Though tired and very jet-lagged at first, the new arrivals quickly adapted to their new home. We learned that they had had a more extended and very different orientation from ours. They actually knew something about the history and culture of Uganda. Their sense of mission, in addition to being that of bringing to our future students the benefits of the British and American education systems, included a strong ideological component. For us, it was somewhat unnerving to realise that we were perceived as the remnants of an oppressive colonial power.

Put crudely, Britain, though claiming that it represented a "new order", hoped to retain a degree of influence over the newly-independent Uganda and the soon-to-be independent Kenya and Tanganyika. By contrast, our American colleagues saw themselves as ambassadors, anxious to share their country's ideals of freedom and democracy. I knew next to nothing about the United States, and I was ill-prepared to debate these issues. Though an enthusiastic supporter of John Kennedy, then the President, I still bore some of my mother's anti-American prejudices. In time, however, I learned a great deal from the Americans with whom I studied and worked during the next three years. Indeed, among my most valued aspects of those years was all that I derived from my American friends.

Our teachers at Makerere were almost all British expatriates, and our curriculum during this 1963-4 period was largely based on what I might have encountered had I been accepted in a B.Ed. programme at home. Of great interest to me were our courses in the philosophy and history of education. Here a stark contrast emerged between the British students and the Americans. Though my studies had been very intensive, they had largely for the last six years been confined to three subjects – English Literature, French Language and Literature, and Music. I'd never read any Philosophy, and, as I've mentioned before, History had been denied me. My American counterparts, however, had received a much broader education. They'd already read some Plato, for example, they knew all about Rousseau, and they were well versed in the thinking of John Dewey. For me, my first reading of such authors was quite a revelation, although the desire to keep quiet about the discovery of an obvious flaw within my education prevented me from talking about it.

Unfortunately, our Philosophy/History teacher was a somewhat austere and remote figure, whose lectures were dull and uninspiring.

By contrast, the man who lectured on English and how to teach it was passionate about his subject. I still remember his enthusiastic advocacy of teaching sentence structures according to structural patterns. Banished were the kinds of clause analyses that had once so plagued my English Language classes. I was also very struck by his pointing out that English classes might often be at their most productive when all was silent. A room of students reading intensely might suggest that nothing was happening, but in reality such an assumption would be quite erroneous. Because there was a school attached to the Education Department and a special classroom with banked seats for us students at the rear, we were able to observe this principle in action. It was difficult for us to remain still and silent watching a class of school children reading for forty minutes or so, but we got the point.

My other main subject was Music. Here was a subject I felt I knew a great deal about. From the very first class, however, I fell afoul of the teacher. From Buganda, the most prominent tribe in Uganda, he was adamant that our task should be teaching students about their own musical heritage. We should not be in the business of imposing European musical culture upon African students. Our time with him, sadly limited as far as he was concerned, was spent learning about the rich musical culture of the Baganda. Wherever we were subsequently posted, he told us, we should endeavour to learn and teach whatever music was indigenous locally.

Those of us in his small class had to try and write down some of the songs he played us. As we gradually came to understand, the rhythms and word-settings could be very complex and were generally accompanied by dance and a wide variety of instruments.

We did not do very well with our dictations, but gradually my initial disappointment with the teacher lessened as I began to appreciate just what he was offering us. Sadly, when I was posted to a school, Music was not on the curriculum and the thick file of material I had compiled at Makerere remained unopened. That file, I now see, represented one of the many roads in my life not taken.

Life at Makerere was very pleasant, and a great deal of spare time was spent in the university bar and at the swimming pool. At the bar it was common to meet African students from all three East African countries. Socializing with them, we learned a great deal about the world we had come to and the feelings, aspirations and political views of some of its brightest representatives. As far as I could tell, they did not in any way resent our brash and noisy presence. After all, we were there only temporarily to be teachers, hardly a threat to their more lofty ambitions. As for the swimming pool, this seemed to have little appeal to African students. For us, however, it was a social meeting place, a relaxed environment where we could gather after classes or at weekends. On our first Christmas Day away from home, a large number of the T.E.A. students spent a good part of the time in the pool, joking about what the weather must now be like in northern climes, and, somewhat ostentatiously perhaps, lining up drinks within arm's reach around the rim of the pool. Anywhere else, no doubt, having glassware scattered about like that would have been considered a dangerous hazard, but I don't think anybody gave it a thought, and, fortunately for us all, there were no accidents.

While we were at Makerere, a group of us formed a rugby team. Our first training meetings were excruciating. Not only had most of us not been very physically active since leaving home, but we had completely overlooked another factor. Kampala has an altitude of close to 1200 metres (4,000 feet). Running up and down a sports field was a noticeable challenge to one's stamina, and it took a few weeks to acclimatize. Thereafter, we managed a series of weekend games at various locations such as Entebbe and Jinja. Between our second and third terms, we even went on tour and played some teams in Western Kenya, in places such as Eldoret, Kitale and Nakuru. Most ambitious was a trip towards the end of our stay at Makerere. This was to the Kilembe copper mines in Western Uganda in the foot hills of the Ruwenzori Mountains (the fabled "Mountains of the Moon"). The Europeans working there were reputed to be a tough bunch and we expected to get a bit beaten up. We were not disappointed. After the game, there was some hard drinking at the Miners' club, and then we were assigned our billets for the night with our opposing team members. I had recently bought a small car and had driven to Kilembe with a fellow student, a delightful Scottish woman, who was happy to entertain me. While I drove, she went through her seemingly inexhaustible repertoire of Scottish songs. She was not my girlfriend, but somehow various wires had become crossed after the game, and the Kilembe people assumed we were man and wife. Upon our arrival at our burly (but by then quite inebriated) host's house, his very proper-sounding wife took charge of us. After conducting us to their guest bedroom, she quickly disappeared. We were for a few seconds completely nonplussed. Were we supposed to share a room?

After a moment of panic, we realised that the room had twin beds. Quickly we agreed that it was too late to bother our hostess with the mistake that had occurred. Furthermore, in order not to embarrass this rather formidable woman, we would pretend the next morning that we were indeed married. By turning one of her rings upside down, my Scottish friend even managed to furnish the semblance of a wedding ring. What we did not discuss was where we met, how long we had been "married" and where the joyous event had taken place, all questions our hostess fired at us over the very nice English breakfast she served us the next morning. It was extremely nerve-racking. To this day, I'm not sure whether we passed this test. Had we been would-be spies or undercover agents of some sort, we would surely have been declared complete failures. Did the formidable matron see through the feeble attempt at deception by these two ingénues? I shall never know.

Only after getting on the road back to Kampala did we begin to see the comic side to our ordeal. Even so, the episode remained a private joke between us and not something we shared with our fellow students. Thereafter, although my Scottish songster accompanied me on other rugby-related trips, we always made sure that no one else mistook our marital status when it came to post-game billeting arrangements.

In later years, I sometimes wondered about the Kilembe Mines. Apparently, they were abandoned in the early 1980s, the result of the fall in value of copper and the political turmoil in the area. In 2012, however, following a rebound in copper prices, a Chinese company announced plans to invest $100 million to revive production at Kilembe. A year later it was further announced that a consortium of Chinese companies had been awarded the concession to manage and operate Kilembe Mines Limited. I doubt, though, that the renewed quest for copper will involve weekend games of rugby.

Whereas our studies at Makerere progressed smoothly and predictably, life was not without its small dramas. There was, for example, an ugly incident concerning food. The Mitchell dining hall served what for us seemed to be a monotonous menu consisting principally of rice and meat stew, this latter a thin liquid affair punctuated with many small bones and very little actual meat. The women had much the same fare in their dining hall, but while they complained that so much rice was causing them to put on weight, we men seemed to be having the opposite problem. A few of us explored two different solutions. First we declared that we were vegetarians. It had not escaped our notice that the scattering of Indian students in hall appeared to have a variety of interesting-looking dishes. They even had glasses of milk with their meals. Joining their table and following their non-meat diet came close to solving the problem as far as I was concerned.

The second part of the solution involved we "vegetarians" driving the short distance to Entebbe for Sunday lunch and a large succulent steak at the Lake Victoria Hotel. At that time, Entebbe, the former seat of government for the Protectorate of Uganda, was a quiet and idyllic refuge on the northern shore of Lake Victoria. Since developed as a major centre for tourism, Entebbe now has a considerable variety of hotels and eating places, and even its own university. The town also became a familiar part of modern history in 1976. Just a few hours after the notorious President Idi Amin had opened a dinner-dance at the Lake Victoria Hotel, Israeli commandos successfully raided the Entebbe airport to free more than 100 Jewish hostages on an Air France flight. The hijackers were members of the Popular Front for the Liberation of Palestine and the German Revolutionary Cells. Personally welcomed by Idi Amin, they had been supplied with Ugandan soldiers and extra weapons. But such things were yet to come in the troubled future of Uganda. By contrast, our much earlier worries about Mitchell Hall food seem in retrospect both petty and mundane.

Those T.E.A.s at Makerere in 1963 who stayed on their meat and rice diet were often loud in their criticisms and an embarrassment to many of the African students who seemed to think that the food was excellent and that they had never been so well fed. One day, there was a near riot in the dining hall when one of the T.E.A. students put his plate on the floor with some leftover food to feed a cat that had wandered in. Pandemonium ensued. The normally reticent African students were outraged. Believing that humans and animals should never eat from the same dish, they felt that they and the University, of which they were so proud, had been deliberately insulted. The culprit and those who came to his defence failed to understand, however, what all the fuss was about. It took several days, some diplomatic intervention by our mentors, and, if I recall correctly, a carefully-worded written apology before the matter was settled.

Quite different in character was another learning experience for some of us, particularly those from Britain. One day I was alone in my room seated at my desk. On top of my desk and against the wall, I had placed my bookcase as a means of saving floor space and giving me quick access to my books. Suddenly, my bookcase began rocking forwards and backwards. I was startled and very alarmed.

Feeling physically quite queasy, I wondered whether I was suffering some kind of mental instability. With some effort, I stood up, holding tightly on to the edge of the desk, because by then the room itself seemed to be moving. That was when I became aware of a lot of shouting outside. When I looked through the window, I saw numbers of African students running from the building. Suddenly, I understood. Earthquake! As fast as I could, I fled too, but by then the ominous shaking was over. Such seismic events were, it turned out, common in this part of the world and rarely caused anyone any harm. Nonetheless, as a precaution I returned my bookcase to the floor. Not for me the grisly end of Leonard Bast in *Howard's End.*

Equally unnerving at the time but also somewhat comical in retrospect was another very different episode at Makerere. One afternoon, I started to feel quite sick and began to suffer from diarrhoea. This had happened once or twice before, but rest, plenty of water and my bottle of anti-diarrhoea pills usually took care of things. But not this time. As the hours passed, I seemed to get progressively worse and the episodes of vomiting and diarrhoea became more and more frequent and violent. Helped by a couple of friends, I managed to stumble the mercifully short distance to the university sick bay. We reached the steps leading up to the main doors just as darkness approached, a rapid process in tropical climes. I put one foot forward onto the bottom step and lurched forward to begin my climb, but I have no memory of what happened next. Nor did I ever have any memory of the night that then followed. When I opened my eyes, I found myself looking into the black face of a figure in white. The face was very full, almost moon-shaped, and the eyes were unusually large, the irises dark and the whites brilliant, almost luminous. Smiling, the face spoke slowly in a warm and deep voice:

"Well, hello, Mr. Young. I'm so very pleased to meet you. How are you?"

I couldn't answer. I had no idea where I was, what time it was, or what had happened. Indeed, at that moment, I was thoroughly convinced that I was dead and that this face and genial voice belonged to the very being my atheist self had vehemently claimed was non-existent. Of course, the truth about my situation quickly became apparent to me. Though a matter for amusement, particularly the idea that God was black, the episode has stayed in my mind, a fleeting thought, however mistaken, that death might not be such a terrible thing, more an awakening than a falling into perpetual nothingness.

Somewhat different but also ingrained in my memory was something that happened very late one evening. A group of us were standing just inside the gate to Mitchell Hall. Suddenly, there was a quite unexpected sound and, turning towards it, we saw an African friend of ours coming through the gate from the direction of the city. He was sobbing and quite unable at first to tell us what was wrong. Had he been attacked? We'd been warned to be careful about walking back from the city after dark. But no, there was no evidence of that? Had there been an accident? Had he received bad news? Shaking his head in response to all our questions, he managed at last to blurt out,

"It's the President! He's dead!"

"King Mutesa?" we asked.

"No, no, not him. Not the President of Uganda."

Then it all came tumbling out, along with more sobs and tears

"The President of the United States, Mr. Kennedy. He's dead. He was shot."

In disbelief and shock, we urged him to give us more details, but he had little to offer other than to tell us that Kennedy had, just a short time ago, been in Dallas in an open-top car when his assassin had fired at him. We were horrified and the overwhelming grief of our friend and the many other African students who gathered round him emphasized the global enormity of what had happened. It was nearly impossible to sleep that night, and the next day, a Saturday, was spent trying to get more information and sharing thoughts and feelings with others in the T.E.A. group in both Mitchell and Mary Stuart Halls.

While at Makerere, there were, of course, opportunities to explore outside Kampala. Early on, one of the faculty offered to take five of us from Mitchell for a weekend trip. It would be our first "safari", the name given, it seemed, to any kind of journey, and not just a journey that involved seeing animals in the wild. On the appointed day, we all squeezed into the teacher's Land Rover, very excited but very vague about where we might go and what we might see.

"I thought we might go east," announced Lloyd (very affably, he'd told us to use his first name). "We'll stop and see the dam at Jinja, and then we'll do a bit of Kenya. How does that sound?"

Leaving Kampala, we passed numerous small villages and trading centres, all flanked by clusters of banana trees. As when we had approached on the train, we were struck by the very colourful dress of many of the Ugandan women. These were not pageant costumes but attractive, everyday clothes, even if they seemed at first glance to be somewhat impractical. Their bright colours seemed to be an assertion of all that was positive about what we were beginning to appreciate was a very beautiful country.

Initially, the traffic was quite heavy, and Lloyd reminded us that, apart from the railway, this road was land-locked Uganda's main link to the sea and the world at large. Indeed, the road served a similar function for Burundi, Ruanda, and the eastern part of the Congo.

It took us about an hour to reach the town of Jinja. Once there, Lloyd drove a very short distance south to show us something very special – the site of the former Ripon Falls at the north end of Lake Victoria. This was the place where water flows out of the lake to form the source of what eventually becomes the White Nile. In 1862, John Hanning Speke was the first European to see this long-sought spot, one that Livingstone had spent years looking for. As a small plaque marking the location explained, Speke's visit at last solved the mystery concerning the source of the Nile.

Forty-five years later, Winston Churchill, who was working in the Colonial Office, went by sea to Mombasa, just as we did. There he took advantage of the newly-constructed railroad and travelled inland to explore Kenya and Uganda. Included in his itinerary was a visit to the Ripon Falls. Writing home, he commented enthusiastically about building a dam across the river to provide a source for electric power. In 1954, some forty-seven years later, Queen Elizabeth II, near the same site, inaugurated the Owen Falls dam and a hydro-electric system, telegraphing Churchill to say "Your vision has become reality." Gone now are the Ripon Falls and the nearby Owen Falls, both submerged as a consequence of the new dam. This last, as we saw, is an impressive and massive affair, through which gushes water that generates power for Uganda and western Kenya before flowing some 4,175 miles north to the Mediterranean.

Lloyd then drove us on towards the Kenya border and the town of Eldoret. For a while, the road ceased to be paved, and we had our first experience of a dirt or murram road. As Lloyd explained,

"Most roads are like this. You'll find out soon enough. Generally, they're just fine as long as they've been looked after. Remember, in dry weather, they get really dusty - much worse than this. That makes it hard to see if you get close behind someone else – dangerous, too, if you want to pass them and can't see if there's any oncoming traffic. Wet weather's worse. Roads can get very slippery. Even four-wheel-drive vehicles like this one can easily slide off the road. I've been off a few times myself."

On this bright, sunny day, we encountered none of these hazards. But being cooped up in the back of the Land Rover was hard going, and we were very relieved every time we stopped for a "rest" break. We were starting to look forward to reaching Eldoret, but Lloyd turned off onto a smaller highway going north.

"We'll have a little break down here. There's something I want you to see – if it's there."

Without any further explanation, he kept on driving. Then, after a few more minutes, he just stopped in what seemed the middle of nowhere,

"OK. Out you get, everyone. But keep your voices down, and don't slam any doors. We're up to about 7,000 feet here. Enjoy the clear air and look around."

Almost simultaneously, we saw why Lloyd had made this small detour. Off to the east, quietly going about their own business, were several giraffes, along with a number of gazelles. It was quite magical. Now it really did feel as though we were on safari. For us, it was a very special moment, even though the animals were some way off, and we needed Lloyd's binoculars to see them properly. This was somehow very different from that morning on the train when we'd seen our first game animals. Here, there was nothing between them and us – no dirty train window to impede the view, no train schedule hastening us on towards our destination, and no crowd of fellow passengers tussling for the best view and making the whole experience feel like some Disneyland spectacle carefully staged for a mob of camera-toting tourists. These were "our" giraffes and gazelles, and, leaning against the side of the Land Rover, we could quietly enjoy their company for as long as we liked. Until, that is, at Lloyd's behest, we reluctantly got back into the Land Rover to retrace our path and return to the main road that would take us on to Eldoret, a place that would in time become very important to me.

"Now you should know," said Lloyd, as we began this next leg of our drive, "this whole area of highlands is made up of a lot of big farms. It all started in the early 1900s when over 120 Afrikaans-speaking families trekked up here from South Africa after the Boer wars. Their post office was Farm 64. It was these pioneers who developed Eldoret. Those in the know still call the town "64". What with the Mau Mau rebellion and the independence movement, a lot of them have left their farms and gone back south. It got too dangerous, and some pretty awful things happened. I'm sure that those animals we just saw were on one of their abandoned farms."

When we arrived in Eldoret, we found a small but bustling place with a hospital, lots of small shops, most of them owned by Indians, a boarding school (attended largely by European children), a cinema, automobile dealers and a tearoom, a great favourite, Lloyd explained, for shoppers and visitors. When we left, Lloyd expressed some concern about the time. He wanted to drive south to Kapsabet, so that we could go a different way back to Kampala. He hoped that we'd be able to stay overnight in Kapsabet in the District Commissioner's guest house (he'd done it before), but he hadn't made any prior arrangements this time.

He was probably right to worry, because when we did get to Kapsabet, it was dark. There were virtually no lights in the small town, just the odd kerosene lamp in some of the roadside buildings. Not surprisingly, he had some difficulty locating the D.C.'s house. As Lloyd had explained, Kapsabet was the administrative centre for the largest segment of the Nandi tribe. Long ago, when the British began building the railway across Nandi lands, the tribe rebelled. Eventually, the Nandi leader, Koitalel Arap Samoei, was invited to meet with the British Colonel Richard Meinertzhagen to negotiate a peace. When the meeting took place on 19 October, 1905, in an infamous act of treachery, Meinertzhagen shot Samoei and the British soldiers gunned down some two dozen of his companions.

When we found the D.C.'s house, we were greeted by a charming younger man. As far as I could tell, he bore no residual hostility towards the crimes of earlier colonialists. Indeed, I never did encounter what would have been quite understandable sentiments of this kind, especially given the brutal British suppression of the Mau Mau rebellion in the 1950s. Our host in Kapsabet, after some polite small talk, then showed us to the guest house. It was quite late, and we were very tired after so many miles in the Land Rover. Doubtless, we settled down for the night very quickly, though I have no memory of this. All I recall was waking up to a sunny morning and the cheerful face of the D.C. when he came to see us off.

Lloyd now took us 30 miles westward from Kapsabet towards Kakamega, the next major settlement. On the way, we passed through the southern end of the Kakamega Forest, Kenya's only tropical rain forest. It was an unexpected change from the wide open spaces of the highlands west of Eldoret and the gentle hills and innumerable small African farms that we had seen between Eldoret and Kapsabet. This was a place where the tall trees pressed close against the sides of the road. Furthermore, the road was relatively narrow and somewhat wet and slippery. Lloyd explained that the Forest, which once was linked to the forests to the west in central Africa, contains a great diversity of plants and trees (some of these latter allegedly more than 100 years old). It's also famous for its many species of birds, animals, snakes and butterflies. However, the forest is under threat because it's adjacent to one of the most densely-populated areas of Kenya. For a long time, it's been difficult to preserve the forest in the face of nearby local inhabitants and their need for firewood, building materials, and plants for traditional medicines. It's hard to know what will happen in the future. Lloyd was right to worry. Much later, the Forest was declared a National Reserve and has now become a major tourist destination, offering guided hikes to see the flora and fauna and an elevated canopy walk to see the different canopy layers of the vegetation. However, the threat to the Forest apparently remains.

Once free of the forest and back into sunlight, we arrived – marvel of marvels – at a hardtop road. To the south, it went to Kisumu, a busy town on the north shore of Lake Victoria, and to the north, after passing through Kakamega, it linked up with the road back to Kampala. About that last segment of our safari, I remember little. I think we were exhausted and glad to be on our way back to comfortable beds, showers, and, yes, Mitchell Hall food. Ever since, I have remained very grateful to Lloyd for taking us on this first safari and for sharing with us a few elementary insights about the world in which we had come to work.

While at Makerere, I experienced two more safaris. The first was with a small group of fellow students, our destination Murchison Falls in north western Uganda, some 300 kilometres (190 miles) five hours drive from Kampala. Winston Churchill, following his visit to the Ripon Falls and the source of the Nile, had hiked, boated, and cycled downstream to get to this spectacular place where the river narrows and gushes through a gorge only 7 metres (23 feet) wide before coming to a waterfall and dropping 43 metres (141 feet). As I later discovered, Theodore Roosevelt came two years later, to be followed in time by Ernest Hemingway, who survived a plane crash there. In 1951, John Huston famously brought Humphrey Bogart and Katharine Hepburn to the area to film parts of *The African Queen*.

Because we arrived late in the day, we had no time to see the

Falls, but this was of no concern because, some miles from our destination, we had been taken completely by surprise by the sudden realization that to our left, walking a few feet away parallel to the road, were two elephants. Words failed us all, our initial excitement, shock, and delight recorded only in a stream of expletives. These were the first elephants any of us had seen in the wild. From where we sat in the car, they seemed very big. Would it be safe to stop and watch them, or should we get the hell out of there? When we'd calmed down a little, we decided upon a compromise – take a few photographs, and then move on away from the magnificent beasts, none of which, we afterwards agreed, had shown the slightest interest in us.

We were to stay at Paraa Safari Lodge, at the time, a quiet spot with a dining room and a number of separate cottages (bandas) beside the river ("Paraa" apparently means "the place of the hippos"). Before going to our banda for the night, we were given some advice: "We ask you to be very careful about walking around now that it's dark. Elephants regularly come right into the Lodge area, so it's best to stay inside. And don't leave any food in your car. We had an incident the other week when someone left some bananas on the back seat of their VW. And everywhere, be cautious about going near the water's edge. Hippos and crocodiles, if disturbed, can move surprisingly fast."

This was exciting stuff, but no one in our group, I noticed, showed any inclination to flirt with danger, and we all spent the night inside.

The next day, after leaving the Lodge, we saw a group of some six or seven elephants emerging from the trees along the opposite

shore of the Nile from us. Both the adults and the several young
elephants with them had come to drink and bathe. We could have
watched for as long as they were there, but time was limited and
we felt we had to move on. Within a few minutes, we came upon
a less expected but equally unforgettable sight – a herd of buffalo,
also beside the river. Then, not too long after this, we spotted a
hippo, standing on a mud flat away from the river bank, allowing
us to view the full mass of his body. This was a formidable creature,
not one that I'd want to encounter when out for a stroll at night.

We then moved on to see the Falls. Without lapsing into
clichés, it is hard to do justice to their magnificence, their power
and their beauty. Unfortunately, there appears to be no satisfactory
terminology to provide an adequate equivalent for what eighteenth
and nineteenth-century philosophers, artists, and poets meant
when they referred to "the sublime", something beyond reason,
comprehension and measurement. Churchill appears to have felt
something of this. In his memoir, he records how "We waited long
at this strange place, watching the terrible waters, admiring their
magnificent fury, trying to compute their force." As he did at Ripon
Falls, however, his thoughts turned to "the steady progress of
development," and he asked himself the following question: "Who
can doubt that the bridle is preparing which shall hold and direct
their strength, or that the day will come when forlorn Fajao – now
depopulated and almost derelict – will throb with the machinery
of manufacture and electric production?" (My African Journey
[Toronto, 1909], 166-7). On this occasion, Churchill's colonialist's
vision of the waters being brought "into cultivated subjection" to
supply something that "civilised industry needs in greater quantity

300

every year" has never been realised. Instead, the area has been preserved as a national park and now serves as one of Uganda's principal tourist sites, complete with campsites, lodges and hotels, boat trips, fishing at designated sites and guided tours. However, no doubt Churchill would have been pleased to hear that further north at the Karuma Falls the Uganda government, with funds from China, began construction in 2013 of a 600 megawatt hydropower development that will be completed in 2018.

The other safari from Makerere was an altogether different affair. Our friend Roland Minor had invited Richard Tonkin and me to visit him in Moroto, the small administrative centre in north eastern Uganda that served a district (Karamoja) of some 31,000 square kilometres (12,000 square miles), populated by some 200,000 people. As a veterinary officer, Roland had principally to deal with the Karamojong, whose main livelihood is their cattle. Practising a kind of pastoral transhumance, the Karamojong typically move their cattle at certain times of the year to search for water and grazing areas. This practice increases the threat of spreading disease among the cattle, and, because the Karamojong measure their wealth and status by the number of cattle they own, the veterinary officer has to battle disease and be a skilled diplomat, recognizing the cultural and financial value attributed to cattle.

Seldom did the Karamojong slaughter their animals for food (they were too valuable). Instead, they took from the cattle only their milk and a limited amount of blood. For meat, they relied on their sheep and goats. Famous for their dress (or lack of it), the male Karamojong generally wore nothing but a short brown or black cotton *shuka* knotted across the shoulders. Its purpose, if it had one, was not clear. It didn't seem to be decorative in function, nor was it substantial enough to serve as a blanket on cool nights. We also were aware of the reputation of the men as fierce warriors whose aggression chiefly involved cattle raiding. When we went to see Roland in Moroto, he had only just been posted there from Kampala, and he was, he admitted, still learning how best to work with his constituents.

To get to Moroto, Richard and I went much of the way by bus. A distance of some 500 kilometres (310 miles), the ride was long and very uncomfortable. The only non-blacks, we were, I was sure, the object of a great deal of good-humoured comment. The seats were narrow and hard, the kind you might find in the typical North American school bus. There were frequent stops with a constant turnover of passengers. Throughout the journey, every available seat was taken, while additional passengers stood in the central aisle. Then there was the baggage to be accommodated – large bags of produce, the odd live chicken and yet more bags, the contents of which were a mystery. The close proximity of so many people only exacerbated our difficulty in coping with our fellow passengers' strong body odour, derived, I suspect, from the particular foods they eat and from cooking over wood fires. Did we smell as bad to them?

The worst moment for me, however, came when one particular man boarded the bus and sat next to me (Richard was on the seat in front to be, like me, next to the window). Once the bus got going, I noticed that the man's skin was shedding flakes everywhere around him, including on me. His hands seemed quite deformed, and generally he didn't look at all healthy. It was somewhat unnerving, but there was nothing I could do. Finally, we reached his stop, and he got off. Looking out of the window, all was explained when I realised that we were passing one of Uganda's leprosy colonies, where my neighbour was presumably a patient. Fortunately for my peace of mind, I was already aware that leprosy is not particularly contagious.

Moroto occupied a spectacular location. A small town with a population at that time of about 1,000, it was situated at the foot of Mount Moroto, an extinct volcano some 3,000 metres (10,000 feet) high on the border with Kenya to the east. Roland's house was one of a number of government houses. Among its various features was a guest room, which Roland assigned to me. Because of the warm, generally arid climate, two sides of the room had no windows. Instead, from waist level to ceiling, two walls were completely open, apart from a wire screen that was intended, I assume, to keep out birds, animals and human intruders. The overhanging roof shielded the room from direct sunlight and from any rain. It was an ideal sleeping place, and I often wondered afterwards why this very pleasant and practical architectural feature wasn't found elsewhere. Almost twenty years later, when I moved into a house in quite another country, I discovered just such a room, perfect for hot summer nights, although I never actually used it for sleeping.

While we were in Moroto, Roland was working, but he generously offered to let us accompany him on various safaris, all involving the Karamojong and their cattle. Richard and I had plenty of opportunities for observing all this, where possible remaining at a discreet distance from Roland as he worked. While we were in Moroto, Roland and some of his colleagues had to deal

with a particularly difficult situation, one he later described in
detail in his book (*A Lot of Loose Ends*, 48-50). Quarantined at
Kopopwa, the eastern end of Iriri, were some 250 cattle that were
considered potential carriers of contagious bovine
pleuropneumonia (CBPP). This was a disease capable of wiping out
great numbers of animals if allowed to spread. At that time, Uganda
was free of the disease, but there would be a dire risk if these
animals came into contact with CBPP-free herds. This might
happen if the animals were traded or used, as was the custom, for
bride payments. The only viable solution to the current situation
was to slaughter the quarantined animals and pay compensation to
their owners. But there were other issues to be considered. First and
foremost was the fact that the cattle represented the principal and
most tangible form of wealth and status among the Karamojong.
Could paper money work as a substitute? The men didn't have
clothes, let alone pockets to stow away a wad of cash. Would they
accept such a deal?

Keeping their intentions secret, the government officer in
charge, together with Roland and his colleagues conducted various
tests on the animals. Then they convened a *baraza* (ostensibly, a
meeting of leaders to discuss solutions to an urgent problem). I'm
not sure that there was much discussion on this occasion. With an
array of policemen armed with Sten guns and rifles to back them
up, the government officer and Roland told the cattle owners of
the decision to slaughter the animals and provide financial
compensation. Richard and I were not present to witness any of
this, but the announcement was met with angry and menacing
ululations among the women. According to Roland's account,

however, the men were more phlegmatic: "Perhaps they thought to take the compensation and recover the cattle later" (50). To thwart anything of this kind, the cattle were immediately moved to a secure *boma* (a livestock enclosure) a few kilometres away and retained under armed guard for the night.

Early the next morning, the slaughter began. Although within sight of it, Richard and I remained too far away to see any of the gory details as each animal was stunned, killed and bled before being skinned. The whole business took most of the day, but when it was over, the women began collecting up all the meat they could carry off. Fires were lit, and as darkness set in, there was singing and the sound of a celebratory feast. I was quite moved by this unexpected outcome and shortly after wrote some verses to try and record my feelings:

"They'll have to go," says the government man.
Behind – the yellowed plain. Vast dizzy flatness.
A cow coughs. The echo seems to strike back
Hard from the rocks of far-off mountains, long since
Stripped by the sun of their earthen veils: this same sun
Which now desires the plain, and made the men
So black. Watch how these naked warriors,
Tall as spears, hold back the sun. Silent.
Standing between him and loved ones, plain and cattle.
Close by in the bush, the women sit
Chattering and laughing, as women do, but
With side-long glances at the men and him.
They know the danger. Tenderly, they finger

Precious cooking-pots and gourds of milk
And blood, given by cows that morning,
Long before the sun and flies had shown themselves.
So the female kind watch on. Chattering still.

In the shade the government man briefly
Removes his sun-helmet, wipes his balding head:
"They'll have to go." Once more a cow's cough.
"Explain about the compensation."

They listen while the other flaps at flies.
They know the cow's cough stands for death, and the
Sun seems to grow more heavy now. One man
Leans against his spear. Is it the sun, do you think,
That makes a man feel thus at mid-day?
"Right, line them up. We'll give out compensation
Now. Be sure to give them a receipt."

The men say nothing, their eyes stare on across
The plain, and mourn with kinsmen, fathers, sons.
The silent grief of warriors and men.

By evening all is finished, even for the vultures.
The government man dines miles away.
Upon the plain, now briefly free from sun,
A camp-fire lights the cheeks of laughing men.
There'll be a smell of meat till sunrise.

Towards the end of January at Makerere, we were all sent off to different schools for several weeks of teaching practice. To my surprise, I was posted to Kapsabet, a place I had already been to on the safari with Lloyd. The Kapsabet Secondary School was a boarding school for mostly Nandi boys. The school taught the four grades after primary school that led up to O-levels. These were a standard set of examinations administered prior to Independence by the University of Cambridge Local Examination Syndicate but now replaced by the Uganda Certificate of Education (UCE). I had not seen the school during my earlier visit with Lloyd, nor had I really looked closely at the town itself, so it was as if I was going there for the first time.

But there was a problem. A day or so before we were to leave, some disturbing rumours began circulating. No trains were arriving from the east, nor was any traffic from Kenya arriving by road. Eventually, it was determined by those administering our programme that there had been some "trouble" in Jinja. Having recently bought a used car, a small Austin hatchback, I was ready and eager to set off on my own. With its back seat folded down, the car was filled with my belongings. Even the front passenger seat area was packed to capacity. Excited by the prospect of getting away from Makerere, I wanted to get going, but there seemed to be some uncertainty and dithering among those in charge. Eventually I was assured that there was nothing to worry about.

The next morning, still not knowing what the "trouble" was and still not fully trusting that those in charge knew enough to make an informed decision, I set off, driving eastwards along the same road that Lloyd had taken us a few months earlier. As the first few miles passed, I was conscious of the very reduced amount of traffic. It made driving very easy but at the same time increased my apprehension. I realised that I didn't fully trust those administering the T.E.A. programme. Their motives might well be political rather than concerned with our well-being. I thought of how we had all been made to participate in the parade to celebrate the first year of Uganda's independence. Out of nowhere had materialized a large float. On top were the words "80 Teachers for Uganda Secondary Schools," and on the sides were "U.S. Agency for International Development" and "U.K. Department of Technical Cooperation." Most of us were told to march in front behind a banner that said "Here Come the Teachers." A number of students, mostly women were placed on each side of the float in front of a large painted map of Uganda. What upset many of us, including the person involved, I suspect, was the prominent placing of the one African-American student in our group on a special seat constructed high up on the float. Such crass political propagandist exploitation of our programme greatly irked me and my fellow students.

Now, as I drove towards Kenya, I found myself pondering the decision-making process that had sent me off. In the face of disturbing rumours and with only the reassurance of a few African government officials, it had been decided that it was safe to leave Kampala. Was a political point being made here by a show of deference to and trust in the Ugandan government officials? Was this kind of thinking taking preference over concern for the welfare of me and others?

I shall never know the answer to this last question, but a few miles further on I was to discover that the decision to let me go had been stupid and wrong. Just before getting to Jinja, I encountered a roadblock manned by Ugandan soldiers who forced me to stop. I rolled down both my windows as instructed and tried to keep calm. This was made difficult because, as I tried to gather my wits, the business ends of two rifles came through the passenger side window and began poking around in the array of possessions that surrounded me. Suffering at this moment from an acute shortage of Swahili, I could only come up with a single word – "mwalimu, mwalimu" (teacher, teacher), by way of an excuse for my presence on the highway and, I suppose, as plea for my own safety. After a brief consultation among themselves, the soldiers waved me through. It had worked. Two more such roadblocks followed, and thankfully my magic password also worked, although, as before, the soldiers were unsmiling and very nervous in demeanour. Anything could have happened.

Once past Jinja and having reached the stretch of murram road that marked a kind of no man's land between Uganda and Kenya, I told myself that I was safe. So why didn't I feel safe? It was then that I realised I was quite shaken up and my nerves were still on edge. Still thinking about those rifles poking around inside my car, I noticed up ahead a large dust cloud on the road. Even stranger was the sight of a small plane circling overhead. When I was close enough, I saw that approaching me was a convoy of trucks led by an armoured scout car (it looked like a Daimler Ferret). I pulled over as far as I could to the side of the road. It was impossible to be inconspicuous, but I wanted to appear as unthreatening as possible.

When I looked up, I was utterly amazed by what I saw. At the tip of one of the scout car's radio antennae was a small Union Jack.

Furthermore, the soldier standing up in the turret, peering from time to time through the binoculars that hung around his neck, was wearing a British uniform. I gave a somewhat tentative wave, but got nothing in return. The officer in the scout car out front and the troops in the trucks that followed had no interest in frivolous waves to passers-by. With their spotter plane to guide them, they were on a serious mission.

Later, I found out what it was. Unknown to us at Makerere, the "trouble" on the road was in fact a mutiny by Ugandan soldiers at their base in Jinja. Following Independence, they had expected their British officers to leave so that a Ugandan officer corps could be created. They also expected a significant pay rise. Frustrated when all such expectations were ignored, soldiers of the 1st Battalion mutinied on 24 January and detained their British officers, together with Felix Onama, the Uganda Minister of the Interior, who had come to Jinja to deal with the situation. Prime Minister Obote then asked for British military intervention in order to prevent the mutiny from spreading to other military bases. What I saw that day on my way to Kapsabet was the British response, as about 450 soldiers made their way to Jinja. There they surrounded the barracks, seized the all-important armoury and ended the mutiny. Knowing none of this at the time, I was nonetheless greatly relieved to have these very determined-looking troops between me and the "trouble" in Jinja.

Once I arrived in Kapsabet, I was assigned to a house temporarily vacated by a teacher currently on leave. This I was to share with two other B.Ed. students from the T.E.A. group. Time passed very quickly while we were there, and I now remember little.

In retrospect I realise that I should have kept a diary, but before coming to Africa I had destroyed the diaries that had accompanied me through adolescence. I suppose I just did not want to risk sharing my inner thoughts with anyone else. Now I regret not taking that risk. The memories that have stayed with me are sometimes suspect, and impossible in many instances to check against any kind of corroborating evidence such as a diary would have provided.

One thing I do recall with some clarity, however, was the realization that teaching could be very hard work, something for which Makerere had not prepared us. In addition to the hours spent teaching the classes themselves, there was the preparation for those classes the night before, along with the marking of tests and writing assignments. Very naively, none of us had anticipated just how much additional work there was to do outside the classroom. Because this was a boarding school, there were other duties such as inspecting dormitories to see that they were clean and tidy each morning, supervising games and athletic activities each day after school ended, turning on the diesel generator each evening as darkness fell, supervising evening homework in the classrooms, making sure all the boys were in bed before the generator was turned off at 10 pm, supervising detentions on Saturdays when malefactors had to work at tidying and weeding the school grounds, attending sports matches on Saturdays, and travelling with the teams, who rode in the school truck to away games. Of course, these duties were shared among the teachers, but invariably each one of us was responsible for something in the course of each week.

There were also all manner of unplanned matters requiring our involvement. I remember two in particular. One morning our American headmaster, John Allen, asked me to go with him to the local jail. The previous evening, one of the students in the class to which I had been assigned had gone into town, where he had had too much to drink and become threatening and aggressive. As a result, he'd spent the night in one of Kapsabet's two jail cells.

When we got there, the scene that awaited us was like something in a wild west movie. The two jail cells faced directly onto the street, the small barred window in each door allowing anyone passing by to see the prisoners. Our student seemed to be the lone occupant of his cell. As we approached, he was standing at the window, his hands grasping the bars. It was hard not to laugh at him, but proper decorum ruled otherwise. Besides, it quickly became obvious that the boy was close to tears, and terrified about what could now happen. To be expelled from school would be a terrible punishment, given the sacrifices that had no doubt been made by his family to give him an education and given the expectations he and his family no doubt had regarding his future. If we informed his father what had happened and sent him back to his village, even for a limited time, he would receive a parental beating, the severity of which we preferred not to imagine. In the end, no charges were made by the police, and the boy was released to us. As I recall, John then took him to the school office and outlined the frightening possible outcomes if the student ever caused problems again. As far as I know, the boy was a model student thereafter.

Another extracurricular episode was of quite a different kind. One day during a soccer game after school, one of the students broke his arm. Putting our elementary first-aid knowledge to work, two of us immobilized the arm and put it into a sling. Then I brought my car up to the playing field so that we could drive him down to the Kapsabet hospital. But now a problem emerged. The injured student, backed up by a small but very vocal contingent of his fellows, begged me not to go to the Kapsabet hospital. They complained that the doctor there was no good. It was a bad place. I had some sense of what they meant. I'd met the doctor, a rather sycophantic Indian, who had given me a brief tour of the facilities. I remembered being horrified when he showed me the operating room and picked up various surgical tools for me to examine. Nothing looked very clean, and I suspected that nothing was going to be properly sterilized before being put to use.

Although there was some concern expressed about setting the wrong kind of precedent, I got permission to take the student the 48 kilometres (30 miles) to Eldoret to what was still being called the "European" hospital. We set off, a colleague and I up front and the injured student flanked by two of his friends squeezed in the back, the injured arm resting on a small cushion. It was a slow journey, because every time I hit a bump, there were screams and groans from the owner of the broken arm. Indeed, twice he passed out. Eventually we arrived. It was now dark, and an orderly took charge and settled our student into a vacant bed. Only then did we learn that the doctor had gone home for the night and would not be able to see our student until the morning. Had we made a bad decision in bringing the student here? I later worried about this, until one day I read in the newspaper that there had been questions asked in the Kenyan parliament about the exceptionally high mortality rate in the Kapsabet hospital.

Immersed in learning how to cope with our workload, we soon realised how vital it was to have the help of servants. With no gas or electricity during the day, water was heated over a wood stove and cooking was done the same way. Having a hot bath, which I found I needed after a day in the classroom and an hour or so on the sports field, would have been very difficult without help. One of the school houses, I observed, had a very good solution to the logistical difficulties of getting enough hot water. Outside the house but adjacent to the bathroom was a tall brick structure. On top of it was a large oil drum placed on its side, and below the drum was sufficient space to build a fire. A water tap fed by a pipe from the house supplied water through the top of the drum. Once the fire was lit and the drum filled with water and heated, hot water could be gravity-fed into the bathtub at the turn of a tap inside the bathroom. But putting this system to work required someone to look after the fire and fill the oil drum with water. Other tasks for which servants, usually two per house, were responsible included shopping, collecting milk from the school farm, preparing and cooking meals, house-cleaning, laundry and garden work. Not at first grasping the intricacies of the system and not knowing more than a few words of Swahili, we inevitably erred on occasion, upsetting the sensibilities of the servants assigned to us. It was, I suppose, a valuable part of the learning experience provided by our weeks of teaching practice. When we received our permanent postings after finishing at Makerere, we would, or so we hoped, be more adept at managing servants.

In spite of all the work connected with the school, there was time to explore our surroundings. Kapsabet was essentially a one-street town, built along the sides of a wide dirt road. There were some administrative offices, a small hospital with a generator, which like that of the school only came on for a few hours at night, a police station with (as already mentioned) a couple of jail cells, two small banks that opened for a few hours once or twice a week, and the Nandi Store run by an Indian shopkeeper, who served African customers at a counter on one side of the building and Europeans at a counter on the other side. Completely unaware of such niceties, I went to the "wrong" counter the first time I visited the store, something the Africans in the store found extremely amusing. In front of the store was a row of gas pumps. Because there was no power, customers had to pump their own gas using the large handle attached to the side of each gas pump. Along the same street was an encampment for askaris, the soldiers-cum-policemen under the command of the District Commissioner. There were also more shops, some bars, and a further set of gas pumps, but they all seemed to be patronised solely by Africans.

Set back from the road in a very attractive grassy setting was the very European-looking Anglican church, a brick affair dominated by a squat square tower. Though architecturally something of an anomaly, it was attractive in its own way, and when I first saw it, I wondered what kind of congregation it might have now that many of the Europeans had left. I soon got an answer. Knowing that I had been playing the piano for morning assembly at the school, one of the remaining European government officers persuaded me to accompany services at the church on the organ that was installed there. Someone from the congregation would pump for me, since the church was without a generator and air for the organ had to be pumped by hand, a strenuous but essential task. Services occurred in the evening twice a month, something for which I was grateful once I got to meet the congregants.

Mostly Europeans and mostly women, those who attended these services weren't like any Anglicans I had met before. A number seemed to be from Northern Ireland and engaged in some kind of missionary work. After each service, I was expected to go with them to one of their houses for a cup of tea. Because they were very vocal about the evils of alcohol, it was clear from the start that I could expect no cool glass of beer or shot of scotch as reward for accompanying their fervid hymn singing. But worse was to come. Following the tea, out came pencils and paper, and a series of (to me) silly games began. Growing up, I had enjoyed the wild and generally risqué games my family played from time to time, but these games were so bland and innocuous that I found myself constantly peeping at my watch, hoping that the "entertainment" would soon come to an end. Ever since, I have, whenever possible, avoided the pencil and paper games that some hosts and hostesses try to impose on their captive guests.

On one side of Kapsabet, the land sloped down to a narrow river valley, from which the town and school derived more or less clean piped water. Part of the grassy slope down to the river, I discovered, had been a golf course. As Independence approached, it had been abandoned for that purpose. Now it served as a common grazing land for Nandi cattle, and it was hard to discern any sign of its earlier use. Here, I decided, was yet another emblem of the sweeping changes that were occurring as colonial rule was replaced by a new order.

Overlooking the former golf course was Kapsabet's version of that most characteristic of colonial institutions, the Club. Intended to provide a social gathering place for European expatriates, it still functioned, its chief feature being a bar. Theoretically open to any would-be member, it appeared to be largely ignored by Africans, and so, with a much-reduced clientele, the Club no longer had regular hours but opened "on demand". We were taken there very soon after arriving in Kapsabet and returned whenever we had a free evening. In its rather dingy interior, we met other expatriates, mostly old timers still hanging on to train their African replacements. Most of them were as happy to give us advice as they were unhappy about the prospect of leaving when their contracts expired. There was one exception, however, a man I got to know quite well. Optimistic about the future of Kenya, he accepted the new government's invitation to become a Kenyan citizen. How many more there were like him and how well they fared in the new country was something I would later very much have liked to know.

Although the Kapsabet golf course was, it seemed, gone forever, two other club facilities remained, though in a rather dilapidated state – a squash court and a tennis court. After a couple of hours work sweeping and clearing out a lot of accumulated garbage, the squash court was ready for use, although it was sadly in need of painting. Somewhere I found a much-used squash racquet and some squash balls, and we were ready to play. The tennis court took longer to clean up. It needed weeding, and the murram surface needed watering and rolling – several times. We found a net. Though in a dilapidated state, it served its intended purpose, and before long, tennis was revived in Kapsabet. To our amusement a small group of boys began showing up. They turned out to be experienced ball boys, having worked in that capacity, we assumed, in the not too distant past.

As already noted, time passed very quickly during our stay in Kapsabet, and following a final evaluation of our teaching skills by our mentors from Makerere, we returned to Mitchell Hall and the last weeks of our courses, now more interesting because what was said could be set against what we had just experienced in a classroom. When the end of the term came, there was a graduation ceremony and a celebratory party.

A week or so before, we had learned where we were to be posted for the next two years. When we had first signed up, the agreement was that we could be sent anywhere in the three East African countries – Uganda, Kenya, or Tanganyika (or Tanzania, as it was shortly to be named). To my delight, having expressed a preference for such a posting, I learned that I was to be sent to Kapsabet. There were plenty of other possibilities, some of them quite exotic and/or remote, but my rather unadventurous choice was influenced by two overriding factors: I very much liked the staff I had met at the school, and I liked the beauty of the region and what I had experienced of its climate. This latter provided enough rain to keep everything green and fresh-looking, and temperatures that were very comfortable. One could count on a high of about 25^0 C (77^0 F) during the day, but a low of about 9^0 C (48^0 F) at night. In addition, though close to the equator, Kapsabet had an altitude of about 1981 metres (6500 feet). This seemed to dispel any humidity. As for the cool night-time temperatures, these provided an invitation to light a wood fire for those who had a fireplace in their house.

It was now time to leave Makerere and once more set off for Kapsabet.

CHAPTER ELEVEN

KAPSABET: COLLEAGUES, FRIENDS, STUDENTS

After all the goodbyes at Makerere had been said and all the promises to keep in touch had been made, it was time to set off once more for Kapsabet in time for the start of the 1964 school year. A trouble-free drive this time – no roadblocks, no guns, no convoys of soldiers. Once there, I met up with two fellow graduates from Makerere: Pete Ryall, an Englishman, who would teach chemistry, and Hal Strom, an American, who would teach biology. During the next two years, the three of us were to become very close, as we steered our way through what was as much a learning experience for us as it was for the students we were entrusted to teach.

Acting as a partial curb upon our often raucous, high-spirited, and immature behavior outside the classroom were three other colleagues. Of key importance at first was John Allen, the headmaster, a bright, intelligent and very good-humoured American, not much older than ourselves. He had considerable gifts as an administrator and kept us in line with a mix of low-key diplomacy and gentle, reasoned persuasion. John was the exact opposite of the old-school authoritarian model that permeated the British school system. When he left at the end of the year, we greatly missed him, especially when his British replacement attempted to impose on the school the (to us) stifling and hierarchical model of order and discipline so familiar from my own school days.

A close friend of John was another American, Harry Stein. He was something of a mystery to us, a quiet man, a non-drinker, content to spend time on his own, a thoughtful person, capable of making Pete and me very uncomfortable when he questioned some of the political assumptions that shaped our thinking or lack of it. Not very interested in the sports (rugby, soccer, and cricket) that Pete and I claimed were so superior, both Harry and John were passionate about basketball and baseball. Some mornings the two of them would come to school having had very little sleep. Each in his own house, they had been hunched over their short-wave radios late into the night, listening to a game in the U.S.

The third person who had something of a moderating influence upon us was also an American. Married and with two small children, Jim Coleman was a few years our senior. Already an experienced teacher, he had been recruited directly into the T.E.A. programme. He and I shared a common interest in music. Indeed, he was the only person at the school who had much appreciation for "classical" music. At one point (it must have been when he was about to leave) he begged me to exchange one of my LPs for one of his. If memory serves, he'd fallen in love with one of Desdemona's arias in Verdi's *Otello*, exquisitely sung by an artist whose name I no longer recall. In return, I believe I received two Beethoven piano concerti. Looking back, I suspect that Jim got the better of the deal. Jim and his wife Barbara were very hospitable to us but didn't hold back from criticism. Barbara once said to me: "You know, the toilet in your bathroom is a disgrace. Don't you know that your housekeeper has probably never cleaned it? That's a job the housekeepers don't do. Don't you realise that Joseph's been leaving that chore to you?"

After she herself had laughingly demonstrated to me how it was done, I took care of things myself. Jim, however, had an altogether different personality. A redhead, he could on occasion live up to the stereotype. One day, when Pete and I had taken Pete's air rifle and walked on to Jim's lawn to shoot at some small birds high in a nearby tree, Jim suddenly appeared. In a state of outrage, he first berated us for shooting at birds and then forbade us ever to come into his garden for such a cruel and mindless purpose. He was absolutely right, of course, and after we'd given some thought to what he'd said, we went back to his house and apologized. To this day, when I think about this episode, I wonder just who those two young men were. They don't seem at all related to the two men I now know.

Two other teachers I remember particularly well. One was a Sikh, a kind and thoughtful man, who no doubt found much to question regarding our attitudes and behaviour. Fully conversant in Swahili, he could be very helpful when it came to dealing with servants. On one occasion, he came to see me to point out that my cook/house servant, Joseph, had set up some kind of business selling beer. His "brewery" was my kitchen, a small brick building constructed, as was the custom, a few yards removed from the house. I had to confess that I had not recognized the pervasive and very distinctive smell of *pombe*, the traditional local beer made from maize meal. I was aware, however, that Joseph was sometimes quite intoxicated when he served the evening meal, particularly on Saturday nights when I might have guests. Although he always managed the job, his staggering about and dishevelled appearance were becoming a problem. At first it had seemed mildly amusing. Wasn't he entitled to a bit of relaxation, particularly on a Saturday night? But now, I could see that something had to be done.

I accompanied my colleague to the kitchen, a place I rarely entered. As if by a common unspoken agreement, this was Joseph's territory. Once we had crossed the threshold, Joseph obviously realised that something serious was afoot. My Sikh friend was a tall man, and with the addition of his turban, he was an imposing figure. I did not understand most of what he had to say, but I noticed that there were plenty of allusions to "Bwana Young" thrown in. By the time he had finished, Joseph looked very chastened, even more so when I asked that he be told that if it (I never specified what I meant by "it") happened again, he would lose his job. To my great relief, "it" did not happen again, and my relationship with Joseph, who seemed to bear no grudge about my closing down his *pombe* business, remained cordial from then on.

The other teacher, who was there for part of my time in Kapsabet, was Dan Fitts, a congenial American Peace Corps volunteer, who arrived in January 1966. No doubt we gave him a difficult time at first, because we had little time for President Kennedy's brainchild organization, however much we liked almost all the volunteers we came across. Blanket policies prohibited Peace

Corps volunteers, for example, from having cars or servants. The intention was that they should live on equal terms with the local people they had come to work with. For too long the stereotype of the "ugly American" had prevailed. The Peace Corps was an attempt to counter that image. Not having a car meant that the two women teachers, who had been posted to a somewhat remote school in the Elgeyo area, some 32 kilometres or so (20 miles) north east of Eldoret, had no easy way of shopping or socializing with others. Laughably, they had been issued with horses, which took a lot of time and energy to maintain and which remained impractical as transportation. The Catholic priest at a nearby mission told us about their situation. Sensing his concern, Pete and I went to visit them. They seemed in good spirits, however, so we assumed all was well. Later we learned that their situation became impossible, so the horses were sent elsewhere, and the two women were moved to a different location.

Then there were the women at a school some thirty miles from us in the other direction. One night, according to the story that we heard, someone had broken into their house. When they had tried to defend themselves, the intruder, who had a *panga,* slashed the arm of one of them, seriously wounding her, before he fled. The woman was rushed to the nearest hospital (not, thankfully, that in Kapsabet) where she was attended to. What angered and upset us was hearing the story that the Peace Corps administrators subsequently rebuked her for not going to the hospital (a considerable distance away) that had been designated by them for emergencies. Following this absurd and unfeeling bureaucratic response, and suffering from what's now known as PTSD, both women resigned from the Peace Corps and went back to the U.S.A.

At about this time in the United States, Sargent Shriver, the Director of the Peace Corps, proposed that the Peace Corps should replace the Teachers for East Africa programme. We thought, of course, that it would be a retrograde step to replace trained teachers with Peace Corps volunteers who had no professional preparation for teaching. The East African countries, it turned out, agreed with us, and they made it clear that they would not accept Shriver's proposal. Eventually, a compromise agreement was hammered out that was acceptable to the Africans. Teachers College at Columbia University was asked to set up a special programme that would train Peace Corps volunteers for East African teaching assignments. With that in place, the T.E.A. programme was then phased out.

The students at Kapsabet School were a delight. Highly motivated, they were willing to work extremely hard. But in their view hard work was measured by the number of hours invested in rote learning. This made them vulnerable regarding problem solving and perceiving connections between the different things they had learned. As the O-level exams approached, students believed that they should be left to themselves to study and that there should be no classes and no official bedtime. Such study had become a well-established ritual at the school, but to us it appeared completely counter-productive. It was the wrong kind of study, a chief effect of which was to create over-tired students who were likely to function below their potential when it became time to write their O-levels.

When John Allen's successor attempted to force a break with custom, there was trouble. To everyone's amazement, the students went on strike. They refused to enter their classrooms, and late at night, as we discovered, they began studying in the latrines. The headmaster became increasingly insistent that his orders be followed, and the students became very agitated at having their all-important exam preparations restricted.

Unfortunately, the Kenya government had earlier issued a directive that there would be zero tolerance for school strikes (there had been some in previous years at other schools). Should a strike occur, the school was to bring in the police to break it up. To our horror, the headmaster did just this and contacted the District Commissioner. Unannounced, the D.C. arrived early the next morning with a truck full of policemen armed with batons, shields and tear gas. Dressed in their protective riot gear, they were lined up in between the school office and the classrooms. They were a formidable-looking sight, as I suppose they were meant to be. The D.C. then gave the students an ultimatum. "Do as you're told, or the policemen will make sure you do follow your headmaster's instructions." After a tense few minutes, the students complied. The D.C. and the police squad then gathered up their gear and left. The school was eerily quiet, and everyone was understandably in a state of shock. Having got his way and having listened to a number of suggestions from his staff, the headmaster then offered the students a compromise solution that dealt with the key issues of classroom hours and night-time study. This was accepted, and the crisis passed. In essence, the students got more or less what they wanted, even though most of us believed it was not really in their own best interests.

While most of my contact with the students was in the classroom, many of my most vivid memories were of encounters outside it. Having let it be known that they should feel free to come to my house if they had anything important to discuss, I was very occasionally taken at my word. One day a small group (they always came in groups of four or five) came to my door. From their demeanour I could tell that this was a serious matter and I was immediately concerned. What had I done? What had someone else done? What was I about to be involved in? Having sat them all down, I waited nervously for someone to speak. Eventually, one of them explained: "Well, you see, sir. There's something we don't understand."

This was followed by a long pause, exchanges of looks among them, and some shuffling of feet. Eventually, the question tumbled out: "We want to know what is love."

I was immediately relieved, but at the same time really puzzled.

"I don't quite understand. Surely you've experienced love. What about your mothers, what about your fathers, or your sisters? Some of you must have girlfriends."

This seemed like safe territory, but why their question? No, that was not it. As we kept talking, and I offered various suggestions, I began to perceive what this was all about. What seemed to be at issue was related to some kind of cultural gulf. On one side were European concepts of love and romance, and on the other side were traditional African ideas about love and sex. My students' question arose chiefly because of the literature they were expected to read, literature they would subsequently be examined on in their all-important O-level examinations. We teachers had assumed there was no such gulf and that our students shared the underlying concepts of romantic love in such literary works as *Pride and Prejudice* and *Romeo and Juliet.* I admit to being floored by my students' question. I tried to answer it, but I know that I quite failed them.

Recently I came across a discussion of this very topic which grew out of a teacher's difficulty in 1962 in answering a Nigerian student's question: "Excuse me sir, what does it mean 'to kiss'?" Some ten years later, without explaining how or if he came up with a satisfactory answer, this same teacher argued that the concept of romantic love was relatively new to Africa and had been introduced by Western influences:

There is at least one whole section of the world where the love story is virtually nonexistent. I can think of no contemporary African novel in which the plot line progresses because of the hero's attempt to acquire a mate, no African novel in which seduction is the major goal, no African novel in which the fate of the lovers becomes the most significant element in the story. No African novel works this way because love as a theme in a Western literary sense is simply missing. Romantic love, seduction, sex – these are not the subjects of African fiction... There are no graphic descriptions of erotic love, there are no kisses, no holding hands. There is, in short, no love story as we have come to think of it in Western Fiction. Not even the unrequited lover pining away. African fiction simply is not made of such stuff. (Charles Larson, "Heroic Ethnocentrism: The Idea of Universality in Literature," *American Scholar* 42, no. 3 [Summer, 1973], 78.)

I was equally at sea when one of my students invited me to his home. When we arrived, he introduced me to his father, but then began a series of introductions to his father's wives, each of whom had her own house. At each stop, we entered through the low doorway of a round thatched-roof structure with whitewashed walls. Inside, I was served a cup of fermented milk, a ritual form of hospitality. Unfortunately, I never got used to such milk. Indeed, I have to confess that I found it very difficult not to gag at the first mouthful. There was also another difficulty. If one finished the drink before the visit was concluded, the cup would be refilled. As I recall, there were four wives to be visited, each offering the not-to-be refused cup of milk. One of them was my student's mother, but all had to be shown proper deference according to a social code that I did not really understand.

On another occasion, I visited the home of another student. He was in my "House". As was the practice in many British schools, the students were divided into different Houses, often corresponding to their dormitories. There was then a ready-made structure for intra-mural sports and athletic competitions. My House, having come top in something or other, was given permission to put on a feast. This would involve slaughtering some poor animal that would then be roasted over an open fire and eaten. The purpose of the visit to the student's home was to collect a sheep, but what I chiefly remember was the journey back in my small car with two students in the back seat, the animal held firmly in place between them. Fortunately, there were no "accidents", but all of us ended up smelling like the beast we were transporting. On this return journey, there was much joking, with the students telling me that testicles and eyes were considered special delicacies. Perhaps I would like a taste when the feast was held. I was pretty sure they were teasing me, since no one seemed offended when I politely declined.

As House Master, I did drop by when the celebration was in progress and I was given something from the animal to eat. Whatever it was tasted fine, but I decided not to ask for any details concerning the choice morsel I'd been given.

Another visit to a student home occurred somewhat earlier during my teaching practice at Kapsabet. One of the students in my class invited me and the other trainee teachers to a special event that was about to take place – the circumcision of his sister and another girl from the community. We knew that circumcision ceremonies were regarded as very important life-cycle events among the Kalenjin (Nandi), a kind of initiation into adulthood, and we understood that it was something of an honour to be invited. Younger boys in the school were routinely given permission to be away for their circumcision, but their ceremonies were secret and not open to outsiders. Female circumcisions, on the other hand, appeared to be far less restrictive concerning who might attend. Very early on the day in question, five of us drove to my student's home. There, somewhat to our embarrassment, a table and chairs were set up, and we were served a small breakfast by my student while the whole community at a discreet distance stood and watched.

The celebrations, as far as I could tell, had been going on all night, and the two girls had been dancing all that time. As we waited, they spent some time in a nearby river. The combination of very cold water and dancing were supposed to have a numbing effect so that the two of them would not suffer too much pain, an important strategy since crying out was forbidden. Wearing colourful ornamental costumes, the two girls then appeared, dancing in the centre of the now large and very excited circle formed by the assembled crowd. They were then conducted to one of the houses, where the deed was done. Apparently, all went well, and an announcement to that effect was then made. A small group of women, who I assumed included the mothers, were so ecstatic and so joyful that two of them appeared to lose consciousness and had to be held upright by the others. I had never in my life witnessed such powerful and unrestrained emotion, almost frightening in its intensity. After expressing our thanks and offering congratulations to my student's family and the community elders, we teachers returned home. The girls remained indoors out of sight. Checking with my student in the days that followed, I learned that they were doing well. Now considered to be adults, they would before long be married.

Today, of course, female circumcision, or female genital mutilation (to use the modern preferred term), is widely condemned for its negative health consequences. The World Health Organization considers it a violation of human rights, and there are a number of United Nations treaties banning it. It is long embedded within many cultures, both in Kenya and elsewhere, and attempts to ban the practice have had only partial success. In 1990, as a result of a presidential directive, Kenya banned the practice. More recently on 30 September 2011, the Kenyan parliament passed an act that criminalized all forms of female genital mutilation, but it would seem that the effect has been to make circumcision something to be carried out in secret. In time, perhaps, some kind of alternative ritual will become accepted, and young women will be able to take their place within their communities as adults without having to undergo the painful and dangerous physical rite of passage decreed by tradition. Such questions, however, were not on the minds of those of us who attended what appeared to be a very joyful day in the lives of my student's family and community. Only years later did I realise that our presence was a tacit sign of approval for what the two girls were going through. They may have been willing participants, but they really had no choice in the face of family and community pressure to follow tradition.

Another reminder of the cultural divide separating me from my students was of a very different kind. For some time, the area around Kapsabet had been hit by a series of cattle thefts. We were somewhat apprehensive about this, because the school had its own farm with some valuable cows that supplied all of us with milk. We had been told to be watchful regarding their security, but somehow cattle thieves came onto the school grounds and managed to round up some of the cows and get them out to the Eldoret road adjacent to the school. This had happened in the middle of the night, but the alarm had been raised almost immediately. When Pete Ryall and I, along with other staff members, had thrown some clothes on and stumbled out of our houses, we discovered the students were already up. Armed with sticks and all manner of other improvised weaponry, they were about to set off in pursuit. It was impossible to hold them back. What's more, we realised that if they caught up with the thieves, they would kill them. In my mind, this threat was related to the warning that various "old timers" had given us about driving: "If you ever hit someone, don't stop. Just drive to the nearest police station and report what's happened. If you do stop after hitting someone, you could be killed."

Pete and I had once observed a somewhat different situation, but one that also revealed the need for wariness when driving. On our way from Kabsabet to Kakamega, we rounded a bend and discovered a growing crowd surrounding a British woman. Standing beside her car, which had apparently broken down, she was endeavouring to write a note and persuade someone – anyone – to go and fetch her husband. By the time we arrived, she was very agitated and increasingly fearful. Though it was hard for us to understand why, the crowd, rather than being sympathetic and helpful, was becoming increasingly hostile. We both jumped out of our car and while Pete – how shall I put it? – barked at the crowd and ordered them to move back, I took a look at the woman's disabled vehicle. It was obvious what was wrong. Her silencer had dropped to the ground and the exhaust pipe had broken. Pete and I had already experienced a similar situation, and I now kept a length of baling wire in the trunk of my car for just such an emergency. One of the Eldoret rugby-playing farmers had given me this tip. Baling wire was thin and flexible, almost like string, but used to strap up a fallen exhaust system it was strong enough to do the job and, unlike string, it would not burn if the exhaust got hot.

But this was not the time for the niceties of baling wire. I felt that Pete's "barking" might not succeed in holding back the crowd for much longer. We told the woman to get in her car and open all the windows. A couple of hard pulls then broke the exhaust system free of the woman's car and we threw it into her back seat.

"You'll be fine now," I told her. "It's going to be really noisy, but don't worry about it. The car's OK to drive. But keep the windows open to get rid of the exhaust fumes."

With that, she was off. She wanted to write down our names so that she could thank us later, but, still concerned about the mood of the crowd, we told her to drive on. After a couple more barks from Pete, we were in our car and on our way. We never saw the woman again, and I often wondered what would have happened had Pete and I not been driving to Kakamega that day

On the night of the cattle rustling, having failed to prevent our students from rushing off and exacting some kind of vigilante justice, Pete and I got into my car and drove as fast as we could to the police camp in Kapsabet. We could find no one awake and no one to report to. Pete then came up with an inspired solution. He ran up to the large metal triangle on the police parade ground and started hitting it as hard as he could with the heavy piece of metal hung up beside it. That got the sleepers' attention. Staggering out of their tents, they began forming up in ranks. When a harassed-looking officer appeared, Pete, in his fiercest manner, told him what was going on and made clear that immediate action was needed. That worked. In no time, a truck full of police was on its way. With luck they would get to the thieves before the students did. Pete's quick thinking that night did, in my view, prevent bloodshed. To our great relief, the police apprehended the thieves, the cattle were returned to the farm and our students came back to their beds, their weapons having mysteriously disappeared.

A quite different matter regarding our students was their prowess in track and field sports. When new students arrived to begin their four-year programme with us, we took them to our sports field and put them through their paces. To our immense surprise, we discovered that we had two students who ran the mile in times that were not far off the magic four minutes. Barely recovered from the shock of that revelation, we turned our attention to the long jump. I still remember our astonishment when one student jumped so far that he landed beyond the end of the sand pit. All the other students were then set to work digging out an extension for the pit. When this was done, we asked the student to jump again. This time, we were able to measure his distance. As I recall, he jumped more than 25 feet (7.6 metres), not far off the world record at the time of just over 27 feet (8.2 metres). That same student further surprised us by running a near 10-second 100 yards (91.4 metres) on our admittedly downhill track.

Born in 1949, he (his name was Julius Sang), along with one or two of his fellow students, were an awesome responsibility. What was required by way of training? Would the newly independent country not be interested in knowing that it possessed athletes who, though untrained, possessed such high-level capabilities? How best could we help and encourage them, apart from sharing what little we remembered from our own participation in athletics while at school? Eventually, help came when we learned of a small training programme that had been set up in Nairobi and that people like Julius Sang could attend during the school holidays.

After leaving Kenya in 1966, Pete Ryall and I met Julius in London where he had come to race. Two years later, he participated in the Mexico City Olympic Games. There he ran in the 100 and 200 metres race. Although he failed to win a medal, the world was transfixed by the performance of a fellow Kalenjin runner, Kipchoge Keino, who won a gold medal in the 1,500 metres race (the metric mile), defeating the world record holder, Jim Ryun. From then on,

Kenyan runners, most of them Kalenjin, became a familiar presence at international athletic events, especially in middle and long distance races. At the ill-fated Munich Olympics in 1972, Keino won a gold medal in the 3,000 metres steeplechase, but it was here that Julius won bronze in the 400 metres and gold in the 4 x 400 metre relay, in which he ran anchor for the Kenyan team.

Because so many of Kenya's athletes have been Kalenjin, there continues to be a great deal of discussion about why this group is so successful. Two possibilities seemed self-evident to those of us at the school. Living at an altitude of 1981 metres (6,500 feet) or so confers a natural advantage over other athletes when an athlete descends to competitions at much lower altitudes. Also, when competitions occur at high altitudes, the Mexico City Olympics being an example, a Kalenjin athlete comes with an advantage over those who live at lower altitudes. Today, it is no accident that the Kenyan High Altitude Training Centre for runners at Iten, which has regularly attracted runners from other countries since its founding in 1999, is situated 32 kilometres (20 miles) north east of Eldoret at an altitude of 2,400 metres (7900 feet).

The second home-grown theory among those of us at the school derived from a common early-morning phenomenon that some of us had observed when setting out on a journey around dawn. Many children lived considerable distances from their primary schools. The fastest way to get there was to run, and that is what many young people did, something that necessitated cautious driving if one was out early in the day, especially just before dawn. Other theories, later explored by scientists, have had to do with diet, genetic and anatomical features peculiar to the Kalenjin, and their ability to withstand pain, something required during both male and female circumcision rituals, and something that is useful in long distance racing. No one has come up with a completely convincing explanation, but it would seem that the answer is probably to be found in the happy combination of some or all the possible causes just mentioned.

Apart from athletics, the principal sports at the school were soccer and volleyball, but there was also a fledgling rugby programme. Pete Ryall and I began coaching rugby, hoping that in time there would be enough proficient players to form a school team. The two of us joined the Club in Eldoret and began playing ourselves. It was an arduous and time-consuming business. There was a practice session during the week and a game most Saturdays, often a bruising affair against one of the clubs from communities within a 160-kilometre (100-mile) radius. After some often raucous socializing in the club bar, we would drive home.

But there was a catch. We soon learned that it was customary to have a second, less formal game the next morning, followed by a lunch. Turning up for the Sunday game, especially if you had a hangover or were tired out from the day before, though not mandatory, was considered good teamsmanship and a sign of one's toughness. Pete and I, eager to be accepted by the other club members, did our best to comply.

The other Eldoret rugby players were mostly farmers, many of them Afrikaaners. Some had had a hard time during the Mau Mau uprising, and, though they had not left Kenya as many of their fellows had done, they remained uneasy and very sceptical about how they would fare under the new government. Many of them held on to their ingrained racist attitudes and resented the fact that the club was now open to all. It was much the same situation in the other clubs where we went for away matches.

I mention this because, after our school rugby players were sufficiently trained, Pete and I took a bold and potentially foolhardy step. We invited the Eldoret players to forgo a weekly practice session and instead come to Kapsabet and play a short game against our students. As we explained, we hoped that this would teach the boys something about the game. Our proposal caused considerable consternation. Several players, it seemed clear, did not want to play against blacks. One even attempted to explain to me that he couldn't face the idea of touching an African in the ways the game required, particularly when there was a set scrum. Others, after giving our invitation some thought, agreed to come. They realised, I believe, that they were being invited to step towards the future. All-white teams were soon to be an anachronism. Furthermore, if the white population in the Western highlands continued to diminish, they would need black players in Eldoret if they wanted to continue playing their beloved game.

The big day came some weeks later. I don't know who was more nervous: Pete and I with our fear of something going wrong, the students who were about to challenge a group of older white men, or the players from Eldoret who were, in a modest way, about to make history. With the entire school, students and teachers alike, cheering the Kapsabet team, the game began. We lost, of course, the Eldoret team being more experienced and having a mastery of strategy and various tricks of the game that gave them a great advantage. However, we posed a real threat on the few occasions that our wingers got the ball. Once they started to run, their impressive speed made them almost impossible to catch.

This was something that did not go unnoticed. After the game, when the students had gone off for supper and the visitors were getting into their cars to leave, the Eldoret captain said to me, "You've got some interesting players there. Those two wingers – with a bit more training they'll be an asset to any team. Some of those Kalenjin can really move. I'd never thought about what they might do on a rugby pitch."

What he then went on to say pleased me even more: "Thanks for asking us to come. I understand more now about what you and Pete and the others are doing here. Some of the fellows don't get it yet, but don't think too badly of them. They'll come around, and I'm guessing that those who don't will probably go south like some of the others who used to be in the Eldoret Club."

Today, rugby is a well-established sport in Kenya, particularly in the seven-a-side version of the game. The white dominance of the game has vanished, and many teams, including that in Eldoret, are composed almost exclusively of African players.

Although sports and athletics were an important part of school life, academic matters were our chief concern. As an English teacher, I was very much caught up in an ongoing struggle to improve my students' language skills. After their native tongue and then Kiswahili, English was their third language and now the key to everything they did. Not long ago, I wrote a short piece about myself for the newsletter published by an organization serving T.E.A. alumni. I apparently implied that I felt that I had not contributed very much to the education of my students. To my great surprise, I received an email response to my comments from Hal Strom, the biology teacher I mentioned earlier in this chapter. Inferring that I felt I had been a failure as a teacher, he reminded me of something that I had long forgotten and that for him had been a great success:

I was struck by your observation that you did not feel "sufficiently mature at the time to fully serve the goals of TEA." I would disagree. I specifically remember that you led an effort to improve the English skills of newly-enrolled Nandi students. You developed a special intensive English programme and converted the rest of the staff into teachers of English for several weeks. The aim was to make it possible for these Kalenjin students (with very limited English skills) to benefit from the science, social studies, etc. that would be taught after the intensive English sessions. My recollection is that this general strategy was pretty effective.

Almost all of the schools I later worked in enrolled some students who struggled to learn in English-medium classrooms. The skills and experiences you provided to me in the mid-1960s worked just as well for Norwegians, Azerbaijanis, Koreans, and so on. I would argue that you not only helped all of your students during your time in Kapsabet, you helped hundreds of the students that we teachers later taught.

Apart from having to grapple with learning the English language, my students and I faced another huge impediment. In all we did, we were very constrained by the demands of a curriculum that was almost an exact parallel of its British counterpart. The literature that the students had to read for O-levels was in most instances culturally far removed from their experience. Only when I got my hands on a copy of Chinua Achebe's recently published *Things Fall Apart* did I begin to understand the full implications of this. This novel, written in English by a Nigerian writer, had an African point of view. It explored the customs and beliefs of an African tribe in the 1890s and the impact of both British colonialism and Christianity upon the culture of that tribe. Such matters resonated deeply with African readers, and within a few years, the book was to become a staple in the curriculum of African schools across the continent. When commenting on the unprecedented success of his novel, Achebe remarked: "...this was the first time we were seeing ourselves, as autonomous individuals, rather than half-people, or as Conrad would say, 'rudimentary souls'." (Interview by Bradford Morrow in *Conjunctions* 17 [Fall 1991], para. 90. See http://www.conjunctions.com/archives/c17-ca.htm).

A steady torrent of other works by diverse authors throughout Africa were to follow Achebe's novel, those by Kenya's Ngugi wa Thiong'o being among the most highly regarded. Nowadays, *Things Fall Apart* is a standard text worldwide in university courses in post-colonial studies.

Such matters were often discussed among the staff at Kapsabet. Harry Stein, with his concern with history, was perhaps the most sensitive and prescient concerning the need in all subjects to have new texts that were more suited to our students' circumstances. Later, he was to build a career engaged in all manner of educational projects, most of which involved schools in East Africa.

Beyond the tight-knit circle of fellow teachers at Kapsabet, there were a number of other people who became good friends. Not far from the school, on the other side of the river from which the town drew its water, was a Catholic mission. It was run by a genial and warm-hearted priest, Father Errity. His domain included a girls' school at the mission run by a small group of nuns, a pair of Catholic brothers to assist him, a large parish church, and, of course, a large territory for which he was responsible. He was not, as far as I could discern, engaged in actively recruiting souls; however, he did find himself in constant conflict with various evangelical Protestant missionaries who not only sought to gather in new converts but viewed him as little better than an agent of the devil. As I gradually came to understand, the Catholics (at least, those of Father Errity's ilk) tended to be tolerant of many local traditional ways, the dancing, the polygamy, and the rituals such as circumcision. Many evangelicals, on the other hand, wanted converts to break from the "old" ways, and actively sought to recruit those willing to be "saved" from such evils.

Father Errity's mission became something of a retreat for Pete and me. Like all the other Catholic mission houses I visited, the priest and any brothers could only have a drink when lay visitors were present. Needless to say, whenever we dropped by, whether at Father Errity's mission or other Catholic missions like it, we were always welcomed inside and offered a drink. But that's not why we went. Father Errity was a wonderful listener. Did years of practice in the confessional hone that particular skill? We could relax in his presence, talk about irritating school affairs, conflicts with colleagues, problems with servants, or anything else, however trivial, that was on our minds. The gentle humour and wisdom of his responses were traits that we came to value. I think that perhaps we gave something in return. In his position of authority, it was awkward for him to be too friendly with the brothers and nuns in his charge. Without ever being inappropriate or stepping outside the bounds of decorum, he sometimes hinted at his own frustrations and difficulties. Talking to sympathetic outsiders like us perhaps occasionally helped him.

I never talked to Father Errity about my conversion to Catholicism and my subsequent loss of faith, but I suspect that he guessed there was something of the sort in my past. A couple of times, he took me into his church and let me try out the organ. He would say: "We could use someone to play for mass on Sundays. I'd get someone to pump for you. Would you like to give it a go? Or just come and see for yourself what it's like here on a Sunday morning."

I declined both his offers. I didn't want to get drawn in, and, besides, there was Sunday morning rugby to consider.

I was very sad when I left Kenya and subsequent attempts to keep in touch with Father Errity never really worked, but I shall always remember him with great affection.

Teaching at the same mission was a small group of nuns. Their duties also appeared to include looking after some of the domestic needs of Father Errity and the Brothers. Because we teachers at Kapsabet, on a rotating basis, were given a weekday afternoon off so that we could do our shopping in Eldoret, I was often able to stop off on the way to pick up a couple of nuns who had similar errands. They were always excited, free from some of the restrictions governing their lives at the mission. They would chatter incessantly both coming and going, trying one's patience to the full. Once the shopping in Eldoret was over, their great delight was to go to the

tearoom that Lloyd had pointed out when I'd first visited the town. There we would meet up for tea and something sweet and tasty before starting the drive home.

On one occasion, the routine trip with the nuns was transformed into something else. Somehow, they had persuaded Father Errity to grant them permission to see a movie. Their delight and exuberant anticipation were so great that it was impossible not to agree to take them. The film in question was *The Sound of Music*, which had only just come out. In time it would become something of a classic, but how the nuns had learned about it so soon I have no idea. And why would Father Errity give his blessing to the sisters' seeing a film about a would-be nun who discovers that the cloistered life is not what she wanted after all? What's more, did he know that in the film the postulant falls in love with a widower who has seven children? Did he know that she marries him, thereby ending her original vocation? Assuming that the nuns did know about some or all of these things, I have to conclude that they conned the good father, displaying a degree of independence that they would not normally have got away with.

Once we were seated in the theatre and the film began, the nuns became totally absorbed. The music was wonderful and there were plenty of comic moments. Once the romance between Maria (Julie Andrews) and Captain von Trapp (Christopher Plummer) began to develop, a different mood set in. When a frightened Maria returns to her Abbey, she talks with the Mother Abbess (Peggy Wood). Maria wants to take her monastic vows, but the Abbess instead tells her to return to von Trapp's home. Maria must face up to her situation and discover whether she and the Captain truly love each other. She must search for the life she was destined to live. As the Abbess suggests in her song, she must:

Climb ev'ry mountain
Ford ev'ry stream
Follow ev'ry rainbow
'Till you find your dream

A dream that will need
All the love you can give
Every day of your life
For as long as you live

Although the sisters made it very clear that they had loved the movie, our ride back to Chepterit was for once a relatively quiet affair. They were, I suspect, immersed in their own thoughts. Today, I wonder what those thoughts may have been. What kind of sacrifices had they made to join their Order? Had any of them had to choose between love for a man and religious devotion to the Being to whom they were now "wedded"?

Not far from our school, and facing the Catholic mission across the river valley, was a very different establishment, a Protestant girls' school run by the Africa Inland Mission, an organization which sent its first missionaries to Kenya in 1895 but which today has personnel serving in some twenty-two African nations. As the current website of AIM explains, its missionary team is "diverse, from outreach workers and church planters, to medical personnel, to a broad network of logistical and support personnel – pilots, teachers, accountants, engineers, IT workers, and more. Together, we're committed to *being* and *making* disciples of Jesus Christ."

My principal contact with the AIM school was with two of its teachers, Frank Laemmlen and his wife Anne. Both Americans, they became very good friends, and I saw a good deal of them and their young daughter Teresa, who was born in the Eldoret hospital in 1964. Fresh out of college and devout Christians, they had volunteered with the Mennonite Central Committee to serve for a three-year term in an AIM school. Frank was very science-oriented and, as far as I recall, taught biology. Anne was different in many ways. She was very creative, always coming up with new projects to pursue. She was also a wonderful cook, and to this day I still remember my first bite of her pumpkin pie. This traditional American dish was completely new to me, along with the celebration of Thanksgiving Day. Today I still use Anne's recipe, which she had received from her mother and which I have in turn passed on to a number of friends.

I never discussed with Anne and Frank how comfortable they felt working for AIM, but I suspect that our dinner evenings and parties may have offered a welcome temporary break from their different world, a stone's throw away on the other side of the Kapsabet-Eldoret road. I always enjoyed being in their company and was delighted on one occasion when they invited me to go on safari with them. They had borrowed Hal Strom's Land Rover and planned to drive some 240 kilometres (149 miles) south east of Nairobi and camp in the Masai Mara Game Reserve.

On the way, we made a brief stop. A Masai woman with a small child came up to us and asked if she could have a ride. Frank agreed right away, but Anne was not happy. It was an awkward moment, and during the brief marital contretemps that followed, I kept quiet. I myself never gave rides unless I already knew the person. Only twice had I broken my own rule, and that was when I had been frantically waved down because a pregnant woman, her time fast approaching, needed to get to the hospital. In the case of the Masai woman and her *mtoto*, there appeared to be no emergency. As we barely liked to admit, however, there would be the familiar problem of body odour if she and the child were in the vehicle for any length of time.

The discussion between Anne and Frank continued for a while, but Frank prevailed, a reminder that this normally reticent man had a very strong will when he believed that something he was doing was right. So we found space for our new passengers and put up with the consequences. The Masai woman was delighted and vociferous in expressing her thanks, and Teresa, who had watched the entire mini-drama with obvious interest, was also pleased. She'd seemed fascinated both by the child, who was not much bigger than herself, and even more by the woman's ankle bracelets, her colourful necklaces and her very long earrings.

Once we had arrived in the park, we set up camp in a grove of trees beside a small river. It was an idyllic spot, quite deserted while we were there. After sitting around our small fire, we retired to our respective tents for the night. It was then that we began to wonder whether we had chosen our camp site wisely. As it soon became obvious, our idyllic riverside spot was next to a major watering place. Throughout the night, there was a great deal of splashing only yards away from us, accompanied by all manner of animal sounds, including ominous grunts and coughs that may well have been leopards or lions. Fortunately, we were completely ignored, but the episode was something of a lesson regarding the choice of such a camp site.

The next day we saw all kinds of game, including lions. During the day, they tended to stretch out in groups, spending most of the time sleeping. If one located such a family group, one could usually drive up within a few yards to observe them and take pictures. The lions would largely ignore one. But step out of the vehicle, and the lions, as if sensing danger, would immediately be on the alert. Ironically, the best way to locate lions was often to do just that. If one stopped in the middle of a grassy area, for example, where the tall grass could be hiding a group of recumbent lions, getting out of the vehicle might result in some heads popping up. Having located the animals, one needed to hop back quickly into the vehicle before causing any more excitement among the lions.

Of course, we saw many other types of animals – wildebeest (gnus), various kinds of gazelle, zebra, impala, giraffe, and topi. The area is also home to buffalo, elephant, rhino and hippopotami, but I don't now recall exactly what we saw during our brief visit. In the mid-1960s, Masai Mara did not have much in the way of facilities, and relatively few tourists went there. Today, it has become much more popular as a tourist destination. The roads have been improved, and there are various kinds of accommodations. Our pleasure in feeling that we had the place to ourselves would now, I suspect, be hard to duplicate.

Another married couple, Tom and Pauline Powell, were also very important to me. They had been in northern Kenya towards the border with Somalia, but it became too dangerous to stay. They had adopted an orphaned baby giraffe that often came into the house. When someone poisoned the animal, they sensed it was time to go. Tom then got a job as a manager on one of the large tea farms in the Nandi Hills, just to the south of us. I believe he'd been let go at Independence but then had found employment with the regional government in Kapsabet as a district cattle officer. He was a generous and affable soul, always with some pet enthusiasm to share.

One day he came to me with a question: "So, how would you like to have a horse? I was just up at this place north of Eldoret. The farmer seems to have abandoned everything, including some horses. It's a shame. There's one very good-looking horse that I could get for you, if you're interested."

My protestations about not knowing how to ride, not having any tackle and not having a stable were brushed aside.

"Look, we'll drive up there, you'll take a look, and then you'll decide," he said.

So when I had some free time, we drove to the farm in question, and Tom showed me the horses he had seen. One of them did indeed stand out, a large animal with a shiny coat. Tom enumerated its many virtues. Then he assured me that he would teach me to ride. As for bit, bridle, and saddle, I would be able to get them from Ishmail, the Somali trader in Eldoret, whose store was full of used items of just that kind. As for a stable, Tom had that all worked out, too. My garage, a free-standing, thatched-roof, open-sided structure, would be easy to convert. When we got back, I talked to the headmaster. He clearly thought I was out of my mind but nonetheless agreed. Tom was elated. This was one enthusiasm that was going to bear fruit.

Some days later, after we'd prepared the stable, he somehow found an excuse to get the use of a government truck for a few hours one morning. Because I was teaching at the time, he and his African assistant went off on their own to collect the horse. When I came back to my house for lunch, horse and truck were waiting for me. As I approached, Tom came towards me, a rueful look on his face.

"I'm afraid there's been a bit of a cock-up. We couldn't get the horse you wanted. It was really wild. We would never have got it on to the truck. I think it's been left on its own for too long. We didn't know what to do, so we decided to take one of the others. This one's a mare and much more docile. Probably, this'll be better anyway for a beginning rider."

There was not much I could say, so we downloaded the horse and put her into the freshly-prepared stable. Thomas, my second servant, had agreed to be in charge of feeding and watering, and, after Tom had shown him how, he was also in charge of grooming with the curry comb that Tom had found. After I'd been to see Ishmail and bought the necessary tackle, my riding lessons began, much to the amusement of many of my students. I also managed to find a couple of books. One, which was on the care and upkeep of horses, had a fascinating chapter on horse psychology that left me feeling guilty for depriving Sally (the rather tame name was all I could come up with) of her life on the farm with other horses. It seems that a key feature of horse psychology is that horses are most comfortable when in the company of other horses. As a substitute, it was recommended that one provide the horse with some other animal for company, perhaps a dog, a cat or a goat. Although I had a dog, I knew that he would not be the answer (more of that later). The best I could hope for was that some kind of bond would develop between Sally and some of Joseph's chickens, which were always pecking about in my yard.

The other book was concerned with the art of riding. I soon realised that the finer points were not for me. The basics, as taught me by Tom, would be fine.

Sally, as I have already mentioned, was nowhere near the size of the horse we had originally selected. She was rather small, and I suspect she was also much older. She was probably a little bit too small for me, but I chose to ignore that. She didn't seem so small when I was up on her back. I was also thankful that she was fairly docile, perhaps because of her age.

It was my ambition to use Sally for small errands. One day I felt confident enough to saddle her and set off down the school driveway. Then a right turn on to the main Kapsabet-Eldoret road, or rather the tree-lined track that ran parallel to the road and which many pedestrians used to avoid the road itself. Sally and I did just fine, and when we reached the Nandi Store, I dismounted, and she was content to let me knot her reins around one of the posts in front. A small crowd gathered (I should have anticipated that) to watch this novel spectacle. Perhaps in days past there had been horses here, perhaps even a proper hitching rail. It would have been interesting to know. Did they, I wondered, consider this *mzungu* on horseback to be some kind of idiotic regression to the colonial past? Nowadays, all Europeans had cars, didn't they? Could this one only afford a horse?

Quickly repressing all such thoughts and ignoring the crowd as best I could, I made my purchase and remounted Sally with all the style I could muster. Tom would have been pleased, I felt. All went well after we left the store until we were back on the track leading to home. Suddenly, Sally started moving increasingly quickly. Who knew that she had it in her? Nothing I did succeeded in checking her. I could only hang on and hope for the best. We must have been an impressive sight as we arrived on the school grounds, pounded past the school office and turned into my yard. What was in Sally's mind? I could find nothing in my books to help. Was she so delighted with her new home that she couldn't wait to get back there? Or was having to carry me such a miserable chore that she wanted to be free of me as soon as possible? Whatever the explanation, after two further such episodes, I began to feel that owning a horse was perhaps not for me.

Weeks passed, and I regularly rode Sally about the school grounds. She also got plenty of exercise giving rides to children, among them Tom's Alan, Cathy, and Rosemary, and the two Coleman boys. One day, however, all activity involving Sally came to an abrupt halt when I received a letter in the mail, which may be paraphrased as follows:

Dear Mr. Young,
Ishmail in Eldoret tells me that you have removed one of my horses. This particular horse has been with our family for a long time and was a great favourite with our children. We are shocked and very angry at what you have done. Although we have been away, we have NOT abandoned our farm, something you could easily have found out if you had bothered to enquire. We have been away for a short time, but that does not give you

the right to do what you have done. As you may or may not know, horse-stealing in this country is a very serious offence. I expect my horse to be returned to my farm within a week. Otherwise, I shall inform the police, and you will have to face the consequences.

The woman's letter put me into something of a panic, especially when Tom didn't know if he could wangle the truck again, and a colleague jokingly suggested that horse-stealing was still on the books in Kenya as a hanging offence. Fortunately, before the police came to arrest me, and before Tom lost his job for using a government vehicle in support of criminal activity, he found some way to "borrow" a truck for the second and last time. On this occasion, I was free to go along and witness Sally's return to her former home. She seemed on arrival to be delighted. She came off the truck without need of the slightest urging, and, without a backward glance, galloped off to join her former companions. Tom, his assistant, and I then left as fast as possible to avoid any possible meeting with Sally's owner, and with that, the entire episode was over, along with my riding career. I sold the tackle back to Ishmail (at a considerable loss, of course) and privately vowed to be wary of any future schemes that Tom came up with.

Pauline, like Tom, was British. She was far more level-headed than her husband. I suspect that she was fearful about their family's future. Tom's job would end once he had trained his assistant. What would happen then? Already their oldest child was about to become a boarder at the "European" school in Eldoret, but soon the two girls would also need to go to school. How would they be able to afford that? For the most part, Pauline kept such worries to herself. Always very good-humoured, she held the family together. Without her, Tom would, I suspect have been quite lost.

I often wondered what happened to this family after I left. I expected them to go "south" like so many other expatriates displaced by Independence. Or perhaps, I thought, they would find their way to somewhere else. Australia? Canada? South America? It turns out, however, that they returned to England where, resourceful as ever, Tom did the appropriate training and became an art teacher.

There were others who contributed to our social life in Kapsabet, such as the doctor serving the tea farming population around Nandi Hills to the south of us, the couple in Kapsabet, with whom Pete and I played bridge on a regular basis, and other T.E.A. workers at the school in Kakamega to the west. Particularly important to Pete and me, however, were Frank and Molly Sprank, the couple we had met on the *Kenya Castle*. Because they lived in Nairobi, some 312 kilometres (193 miles) away, we did not see them very often, but whenever we were in the city, we had the warmest of welcomes in their home.

Frank had a business making bottles, best known for an innovation for which Frank was responsible. One day, he had decided that he would provide square bottles for orange juice, in place of the customary round ones. The novel shape and the floral motif on the sides of the bottle created a very distinctive and successful marketing device, and people found that square bottles were somehow easier than round bottles to store in a fridge. A flamboyant figure, Frank drove a large American car, its steering wheel on the "wrong" side, its rear sporting elaborate chrome fins which Frank kept well polished.

Frank and Molly lived in Karen, a suburb of Nairobi built on land some 10 kilometres from the city centre. The land had formerly been part of the coffee plantation established in 1914 by the Swedish Baron von Blixen and his Danish wife Karen (formerly Dinesen). The Blixens separated in 1921, and Karen Blixen then had a long-term love affair with Denys Finch Hatton, who died in the crash of his small plane in 1931. Blixen then returned to Denmark and soon became an established and highly admired writer, her *Out of Africa* (1937) being the best-known of her works. Frank and Molly introduced me to this work, since made very popular following the 1985 movie with Meryl Streep and Robert Redford. Frank pointed out Karen Blixen's house, not far from his own, and on one occasion drove Pete and I out into the Ngong Hills, a beautiful area mentioned in *Out of Africa*, the famous opening of which states:

I had a farm in Africa, at the foot of the Ngong Hills. The Equator runs across these highlands, a hundred miles to the North, and the farm lay at an altitude of over six thousand feet. In the daytime you felt that you had got high up, near to the sun, but the early mornings and evenings were limpid and restful, and the nights were cold.

The geographical position and the height of the land combined to create a landscape that had not its like in all the world. There was no fat on it and no luxuriance anywhere; it was Africa distilled up through six thousand feet, like the strong and refined essence of a continent.

There follows a sequence of exquisitely-written paragraphs describing the Ngong Hills, which play a significant role in the lives of Blixen and Finch Hatton as recounted in the book. As she leaves Kenya at the end of the book, the train taking Blixen to the coast stops at Samburu to take on water. In her final paragraph, she looks back and sees the Hills for the last time, slowly being "smoothed and levelled out by the hand of distance".

It was obvious that the Ngong Hills had a special place in Frank's heart, and I remain grateful that he shared this with us. During our drive, he did not take us to the spot where Finch Hatton was buried and upon which, according to the book, lions were often observed as though they were keeping watch, like those in Trafalgar Square around Nelson's Column. Frank always claimed that he didn't know where the grave was and that anyway it was said to be completely overgrown. Sometimes I wondered about that. Perhaps Frank wanted to keep the location a secret. I also used to wonder how Frank felt when, like Karen Blixen, he took the train to Mombasa to leave Kenya for the last time. Did he, too, turn his eyes back for one last look at the Ngong Hills?

And what of Molly? She was very level-headed and practical, the last person one would expect to see driving about in a flashy American car. She had a fine sense of humour and at times displayed an unexpectedly caustic wit. Unfortunately, her work in the British Passport Office gave her a somewhat racist view of the world. Following Independence, not only were there hundreds of expatriates who were anxious to leave, but there were even more Indians. Never having been to India, this latter group thought of themselves as British and hoped to use their British passport (or obtain one for the first time) so that they could leave Kenya and join the many other Indians already in Britain. This exodus was nothing to that which occurred in the late 60s and early 70s in response to the growing animosity of Africans. Even so, when we knew her, Molly was at the sharp end of these painful developments, and she was not happy about it. Just how she herself felt about going "home" I never learned, but I could tell that she was increasingly aware of the isolation in Karen of herself and Frank and their growing need to be security conscious, as evident from the high fence around their property and the watchman they employed. This was not the Kenya they had known, and, unlike Frank, she was not prepared to make compromises or show understanding towards the new regime and its "Africanization" policies.

I will mention here one last friend - a good companion, handsome, friendly, even loving, eager to join any ongoing activity, and equipped with a sixth sense that seemed to draw him to me whenever I felt down. But there was another side to him. He could be quite wayward and undisciplined, ignoring my presence, pursuing his own pleasures, and often staying away for long periods of time. This was my Irish setter, Brutus, who was with me for most of my stay in Kapsabet. He turned up on my doorstep one day and attached himself to me. He was a delight when his good qualities were on display, but otherwise he could be something of a nightmare. He needed huge amounts of exercise, which I wasn't always able to supervise. If he got the chance to set off on his own he had the entire school grounds to wander in, but he had other haunts throughout the area, including down in Kapsabet itself.

After some of his jaunts, he would return hungry, tired, and filthy. Before he was fit to come back into the house, I'd have to give him a bath and comb and brush him to bring back his beautiful ginger self. In desperation, I began to tether him on my front porch while I was away teaching, and at night I would bring him indoors but again tether him when I went to bed, this time in the closed-in back porch where I kept my kerosene fridge and my water filter. There in the middle of the floor I installed a metal ring and chain that ensured my four-legged companion stayed at home. I paid a price for this. Every night I was sure to be awakened several times by my restless dog dragging his chain about the room or shaking it when he explored a new position to sleep in.

Sadly, Brutus brought about his own demise. Having somehow escaped for the day, he went down into Kapsabet, where he was run over and killed by a police truck as it exited the police camp. Joseph, who'd always shown great affection for Brutus, brought me the horrible news. Barely able to think straight, I asked him to go with my garden servant and bring back Brutus in our wheelbarrow. This they did, while I tried to sort out my own grief. When they got back, I had the gardener dig a grave in my yard. It was a very sad occasion, but, given the free-spirited Brutus's behaviour, it marked an event that could well have occurred many times before.

After the "funeral", Joseph made clear that it was incumbent upon me to go down to the police lines and demand an appropriate financial recompense. I didn't believe that the truck driver could be held accountable, and I made clear that I would not be going after anyone for money. I don't believe Joseph ever quite forgave me for this. Clearly, I was not following the African way of doing things.

For me, Joseph and Thomas were not "friends" as such, but our association was a close one. Every morning before I went off to work the three of us would have a brief meeting. Joseph needed to know what to cook for supper, and he might well have a shopping list.

Having settled Joseph's concerns, Thomas and I would then walk out into the garden and discuss what needed to be done.

There was a considerable disparity in age between the two men. Joseph, an older man, had the honorific title of "Mzee", meaning "old man" but imbued with the very positive connotation that because of age he is to be respected, even venerated. There is no English equivalent to the term, because culturally the special respect accorded to the elderly in East Africa has no English counterpart. Thomas was, on the other hand, quite young, little more than a teenager. There were constant problems between the two of them, chiefly arising from Thomas's resentment at having to accept Joseph's authority.

One day, things reached a climax. I was having my customary bath before supper when there was a considerable ruckus just outside. Minutes later, Joseph knocked loudly on the bathroom door. I must come immediately! So, dripping wet and draped in a towel, I came outside and hurried round the side of the house. There was Thomas shouting incoherently and emptying a large can of kerosene onto the lawn. Not knowing what to do, I yelled at him to stop. To my relief, he did, dropping the can beside him. It was then that I realised he was drunk. Everything was now very quiet, but I now had to act. I told Thomas that he was fired. His response was to burst into tears, but I'd made up my mind. Tomorrow morning I would give him the pay I owed him and then he must leave. It was all a disaster. Thomas was good at his work, and in dealings with me he was generally cheerful and compliant. What had gone so wrong that he had behaved so badly?

The next morning, with Thomas's pay in my pocket, the three

of us convened almost as though it were our regular morning meeting. But the mood was very different. Thomas looked miserable and dejected. He began a profuse but very disjointed apology. I was quite determined to stick with my decision to let him go, but then to my surprise Joseph, who had been very angry at Thomas the day before, now spoke on his behalf. It was a warm and tender plea, like that of a father defending an erring son. Not really sure if I was doing the right thing, I accepted the mzee's advice, and, trusting in his wisdom, I said that Thomas could stay. The cost of the kerosene would be deducted from his pay, and, of course, there could to be no such behaviour in the future. With that, I had us all shake hands in European fashion to signify that we were all in agreement. As far as I was concerned, Thomas was an exemplary worker thereafter.

Although I never learned much about Thomas, I gradually got to know a little about Joseph. When I first met him, his name was Matefari (I believe that's how it was spelled), but shortly after he announced that he was now Joseph. In a pattern that was common among my students, he had discarded his original African name in favour of a Christian name, perhaps at the instigation of a missionary. But his new-found faith, if that's what it was, did not prevent him from following certain traditional African customs. He had, for example, at least two wives. The older wife managed his farm some distance to the west of Kapsabet. Occasionally, she would visit. During her brief stays, all was very quiet in the direction of Joseph's house that was situated only a few yards from my own. When the younger wife came, there was music from Joseph's radio, laughing, and noisy chatter with the wives of other house servants.

Often small children would appear, though which child belonged to which wife I could never quite ascertain. Often small groups of children would play together in my garden. Another teacher "borrowed" one of the school's basketballs, and the children delighted in inventing games to play with it. If things got too loud, I would sometimes hand out pencils and paper. They seemed to like that and would immediately sit down on the grass and attempt to draw. Once, however, one little boy wandered into the garden and did something that I hadn't bargained on, something that angered me but that perhaps taught me a little bit about African values:

> *"The bloody kid's pissed on my car!"*
> *Rushing from the house towards the child*
> *He stood there in his shirt*
> *(Six inches too short at least),*
> *A naked, black-skinned boy, eyes upturned.*
> *Just passing by, he'd seen the car –*
> *Grey, inanimate object.*
> *So there we stood, confronting*
> *One another – this child and I.*
> *I swear I was the guilty one.*

That such a moment provoked me to try my hand at verse is an indication of its significance to me. Sadly, perhaps, this moment and others like it did not always receive the reflection on my part that they deserved. Life seemed at the time just too busy and hectic.

CHAPTER TWELVE

SAFARIS AND GOODBYES

Apart from the busy and sometimes hectic life in Kapsabet, there were regular school holidays when we teachers could go on safari if we wished. Mombasa and its nearby beaches were a favourite destination. At Diani Beach, there was a government rest house beside the ocean. Pete and I visited on several occasions, staying in other similar very basic accommodations if the rest house was being used by someone else.

Walking along the almost white sandy beach on one occasion, I came across an apparently deserted and ancient-looking mosque, its three arched entrances opening directly on to the beach. I stepped inside. Away from the glaring sun outside, it took some time for my eyes to become accustomed to the shadowy interior. It was a strange and other-worldly experience. The Arabs who had constructed this (in the 14th century, I later discovered) knew what they were about. It was a place to be alone with God, if one believed in such a being, and, if not, it was a place that tempted one to feel that there was something greater than oneself, what

Wordsworth in very different circumstances referred to as "a presence that disturbs me" and "a sense sublime/Of something far more deeply interfused."

Of course, the beach, the blue waters of the Indian Ocean and the temporary release from all the burdens of our work in Kapsabet were wonderful in themselves, but it is my experience in the mosque that remains uppermost in my memory. Today, the whole area around Diani Beach has been developed to cater to a thriving tourist industry. Access to the mosque, now much frequented by tourists, is via the Indian Ocean Beach Club. In the surrounding area are hotels, villas and cottages. The place we knew has gone, and I doubt that the Kongo Mosque, as it is now named, still offers the kind of powerful spiritual experience I had almost a half century ago.

Another place I visited was Hell's Gate, named after a narrow break between towering cliffs. Situated to the south of Lake Naivasha and the Eldoret-Nairobi road, it was a desolate place with relatively few animals, but striking for its beauty. On one occasion, Pete and I took Jackie Heaton there on a camping trip. A teacher at the time, she was a former professional Outward Bound School instructor and an enthusiastic companion on any outdoor venture we cared to come up with. After setting up the small tent that the three of us would share, we ate our supper and watched the sunset. The ensuing darkness, the proximity of the tall cliffs and the emptiness all around contributed to an eerie sense of dread. This was not a place, I felt, that would evoke the kind of uplifting visionary feelings I had experienced at the beachside mosque at Diani. What exactly had the explorers Gustav Fischer and Joseph

Thompson been thinking when they named this place in 1883? Had they felt any of the fearful awe that I had?

Once again, this is a natural wonder that has since been "discovered". Now a national park, it is home to three Geothermal Power Stations (Olkaria I, II, and III) with a fourth that will be completed shortly. Amenities at Hell's Gate support bicycle tours, rock climbing and hiking, and there are three official camp sites with picnic benches, shower blocks, sheltered picnic regions, pit latrines, water taps and garbage cans. Close to the park are all manner of hotels and accommodations for visiting tourists. Hell's Gate also has attracted movie makers. The setting of *The Lion King*, for example, is based on Hell's Gate, and parts of the movie *Lara Croft Tomb Raider: The Cradle of Life* staring Angelina Jolie were shot there. The place we saw in the early 60s was probably little changed since Thompson and Fischer had been there, but today it has been transformed into a popular playground, still scenic but bereft of those qualities that inspired its name.

Other safaris took me to a variety of other places: Amboseli Game Reserve, where with Pete and Harry Stein I saw, close up, ostriches, elephants, and rhino; Ngorongoro Crater (in Tanzania), the steep interior walls of which keep the rich assortment of large animals penned in; Lake Nakuru, a shallow alkaline lake famous for its flamingos; Lake Naivasha, a freshwater lake where I often camped; Masai Mara Game Reserve, adjacent to Narok, where Richard Tonkin taught, and the place to which Pete and I took his then girlfriend and my fiancée-to-be, who had come on a brief visit from England; and Dar es Salaam, the capital of Tanzania on the coast, which I visited after attending Hal Strom's marriage to another T.E.A. teacher. Particularly memorable to me, however, were the climbs I did of East Africa's three tallest mountains: Mount Elgon, an extinct volcano, which straddles the border of Uganda and Kenya, the highest point of which is 4,321 metres (14,176 feet); Mount Kenya, another extinct volcano (5,199 metres or 17,057 feet); and in Tanzania, though adjacent to the border with Kenya, Mount Kilimanjaro, the highest mountain in Africa (5,895 metres or 19,341 feet) and also an extinct volcano.

Mount Elgon I could see from my doorstep on a clear day. Lit up by the morning sun like some distant jewel, it seemed to invite a visit. During the time I was at Kapsabet, I accepted the invitation on several occasions. Two expeditions have remained in my memory. One of these was my first ascent with Pete, Tom Powell and his house servant. Tom was our leader, and all went well until about halfway up we came upon the prone body of an African, spread out across the path we were following. At first I thought he was dead, but there was a pulse and he seemed to be breathing, though barely. All attempts to wake him were futile. Tom, being in charge, as it were, now wrote a brief note about the near dead man and instructed his servant to go back and get help. Who the note was supposed to go to and who Tom expected to come I never found out.

We all then continued our climb, since there was nothing more to be done. Once at the top, and feeling exhausted from the effects of the altitude, we were able to look down into the crater. Although there were telltale signs of game around the rim, we didn't see a single animal. After eating our lunches, we started our descent, our thoughts now on the fate of the African we had found on the way up. Before we reached the spot where we had left him, Tom's servant appeared on the path in front of us. None of us, except Tom, could follow the servant's Swahili, but Tom summed it up for us: "He couldn't find anyone to come back with him. He says he's sure the man was just drunk and asleep."

It made sense to me. While on our safari with Lloyd, in the darkness as we approached Kapsabet, Lloyd had suddenly braked very hard, and we had narrowly missed running over an African lying in the road. We all clambered out and stood around him while Lloyd checked his pulse and breathing. Attempts to wake the seemingly unconscious man were of no avail. Lloyd diagnosed drunken stupor. With that, he had us drag the man to the side of the road where he would be safe, and then we were on our way once more. Why hadn't I thought of that on Mount Elgon? Why hadn't Tom?

The other climb of Mount Elgon I remember well for very different reasons. It was with Frank Laemmlen. Our plan was to drive to the end of a track that petered out about halfway up the mountain. Then we would continue on foot and camp overnight. This we did, pitching our small tent on the path itself, there being no other flat open spots around. As darkness fell, we lit a fire, cooked a meal, and then sat talking in a desultory way until we turned in for the night. Some time later, I woke up, startled by noises outside. To my somewhat uneducated ear, it sounded like elephants. What's more, the sounds were getting closer. I realised with horror that we had set up our tent in the middle of a game trail. Humans may have used it, but it had been created by animals, who were responsible for its well-worn features.

I shook Frank and told him what was happening. We had to decide what to do. But in response, he gave a couple of grunts and went back to sleep. I'd never encountered anyone who could sleep like that. Though I had a strong impulse to get out of the tent and off the trail, there was no way I was going to leave Frank, so I stayed and waited for fate to play itself out. Perhaps the remnants of our fire and the unfamiliar presence of the tent would keep the elephants from tramping over us.

As the minutes passed, I began to sense that the sounds were no longer getting nearer. Before long, everything was quiet again, except for my heart, which was still pounding away.

Eventually, I was able to get back to sleep. But not for long. Again, I woke suddenly. Something was close by in the darkness. Then I heard its peculiar but distinctive rasping cough. It had to be a leopard. Attempts to rouse Frank again failed. To my relief, however, the animal passed right by the tent, seemingly more interested in our dirty cooking pots than the potentially tasty morsels in the tent. After much banging about with our cookware, the leopard (if that's what it was) then went on its way, leaving me to try and get back to sleep yet again.

In the morning, Frank seemed quite unperturbed when I recounted the events of the night. He admitted to being a heavy sleeper, and he agreed that something had disturbed our cooking pots, but any suggestion that we were lucky to have survived the night was gently dismissed. Although he never expressed his thoughts on the matter, I suspect that he probably considered my fears irrational and needlessly dramatic.

Climbing Mount Kenya was an altogether different affair. Pete,

Jackie and I, after staying overnight with a friend close to the mountain, set off early one morning. We had no intention of attempting any rock climbing. Our intention was merely to trek as high as we could in the space of a single day. As the three of us passed beyond the tree line and approached the steep rocky incline leading up to the summit, we began to feel the effects of the altitude. Pete and I decided that we should rest for a short time where we were, enjoy the spectacular views of the snow-capped summit and then go back down to the car.

Jackie, however, was not happy with this. She wanted to press on. We knew that she was very fit, and, as a former professional instructor in the Outward Bound programme, she was far more experienced than we were. The three of us argued for a while, but Pete and I would not change our decision. Somewhat haughtily, Jackie suggested a compromise. She would walk on for half an hour and then come back. We agreed to this, and off she went. After three quarters of an hour, with Pete and me becoming increasingly concerned and still feeling the effects of the altitude, Jackie appeared. She was walking very slowly and staggering a little from side to side. Once we got to her, she seemed to be in a state of near collapse. One on either side of her, we got her back to where we had left our bags and sat her down for a brief rest, knowing that as soon as we descended the mountain towards our car, she would probably recover.

For the present, however, not only was she quite sick but deeply upset with herself. As a woman and a professional outdoors person, she'd failed in front of these two male amateurs. However, whereas Pete and I had been somewhat annoyed by her going on alone, now we felt very sorry for her. She was a good friend, and we did not want her to feel any less of herself concerning something that could have happened to anyone. And look at us - we had run out of gas long before she had done. Uttering such crumbs of consolation, Pete and I began to help her down the mountain, taking it in turns to carry her bag in addition to our own.

Everything turned out fine in the end, and the three of us, though very tired, were quite ourselves again by the time we arrived back at our friend's house. In retrospect, I realise that the three of us agreeing to let Jackie go off alone was a dumb decision. It broke an important rule, one that is today implied by the Mount Kenya park authority's regulation that forbids those who are alone from entering the park.

Climbing Mount Kilimanjaro was for me an integral part of an experience I had during my first summer in Kapsabet. Hearing that there was an Outward Bound School in Kenya that sometimes took on additional instructors, I offered my services for the summer holiday period. I didn't know much about the organization, but I knew that it had been set up by the German educator Kurt Hahn. His progressive views on education stressed the idea that it should involve experiential learning aimed at developing self-esteem, discovering an individual's innate abilities and developing teamwork and leadership.

The school in Kenya was located in Loitokitok at the base of Kilimanjaro but on the Kenyan side of the border. Somewhat to my surprise, I was offered a position as a Temporary Instructor and told I would be met in Nairobi and driven to Loitokitok by one of the permanent Instructors. Jackie, who'd worked at an Outward

Bound School in the U.K., was, I sensed, somewhat sceptical about my abilities, but she offered to drive me to Nairobi so that she could meet the instructor who was picking me up. It turned out that they had earlier taught at the same school, so before I got out of Nairobi, I first had to listen to an extended exchange of news between two long-term friends. I was quite irritated by this, I suppose because I now felt even more of an outsider. In addition, my self-confidence was already quite low, and the easy banter and shop talk between these two only made things worse.

The drive south to Loitokitok was very pleasant and my companion turned out to be easy to talk to and reassuring about what I had let myself in for. As we drove south, the view of Kilimanjaro became less and less hazy. At the same time, its size became increasingly impressive the nearer we got. When we arrived at the school, I saw that the grounds had been carefully tended. There were flower beds and well-kept paths and grassy areas. Marking the driveway were whitewashed rocks, reminiscent of many a colonial era government building.

I was introduced to the school's director, a pleasant, no-nonsense man, who showed me to my quarters. I had been allotted a small stand-alone cabin. Stepping inside, he urged me to be sure to use the mosquito net hanging above my bed. Then he explained that I would be assigned to a "patrol" of about ten students. My job was to observe them and write reports on their progress as they dealt with the various challenges that would confront them. I should also note how the patrol functioned as a team and who emerged as possible leaders. I could encourage my patrol, but I was not to do things for them. To develop a degree of kinship with the members of my patrol, I was expected to do many of the same activities required of them.

I then met the incoming students, most from secondary schools in the three East African countries. Most of these were Africans, but there were a number of Indians and several whites, one of whom was from the United States. He was a student at Exeter (New Hampshire) and was in my patrol. Later I found out that Exeter was an elite and prestigious high school. Much was expected of its students, a point relevant to something I will mention a little later.

At 6:30 the next day, reveille was sounded and everyone formed up in the cold morning air as though on parade. As instructed, we all wore bathing suits. Then, on the Duty Instructor's command, we set off on a brief run through the adjoining forest. This ended when we returned to a clearing where there was a pool fed by water coming directly from the mountain behind. As we entered the clearing, we were told to jump in at one end of the pool and swim to the other. The water, needless to say, was extremely cold. It was a thoroughly miserable experience. I suppose in the spirit of Kurt Hahn, this early morning dip was considered character building. For a couple of days I went through the routine, but then the instructor who had picked me up in Nairobi quietly let me know that this was something I could skip. I'd set a good example for my patrol and that was enough. What ecstasy it then was to remain in my warm bed for an extra fifteen minutes or so after reveille!

During the ensuing weeks, there was a packed schedule to follow. Everyone attended classes on map reading and the use of a compass, first aid, knot tying, rescue procedures and survival skills.

A series of expeditions in the bush north of the School then put some of these skills to the test. One expedition, for example, involved following map and compass bearings from point to point. Each patrol was assigned a different route. If carried out accurately, a patrol would eventually arrive where we instructors waited with an all-important prize – water. It was no easy task navigating through this hot, arid landscape. Close to both the Tsavo and Amboseli Game Reserves, the area was home to a good many species of animals. Anyone venturing into this world of tall grasses, thorn bushes, and flat-topped acacia trees had to be on the lookout for potentially dangerous animals such as lions, buffaloes or elephants. The students were not too happy about this. Suddenly, the normal excitement and pleasure of spying such game from the safety of a vehicle had been transformed into a wariness tinged with a measure of fear.

To my considerable relief, my patrol successfully navigated its way to our waiting truck. Other patrols arrived sporadically, some having been delayed by straying from the assigned course. Mercifully, none of the patrols had encountered any dangerous animals, though there had been plenty of sightings of giraffe, zebra, gazelle, and the like.

Another exercise out in the bush required students to be completely isolated from each other. They each had to build a bivouac and light a small fire to cook a meal, and then each student was required to spend the night in the bivouac he had built. The only assistance we provided consisted of four matches per student. As I carried out an inspection of the students in my patrol in order to ascertain their initial progress, I was very surprised by what I found. Most of the African students did very well in finding natural materials for their bivouacs, and these same students had no apparent difficulty in lighting a fire. Some of their skills, I suspected, had been acquired during their life at home. The other students, particularly the Indians, were without expertise in these matters. Some of them used all their matches and ended up without a fire, and as for bivouacs, some were obviously going to have an uncomfortable night. Far more surprising, however, was my discovery that most of my Africans were very fearful about spending a night completely alone. All their lives they had slept in the company of others, either family members at home or fellow students in school dormitories. No wonder one of the rules for this exercise was that no one was supposed to call out or attempt to make contact with anyone else.

Other exercises involved rock-climbing and abseiling. These were preceded back at the school by practice on a somewhat daunting ropes course. Designed to build confidence in those who mastered its bridges and ladders, its zip line, and its swings (Tarzan would have loved those), its biggest challenge was the height one had to climb at certain stages. I was not at all comfortable about negotiating some of the obstacles high above the ground, but I forced myself to do it as a means of encouraging my patrol. The follow-up to this was a rock climb up a 30-metre (100-foot) cliff face. It was not as high as the cliff in Bristol I had fallen from and not as difficult a climb, but it was still something of a challenge. Again I had to go up in front of my patrol to try and inspire some confidence in them. I managed to reach the top without too much difficulty, and then members of my patrol began taking turns to follow me. All went well until the student from Exeter briefly lost his footing before grabbing his rope with both hands and wedging himself on a narrow ledge. He froze, and all attempts to get him to take his hands from the rope and resume climbing were of no avail. He wouldn't listen to me or any of the other instructors.

After a whispered discussion, one of the instructors abseiled down to the unfortunate fellow. Another rope was attached to the student, who was then eased (some would say pushed) off his ledge and lowered to the base of the cliff. He was distraught and inconsolable, deeply distressed at letting down the patrol and no doubt thinking of the expectations of those at Exeter who had sent him. But then something extraordinary happened. Seemingly oblivious to all consolation, he wiped his eyes (yes, this strong-looking figure had shed a few tears) and stood up. Addressing me and the other instructors, he said, "I want to do this. Can I have another chance? Let me do this. Please. I can't screw this up. I've just got to do it."

Accompanied by encouraging words from all of us, he walked back to the bottom of the cliff, attached himself to the waiting rope, called up to the patrol member at the top who would belay him, signalled that he was coming, and then began to climb. His fellow patrol members cheered him the whole way. It was a memorable and happy moment when he reached the top, a wonderful smile on his face.

This, I mused later, was presumably what Outward Bound was all about, an individual discovering his personal limitations but then finding the inner means to overcome them, and, as in this case, drawing further strength from a supporting team. Though somewhat corny when one first encountered it, the organization's Tennysonian inspired motto on this occasion seemed quite apt: "To serve, to strive and not to yield."

On another day, we hiked to a different cliff which was approximately the same height. The task this time was to abseil down from the top. Again, I had to go first and show my patrol how it was done. As with climbing, I had no relish for standing with my back to a thirty-metre drop, leaning out into the void almost horizontally, feet planted firmly on the rock face in front and then "walking" down the cliff face as I let out the rope. I had been warned that halfway down there was an overhang, and once below it I would not for a while be close enough to the rock face to have any contact for my feet.

The beginning of my descent was slow and quite nerve-wracking, but gradually my confidence increased. That is, until I reached the overhang, and found myself floating in mid-air. Remembering the instructions I'd been given, however, I kept letting my rope slide through the hand that was extended to my right. I soon realised that I had nothing to worry about, and I began to experiment by letting the rope out more quickly. This was quite exhilarating, and before my feet came in contact with the cliff once more and I reached the ground, I began to feel increasingly confident.

The members of my patrol then followed. The majority did well, but two of them committed the standard beginner's error of letting go the rope in their right hand and grabbing the rope above their heads. Luckily, these two were each attached to a safety rope, and they could then be lowered to the ground. I was very pleased when, with the encouragement of their fellow patrol members, both accepted a chance to try again. This time both made flawless descents, something I was able to describe in very positive terms when I wrote my report on the day's activities.

By now, I'd come to the view that students who had failures of nerves but who then faced their fears and repeated their assigned task should be given extra points rather than being marked down for their initial "failures". I argued this quite strongly with the full-time instructors, but I'm not sure that anyone got the point I was trying to make.

The climax of the Outward Bound course was now approaching – the climb of Kilimanjaro. But first there was a preparatory exercise in the form of an extended hike on the side of the mountain at about 3,350 metres (11,000 feet). The purpose was to help us prepare for the even higher altitudes we would encounter on our coming climb.

During our hike, I began to feel more and more fatigued. When we began our descent back to the school, my patrol was at the rear, and I was behind my patrol. Before too long, they were far ahead of me, and I could no longer hear their voices. After some time and still in the open above the tree line, I felt so tired that I dropped to the ground with an overwhelming urge to go to sleep. I knew this would be a bad thing to do but physically I seemed incapable of moving. This, I came to realise later, was my Outward Bound moment. As I was alone and the last person on the mountain, it was not likely that my absence would be noticed for some time.

My foggy brain had to decide what to do. Could I even get on my feet again? Why couldn't I have a short sleep? Or would I just pass out like the man I had encountered while on safari with Lloyd or the man we found on the track up Mount Elgon? Dragging my backpack towards me to make some kind of headrest, though I had still not decided whether or not to sleep, I remembered something. I opened the top and took out the last of the food I had brought with me – a small orange and some chocolate. I devoured both, and to my amazement soon began to feel that I might after all be able to stand up. This I did. With my pack once more on my back, I staggered forward down the trail. Later, I was ashamed to remember that I'd contravened a major Outward Bound rule. I'd left litter behind, in the spot where I had been sitting - the chocolate wrapper and the orange peel.

After about twenty minutes, I heard voices in front of me and soon came upon several patrols and instructors resting in a small clearing in the forest. There were a few jibes at my expense, at which I smiled without offering any explanation or excuse. Indeed, for the rest of my time at the school and up to the time of writing this account, I never talked to a soul about the incident. There was something unresolved about it, something that still troubles me. By not going to sleep and by getting to my feet and resuming my hike along the trail, had I mustered the resolve to overcome my personal weaknesses in true Outward Bound fashion? Or did I owe my little triumph to the fortuitous help of a piece of chocolate and an orange?

Within a day or so of our high altitude venture, we set off to climb Kilimanjaro. Before leaving the school, the Director made one thing very clear. Each patrol was to function as a single unit. No one could drop out. It was every member to the top or none. Each patrol was to choose a leader from among its members, and he would be in charge of helping his patrol members to work as a team and collectively get every member to the summit. I was mildly surprised but quite pleased when my patrol selected the student from Exeter as leader.

The Director's briefing also included advice about the clothing we should take: warm sweaters and jackets, gloves, balaclavas, heavy socks (take extra pairs), and boots. In addition, we needed our sleeping bags, our water bottles, and the snow goggles that belonged to the school. Everyone was excited as we set off, first through the forest and then out above the tree line, the snow-capped summit of the mountain in the distance. By the time we reached our destination, the so-called Second Caves where we would camp overnight, we were very tired and were beginning to feel the effects of the altitude.

The next day, about an hour beyond the caves, we came to a stream where we filled our water bottles for the last time. As we pushed on ever higher, some students began complaining about headaches and two of them, together with one of the instructors, began suffering from diarrhoea and vomiting, those other familiar symptoms of altitude sickness. Our goal on this second day was the relatively small hut owned by the school. Situated at an altitude of about 4,570 metres (15,000 feet), the hut was an ideal staging point for the last leg of the climb. At this altitude, it was very cold once darkness set in. The hot soup, cooked on Primus stoves, helped a little, as did the close proximity of other sleepers when we wiggled into our sleeping bags.

After a few hours of sleep for those not too troubled by debilitating headaches, we struggled into our clothes and stepped out into the darkness. It was about 1 am. There was a brief breakfast (oatmeal, I think), and then we set off in single file, climbing steadily behind the lead instructor, whose flashlight illuminated the trail for him, though not for us. We trudged forward in the dark, doggedly putting one foot in front of the other. There was none of the normal chattering. Everyone was saving each oxygen-depleted breath for the task at hand, zigzagging upwards on the largely scree surface of this part of the mountain. I followed at the back of my patrol to make sure that everyone stayed safely together.

As we approached the final pitch, where we would be walking on snow, a problem developed involving two of my patrol members. They had stepped off the path and were sitting on a rock, saying they could not go a step further. Our patrol leader halted and came back down the line to see what was going on. This was the kind of moment we all feared. Without these two, the patrol could not go on. I was the one who would make the final decision, but first I had to see what the patrol leader would do. Stepping over to the two on the rock, he first reminded them that the patrol could not go on without them. Not getting any response, he then did something that caught me by surprise. Raising his voice and acting like a stereotypical angry sergeant major, he came out with the following:

"Now stand up and get your asses over here. Get in the line and start moving. You hear me? I'm gonna be right behind you. If I have to, I'll damn well kick you up there. So just get going."

All this was laced with a few expletives that I won't record here. Silently, the two (both Africans) complied. Should I intervene? Were they genuinely too exhausted to continue? What kind of repercussions would there be regarding a white American addressing

Africans like that? Certainly, there was no display here of the mutual respect that was expected in Outward Bound team projects.

After appointing someone else to take his place at the front of the line, the Exeter student placed himself directly behind the two Africans, and we were on our way once more. The last 100 metres or so were the worst. Pausing between steps and breathing six or seven gasps between steps, I found it a considerable challenge to keep going.

At last we reached Gilman's Point on the rim of the crater. At 5681 metres, this was not quite the highest point, but the School considered that this was far enough. Walking a further 45 minutes around the crater rim to what is now called Uhuru Point was not a school requirement. None of us had any objections to that. Sitting on rocks in a state of exhaustion, we were happy with our accomplishment. Few people, however, outwardly displayed any joy or elation. Like me, they seemed dazed and expressionless.

I was aware of the stunning views revealed by the rising sun, but only had sufficient energy to lift my camera and, still sitting, to photograph the sights around me. Most impressive was the view of Mount Mawenzie, another volcano but connected to the tallest volcano, Kibo, by a saddle used by climbers coming from Tanzania. There was also the view down into the crater. Great cliffs of ice had accumulated to produce a strange and other-worldly landscape. Today, climate change has apparently reduced the ice, along with the amount of snow on the upper slopes of the mountain. Knowing this, I'm glad the students saw these things when they did, particularly those who'd never been in contact with snow before and might never walk on it or touch it again.

Coming down the mountain was very different from climbing it. Using the long poles we had been issued with for the climb, we were shown how to descend through the scree, digging the pole into the scree behind for balance and sliding with both feet as though we were skiing. The technique was very dirty but very effective, and in no time that segment of the descent was over.

Soon we had passed the school hut. After refilling our water bottles at the stream, we kept going until we arrived at the caves where we had spent a night two days earlier. My headache was now gone. All I wanted was a good sleep. First, however, something happened which troubled me greatly. With us had been two of the permanent instructors, one of whom had not participated in the final climb because, as he explained, he was sick! When we all reached the caves, these two jokingly told me that they were leaving. They couldn't wait, they said, to get back to the school, where there would be cold beers and hot showers. I didn't like this, but I was in no position to object, especially as this was done all the time, or so they claimed. It particularly troubled me because I was aware that descents, when a person was fatigued, affected by altitude, and perhaps dehydrated, could prove hazardous. Surely the instructors should be at the rear throughout the descent, making sure that no straggler got left behind and that any sick student received appropriate assistance?

A month or so later, I read in the newspaper that an Outward Bound student had died from a sudden onset of pneumonia while descending Kilimanjaro. If I remember correctly, it was the students who had brought him down. Where had the instructors been, I wondered? Were they back at the school, enjoying their cold beers?

In spite of my initial misgivings and some of my criticisms when I left, working with Outward Bound as a temporary instructor was one of the most important parts of my African experience. Like the students who came to take the course, I was tested in many ways, both physical and psychological. From being placed in demanding situations that did this, I learned a great deal about myself, about self-reliance, and about different styles of leadership, not all of which I approved of. I also learned many practical skills in the classroom, but came to realise that such knowledge was always incomplete until put to use outside it.

In placing this account of my Outward Bound experience at the end of this chapter, I am taking a certain amount of literary licence, since the events depicted happened two years before I left Africa. I have done this because during the weeks I spent at the Outward Bound School I was confronted by some of the most intense experiences I was ever to encounter during my three years in Africa. Those experiences, I like to think, encapsulate many aspects of my three-year sojourn.

When the time did come to leave, Pete and I discovered that we would be flying out of Nairobi. For us, there would be no gradual adjustment, with a train ride to Mombasa and perhaps a last glimpse of the Ngong Hills, and no voyage home on the *Kenya Castle* or one of its sister ships. Instead we would be travelling home on a VC10, a relatively new type of passenger jet operated by BOAC. Within a few hours (about 8½, we calculated), we would be back in England.

Pete had flown once before. He'd had to race home at the time of his father's death. His worries about the very idea of flying were made worse on this occasion by the fact that his plane, a De Havilland Comet, had been delayed in Entebbe on account of some mechanical problem. I had only flown once, in a small East African Airlines plane from Dar es Salaam to Mombasa with a quick stop in Zanzibar. I had enjoyed the experience and was now quite excited by the chance to sample the comfort and speed of this (to us) technological marvel. Pete, however, was apprehensive. Like Frank crossing the Bay of Biscay, his fanciful preference would be to sleep the whole way. Where Frank had wanted to wake up only when the *Kenya Castle* arrived in Gibraltar, Pete wanted to sleep until we were on the ground in London.

While we were talking about this, he reminded me that the house we planned to stay in while we were getting our clearance to leave Kenya was owned by Gordon and Ursula Perrins, an older couple who were currently away. Gordon's first wife had been killed when the Comet she was in crashed near Elba. Indeed, there had been two other crashes of this first commercial passenger jet in the early 1950s. The VC10 to which we were going to entrust our lives had been introduced only two or three years before. Joking with Pete about his concerns only seemed to make things worse, so I quickly learned to keep quiet about the issue.

Meanwhile, as the end of the school year approached, there was, we began to see, a lot of paperwork to be done in Nairobi, chiefly at the Ministry of Education and at the offices of the Kenya Revenue Authority. Someone had warned us that we should set aside two weeks for this. To do so we insisted on leaving just before the school year ended, something that annoyed the headmaster and meant that there would be no ceremonial send-off to mark the end of something that would influence the rest of our lives. At the same time, I was well aware that Pete and I had different views about our three years in East Africa.

Later, after he had been teaching for a term in London, the Ministry of Overseas Development offered Pete a contract to teach at Shanzu Teachers College in Mombasa. Pete responded positively to this chance to go back, especially as he would be charged with opening up a new science faculty, but I had had enough. Some latent puritanical trait led me to reject the offer. Life had physically been too pleasant, providing a near perfect climate; a "free" house to live in; servants to take care of all the chores involved in cooking, house-keeping, shopping, and gardening; a network of good friends; and a beautiful landscape that always invited further exploration. But I'd seen too many expatriate old timers haunting the former European clubs that still existed in most communities. I'd seen enacted too many repetitions of the sundowner joke. Sitting on a porch with a drink in hand at the end of the day, a common social ritual, a slightly inebriated man would watch the sun lunging towards the horizon: "Go on. Go down, ya bugger. Don't ya hear me? Go down." Then, after the sun had fallen below the horizon, leaving only a patch of bright sky that would very soon be replaced by darkness, "There, see. I bloody well did it again. Never fails."

I didn't want to end up like that man, and I feared being trapped by the many physical comforts and pleasures of life in a place like Kapsabet. There was something lacking, something that I would never find there.

There was also another matter that made we want to leave. I

had developed grave doubts about the educational system. In essence, we were taking the very brightest students, none of whose parents had been to secondary school, and training them for jobs in schools, in government, in banks and in commerce. Already, as Africanization progressed, fewer and fewer of those jobs would be available. Already too, students who had completed their education and who now expected their dreams of a good job to be fulfilled quickly became disillusioned and angry whenever they failed to find employment. If their numbers grew, they would pose a potential threat to the social fabric of the newly-independent country. Perhaps I was over-fanciful in imagining that in the near future there might be crowds of educated but unemployed young men hanging about on Nairobi street corners. Wasn't this how revolutions began? What Kenya and the other East African countries needed was not the British colonial system of education that I had helped to maintain, but something that also served the broader needs of the economy, a chief segment of which was agriculture. But without some kind of cultural shift that would lead young men like my students to see, for example, that farming was not a demeaning career, there would be little change. My thoughts on such matters were probably ill-formed, but I cite them here because, rightly or wrongly, they influenced my decision not to return.

When Pete and I arrived in Nairobi in the summer of 1966, we began moving from office to office, confronting an unbelievably clogged bureaucracy. According to the unofficial advice we had been given, the trick was to be patient and not reveal any anger. Be polite, and smile. It was something of a cat-and-mouse game, I suspected, but we followed the "rules" and finished the process with a few days to spare.

Just before that magic moment occurred, we were witnesses to a display of the kind we had been warned about. Entering one of the offices, we had to wait while another teacher (not a T.E.A. person) began the process that we had started almost two weeks earlier. He was going to be on the same plane as us, we realised. Now he wanted his papers. The more the clerk behind the counter tried to explain how long the process would take, the more angry the American teacher became. His voice was increasingly loud, and his face turned an ugly red. Sweat broke out on his forehead, and his fist pounded the counter to emphasize the points he was making. Having given the clerk the necessary documents to begin his application for permission to leave Kenya, he turned on his heel and pushed through the door close to where Pete and I were sitting. He showed not the slightest acknowledgement that we were even there.

Approaching the counter, we found the clerk apparently quite unperturbed. We smiled and asked how our file was doing. "You should have everything very soon now," he assured us. And so it was. Later I wondered if the irate American's behavior had helped move things along in our favour while ruining his own chances. We never saw him again, and there was no sign of him on the plane when we left Nairobi.

Of our remaining days, I remember three things. On one of the days, we took the two-hour drive to Lake Naivasha in the car we had been loaned by someone on leave. Hiring a small rowing boat, two fishing rods and some tackle, we went fishing for bass. It was a memorable day, and we caught a number of fish. Under Pete's tutelage, I began to see why some people were so passionate about sport fishing. I wasn't quite so sure about the messy job of cleaning the fish so that we could eat them later. Being out on the water in a boat would probably have contented me.

On another of our days, I was invited to meet Jackie for dinner at the hotel in Nairobi where she was staying. When I arrived, I was somewhat taken aback to see her in an attractive dress. I'd never seen this rather tough outdoorsy woman dressed up like this. After finishing our meal, we stayed at our table, sipping on drinks and intermittently stepping out on to the dance floor. Who knew she could dance? When it was quite late and it was time for me to leave, I sensed that I could stay on at the hotel if I wanted. Reminding myself that I was soon to be a married man, I rejected the idea and moved on to saying goodbye. After an extended hug, we parted, and I never saw her or heard from her again.

My third memory of those emotionally-charged final days was of Pete and me standing in the living room of the house in Nairobi where we were staying. We began stripping off our clothes and piling them on the floor in the middle of the room, engaging in a spontaneous invented ritual to mark the end of our stay in Africa. First we took off our short-sleeve khaki bush shirts, made for us, like most of our African gear, by an Indian tailor in Eldoret. Then off came our shorts, quickly followed by the long white socks which were a required part of this unofficial uniform. In the bedroom, I gathered up more clothes for the growing heap – one more pair of shorts, more pairs of white socks and my beloved khaki bush jacket, with its epaulettes, its four large pockets, and its belt. Other clothes then joined the pile, all things that we would not be needing, we told each other, in the miserable climate to which we were returning. We agreed that we would give everything to the house servant who had been looking after our needs for almost two weeks. This would be in addition to the monetary payment we would give him. The man seemed delighted, though what use he would make of the clothes I could not imagine.

The next day, together with most of those who had come with us on the *Kenya Castle* three years before, we boarded the plane home. After a quick stop in Entebbe, where the remaining British T.E.A. joined us, we were on our way. Pete and I were not seated together, but that didn't concern me too much. I had plenty to occupy my thoughts. Only once did I walk to the rear of the plane to see how he was doing. He looked miserable and wasn't interested in talking, so I left him to his own thoughts and his fears about flying. Like me he would be getting married soon after we returned. Indeed, we were each to be best man at the other's wedding.

As for me, I was thinking about the welcome party that would be at the airport. There would be my parents, with whom I'd kept up a fairly steady correspondence, though I had not written frequently enough, according to my father. He had urged me to write at least once a week, not something I'd found easy to achieve. Always very organized and methodical, he was probably the reason I received without fail a weekly letter. He himself, in his small but very legible and distinct handwriting, always added a few cryptic sentences to my mother's more effusive and rambling missives. It was here in these expanded postscripts that he would politely suggest that I should communicate more frequently. He was right, I now realise. The adolescent who draws back from his mother's emotional outpourings and who finds his father unnecessarily demanding was very slow to die in me. Apart from the issue of letters, there was that of telephone calls. There had been none. As I had tried to explain to them, although the school had a phone, it was understood to be for emergencies only. Getting a line out and then getting connected through a series of operators, north through Africa and then across Europe to England, was not a task worth thinking about. At least, that was my understanding, so I never attempted it. Should I have tried? Would I have succeeded? What then? Would my father have tried to get me on to some kind of regular schedule?

Alongside my parents, I expected to see my future father-in-law in the welcome-home group. He was someone I had come to like a great deal in the short time I had known him before leaving England. He would no doubt have all the latest cricket scores to tell me about, an interest that we both shared, although he was far more passionate about the game than I would ever be. With me, he had been relaxed and easy-going, happy to share his thoughts, happy to show me around his garden, and always delighted to have my company when out walking his much-loved spaniel on the South Downs or along the Sussex seashore close to where the family lived.

Then, of course, there would be my fiancée. Though it was quite irrational, I had had increasingly persistent fantasies over the previous two weeks that I would not recognize her. How much would she have changed since I had last seen her? What would she make of me? I certainly felt that I had become a very different person since arriving in East Africa. Would she be put off by this? I suppose all such anxieties are typical for those returning from long periods away from home, but sitting in the plane and heading across the North African coast towards Europe, I didn't think of this at the time.

Mixed in with thoughts about my impending welcome home was something else. Realising that it would be virtually impossible to snag a teaching job while still working in another country, I had applied to do an M.A. in English at the new University of East Anglia. Somewhat to my surprise, I had been accepted. Once settled in Norwich, I told myself, I would be able to look for a job and make myself available for interviews. Something was sure to turn up. Above all, by going back to university, I would be returning to the world of books, from which for the last three years, I'd felt cut off.

But thinking about this produced new anxieties. My reading and book buying had been very limited. Apart from a few conversations with people like Jim Coleman, I had had few opportunities to exchange ideas about literature. Inevitably I felt quite out of touch with the literary culture I had left behind. How would I fare in a graduate programme, where other students were bound to be better prepared than I?

With all these thoughts and questions tumbling around in my mind, the closer we got to London, the more agitated I became. But once on the ground, a new problem confronted me - Customs. Stupidly, I had with me back-dated vendors' receipts for items like my watch and camera that I had bought in Aden. Naively, I had accepted the Arab traders' assurance that this would ensure that I would pay no duty. The customs agent was all too familiar with such tricks and kept me waiting while he slowly and methodically went through the rest of my luggage. Glancing around me, I realised that most of those who had been on the plane had already been cleared. Feeling very alone, I now began to worry about the welcome party out in the waiting area. What would they be thinking when I failed to appear?

After a considerable time had elapsed, and after I had confessed my sins to the customs officer and apologized for what I had done, he let me go. I gathered up my bags, took a few steps forward, and passed through the exit doors into the new life beyond.

AFTERWORD

Writing this book has been a surprising act of self-discovery. I began with an initial foundation of memories from the Second World War to the summer of 1966, when I returned to England after three years in Africa. I found that writing down those memories set off a quite unexpected evolutionary process. Each specific memory almost invariably seemed to trigger additional memories. Rather than worrying about whether I had enough material for a book, I began to be concerned about overtaxing my reader's stamina with too much detail.

At the same time, I became increasingly aware of something else. Those memories that I was able to check against documentary records or the memories of other people often turned out to be either completely inaccurate or not in accord with what others, family and friends, remembered. For example, the factory close to my home in Chelmsford which had been a regular target for German bombers, according to my seemingly clear memory, was Marconi's. Research in books and on the internet, however, revealed that this manufacturer of radios was located elsewhere in the city. The factory that led to our home being threatened by any ill-aimed bombs was not Marconi's but Crompton's, a manufacturer of electrical parts and a quite separate German target. Such errors on my part greatly disturbed me when I uncovered them, but they could easily be corrected. Whenever my memories conflicted with those of family or friends, however, the issue was more complex since I could not always determine what the truth was. For the purposes of my narrative, I had to make a choice, knowing it might be in error.

As lawyers have long recognized, memory is a very treacherous component in determining the factual truth, and witnesses to the same event will often have different and contradictory memories of that event. But there is perhaps a larger issue involved, one deftly handled by Gore Vidal in the opening of his *Palimpsest: A Memoir*, where he distinguishes between a memoir and an autobiography:

"A memoir is how one remembers one's life, while an autobiography is history, requiring research, dates, facts double-checked. I've taken the memoir route on the ground that even idling memory is apt to get right what matters most." (Palimpsest: A Memoir [Penguin Books: Harmondsworth, 1996], 5.)

What I have written leans in the direction of memoir. It is a construct of the first twenty-five years of my life, built from my memories, no matter how unreliable and selective they may be. The material in these chapters represents the person I believe myself to have been fifty years and more ago. With luck, I get right, as Vidal has suggested, "what matters most."

Shaping my narrative required me to contemplate a number of choices I made or which circumstances made for me. Dominated initially by my love of music and books, these "roads taken" in retrospect appeared to be leading in the direction of one or other of these two great loves. Boarding a ship for Africa, however, was in many ways a turning of my back upon so much of what had led up to that moment. The three years I spent there, first in Uganda and then in Kenya, undoubtedly changed my life for ever, but not in any grand dramatic way. The *Kenya Castle*, as it made its way towards Mombasa, was not, in my view, on some kind of voyage into Conradian darkness. But nor was it, contrary to what my "Colonel Blimp" at the Commonwealth Office appeared to believe, the bearer of a new youthful order, lighting the way to a brave future for the three newly-independent countries of East Africa. Yes, my life was changed, an unexpected road was taken, and new roads then beckoned, but not to Africa.

Writing this memoir is, of course, an attempt to recapture the past. But that past, like childhood and youth, is irretrievable, a dream world, to which one may at times long to return but which remains elusive. The presence of this dream world in literature has been a recurring study of mine. To discover it as part of my own psyche was a surprise, though one that I of all people should have anticipated.

Nostalgic contemplation of the past is in the main a pleasant pastime, but when comparisons are made with the world as it is today, the results can be painful. It distresses me to see the commercialisation of many of the places I visited on safari in Africa which are now fully developed as tourist destinations. It distresses me that the place I once taught in is now a rather dilapidated primary school, the original secondary school having been moved to a new building. It distresses me, too, that the house I lived in, of which I have many joyful memories, is now reduced to a filthy, barely inhabitable shambles, desperately in need of repairs and renovation. To explore the significance of such changes would require another chapter or so. I note them here because they are part of the inevitable process of change.

In spite of such matters, I remain positive about what brought me and my fellow T.E.A. members to Africa. Our task was to contribute to a new order. In our own fumbling way, we did make a mark, and, judging from their ongoing activities, many T.E.A. members continue to this day to offer help and support to schools in East Africa through the alumni organization.

As a final note, I would like to acknowledge the encouragement and help I received from my wife, Wendy Katz, during this latest writing project. In addition, when writing the final three chapters of this account, the section concerned with Africa, I also received encouragement and help from a number of people who need to be acknowledged here. All but four of those I shall name were with me as part of the Teachers for East Africa project. I list them in alphabetical order: Rosamunde (Roz) Blanck, who now lives in Manhattan after years in the far east, a lively and witty woman whom I wish I had got to know better; Dan Fitts, a Peace Corps volunteer, who taught with me at Kapsabet and who by chance "discovered" me in Nova Scotia when he came to visit his son, a student at Saint Francis Xavier University; Anne Laemmlen, who generously allowed me to read her memoirs of that time, and her husband Frank Laemmlen, both good friends who worked at a different school in Kapsabet; Louise Laemmlen, who was born shortly after her parents left Africa and who herself has published a memoir; Roland Minor, the veterinary surgeon I met on the *Kenya Castle*, (who now has a house in Lamu on the coast of Kenya) who recently published his memoirs and generously gave me permission to quote from them; Pete Ryall, a close friend while we were both in Kapsabet, who now lives on the west coast of Australia; Frank Smith, who like me was recruited from the University of Bristol, and who now lives only an hour or so away from me, having only recently retired from teaching in Qatar; Harry Stein, who taught at Kapsabet, whose world view was wiser than I was initially willing to acknowledge, and who visited my parents in England while he was on leave and so impressed my mother that she put away her anti-American prejudices for ever (Harry has continued to revisit East Africa as a valued expert on education); and Hal Strom, who taught at Kapsabet and later taught at schools in many different countries before working as an educator near Idaho Falls.

14239121R00244

Printed in Poland
by Amazon Fulfillment
Poland Sp. z o.o., Wrocław